THE E-COMMERCE ARSENAL

Arsenal

THE E-Commerce

12 Technologies You Need to Prevail in the Digital Arena

ALEXIS D. GUTZMAN

AMACOM

AMERICAN MANAGEMENT ASSOCIATION

New York • Atlanta • Boston • Chicago • Kansas City • San Francisco
Washington, D. C. • Brussels • Mexico City • Tokyo • Toronto

This publication is designed to provide accurate and authoritative information in regard to the subject matter covered. It is sold with the understanding that the publisher is not engaged in rendering legal, accounting, or other professional service. If legal advice or other expert assistance is required, the services of a competent professional person should be sought.

Library of Congress-Cataloging-in-Publication Data

Gutzman, Alexis D.
   The e-commerce arsenal : 12 technologies you need to prevail
   In the digital arena /
Alexis D. Gutzman
      p. cm.
   Includes index.
   ISBN 0-8144-0623-8
      1. Electronic commerce. 2. Web sites—Design. 3. Internet
advertising. 4. Internet marketing.

HF5548.32.G88 2001
658.8′4—dc21

                                                        00-049579

Printing number
10 9 8 7 6 5 4 3 2 1

TO CONSTANTINE

CONTENTS

PREFACE

E-commerce technology is changing daily. This book is designed to tell you what the must-have technologies are for your Web site, with resources listing vendors for each technology. However, new vendors are entering the field daily. For example, for the technology I discuss in the Epilogue, alternative payment systems, I received three press releases in the week before this book went to the printer. In fact, this book has been difficult to write because I have never felt that any chapter was finished.

When you get through here and you understand how all the technologies work and why you should implement them, you can get a weekly update of sorts by subscribing to one of my newsletters, hosted through the ECommerce Guide (ecommerce.internet.com) at Internet.com. I also write two weekly columns: EC Tech Advisor and eBusiness Illuminator. In fact, most of the research for this book came from interviews I conducted for the EC Tech Advisor columns. After interviewing hundreds of technology vendors, ASPs, and consultants, I wanted to be able to put it all into context for my readers. A column is no place to do that, and this book is the result of that desire.

ACKNOWLEDGMENTS

The contributions of many people went into making this book. First of all, I want to thank the many readers who have followed my columns since I started writing for Internet.com in August of 1999. Their feedback and questions helped me see that despite all the free e-commerce resources available online, a book like this was still needed. Laura Rush and Gus Venditto of Internet.com have given me a forum for my writing, for which I am grateful. They even run my controversial columns.

I deeply appreciate all the assistance of the many people who have helped me directly with the book. Paul Bates, Vice President of Research at BizRate, was extremely generous with his time and data. Without naming them all, the executives at the many vendors I interviewed were very helpful. Several were kind enough to review chapters and answer my questions—at all hours. They include—Scott Moehler and Awele Ndili (MobileShift), Lee Gerdes (Net Perceptions), Rich Clayton (Angara), and Michael Murphy (Siebel Systems). Professional colleagues who have become friends over the years were the most reliable sources of criticism of the original outline and early chapters. They didn't worry that I might write ill of their technologies or their companies and told it like they saw it: Howard Schwartz (who enjoyed his critical role, perhaps a bit too much) and Jay Sanne (iXL), Steve Sabatini (In2a.com), Julie Rutherford, (Boxer Learning), Tom Herrick (The Museum Company), and Tom Starnes. Michael Givens (Accelerus.com, Inc.) and Richard M. Cavagnol (the Center for Performance Improvement of PricewaterhouseCoopers) made the mistake of sending me e-mail about columns I had written and knowing more about the technologies than I did. They assisted me with the chapters on content management systems and on real-time access to inventory and order status, respectively. D.R. Peck of GreenFlash Systems was very helpful in reviewing the chapter on search engines, and Cameron Barrett was kind enough to review the chapter on content-management systems. Both of them responded to my requests for assistance, not knowing anything about me.

Personal friends and family also gave me valuable insight into a layman's understanding of my material. They include Andrew and Theana Vavasis;

my sister, Patrice Dalianis; my brother, Ares Dalianis; and my father, George Dalianis.

My agent, Carole McClendon of Waterside Publications, encouraged me and found me an excellent press for this book, for which I am grateful. Many, many people at AMACOM burned the midnight oil for this book. I'd like to thank the ones I know—Jacquie Flynn, Senior Acquisitions Editor; Andy Ambraziejus, Managing Editor; Lydia Lewis, Production Manager; Irene Majuk, Director of Publicity; Jim Bessent, Associate Editor. Then there are Scot Amerman and Ruth Mannino, copyeditor and proofreader, respectively. Thanks also to Nate Ouderkirk of TenBelow Design for the design and for his expert page makeup under grueling deadlines—including the ones I didn't meet.

I am grateful, finally, to my husband and children—one of whom arrived halfway through the project. A book like this is a social project because so much of the research has to be conducted on the phone during the day. My children seemed to understand that there were moments when I couldn't get them band-aids or pour them milk. My husband encouraged me daily. When I first suggested the topic, he insisted I submit it to my agent. Once I'd committed to dates, he helped me find the right noun to be the object of "mitigates" when I was bleary-eyed from writing, and let me sleep in (no small task with three children under four) when I'd stayed up all night to meet a deadline. This book is not among the three most important things I've produced in my life, but like the other three, it wouldn't have been possible without him.

If you have any questions or want to send comments about this book, please write to me at alexis@overtheweb.com.

PART I

THE E-COMMERCE CLIMATE

Online

THE WEB is perhaps the most competitive environment the world has seen since the gladiatorial ring of ancient Rome. Many sites compete for the same customers. Merchants frequently sell at or below cost.[1] Marketing standards are still in the formative stages; high-profile run-of-site banner ads have been widely discredited.[2] There are many shoppers and few buyers.[3] Shopping carts are abandoned three times as often as purchases are completed.[4] Almost one-quarter of purchases involve customer service contact, and those customers who do contact customer service are *less likely* to return to that merchant![5]

Nevertheless, there is still hope, both for the already-online and for aspiring online merchants. Implementing the right high-value technologies today can help to improve many of these negative statistics and help a site build a large base of repeat customers who keep coming back. There is a lot of money to be made on the Internet. This book will help you catapult your site into the ranks of those that thrive in the competitive environment online by showing you how to implement the key technologies that attract and retain quality customers. Before getting to the heart of the matter—the technologies that address the challenges of the Web—we need to uncover what the underlying causes of the problem are, because the technologies need to tackle those head-on.

The major cause of problems for the online merchant is also the major appeal of the Web to the online shopper: competitiveness.

THE CAUSES OF COMPETITIVENESS

The symptoms of competitiveness are apparent to all, but what makes for such a competitive environment? Three forces are responsible, all of which are interrelated:

1. Lack of geographical constraints when shopping on the Web

2. A superabundance of readily available information about products and services

3. The absence of customer loyalty

NO BOUNDARIES

The Web is truly global. If you move from Austin, Texas, to New England and find that your favorite hot sauce is not carried by your local grocery store, you can probably find it online. The same goes if you move from Austin to New Guinea. When consumers shop for products online, especially in the United States, there's often an incentive to purchase from an out-of-state merchant, because sales tax won't be applied. Rather than being locked into the inventory and pricing of local merchants, customers are free to shop from any of thousands of merchants from around the world who offer the same or similar goods.

Shipping costs within the United States are rarely differentiated by state. Most sites charge the same shipping cost (if, in fact, they still charge for shipping[6]) regardless of the destination in the continental United States. Merchants in high-cost-of-living states like New York, Massachusetts, and California have to compete with merchants in low-cost-of-living states like North Dakota, Tennessee, and Iowa.

ABUNDANT INFORMATION

It was once the case that if you wanted to buy a faucet, you went to the local hardware store or home improvement superstore, looked at the choices, talked to the salesperson, and came home with a faucet. Today, faucet shopping might involve visiting eight or ten different home improvement sites, reading articles about "fixing up your bathroom," and selecting from a wider variety of faucets, with more information about the faucet you ultimately purchase than you probably need. Mary Modahl, in *Now or Never: How Companies Must Change to Win the Battle for Internet Consumers*, describes this phenomenon as an "increase in apparent supply."[7] The logical result of greater apparent supply is lower prices, because customers are willing to shop around to find the great deal they believe is out there.

NO CUSTOMER LOYALTY

It's a common lament of Web merchants that customers aren't loyal. Few merchants can count on repeat customers without heavily marketing them via e-mail or other means. The real question is why any online customer would be loyal in the first place. There are none of the usual costs associated with visiting multiple merchants—loading the kids up in the minivan and driving from store to store, checking store hours and locations, and so on—and none of the advantages of shopping from the local merchant—being recognized, friendly neighborhood chit-chat, helpful personal service, and so on.

One of the keys to success for the online merchant is overcoming the natural lack of loyalty endemic to the anonymous shopping experience by creating loyalty-inducing, personalized experiences. But few online merchants have either mastered the techniques for doing this or implemented the technologies to facilitate the techniques. Most of them simply send the same e-mail message to anyone who's ever shopped with them, hoping they are developing a relationship with the customer. For customers to perceive value in such relationships, sites should answer questions that are likely to be on the customers' minds. An excellent example is what LifeMinders.com (a newsletter service) does: It sends e-mail that's appropriate to the season and the geographic region of the recipient, giving instructions on such things as what seeds to plant this month or season-appropriate landscaping. Chapter 6 discusses effective use of such targeted electronic direct mail (EDM) in detail.

INCREASED CUSTOMER EXPECTATIONS: THE CONSEQUENCE OF COMPETITIVENESS

For the merchant, the competitive environment is going from bad to worse. Despite the fact that shoppers will click away from a shopping cart more often than they'll give you their payment information, these price-conscious, disloyal potential customers are expecting more from every merchant!

What kinds of things do they expect? According to BizRate.com, the premier post-sale consumer research firm, they expect a powerful search tool on your site.[8] According to Forrester Research, a leading independent research firm, they expect free shipping.[9] You can add to that list a complete purchase history, expedited check-out, special deals, and up-to-date shipping status. It's not good enough, however, to be prepared to offer what they expect today. If you're going to win in this "keeping up with the Joneses" battle, you need to add what customers will be expecting in the near future. Add real-time presales assistance (the kind customers can get without disconnecting from the Web via their dial-up access), to-the-day shipping estimates by product based on customers' zip codes (next day to every zip code for no additional charge is optimal), access to special members-only sales via e-mail notifications for only those categories of products about which they care, and wireless access to purchasing.

DON'T HURDLE; POLE-VAULT

The bar has definitely been raised from only three short years ago, when major merchants debated the need to accept credit card payments online in real time, and when some major sites, while appearing to perform real-time automated processing of payments, were actually keying all payments by hand behind the scenes.

The three-guys-in-a-garage model of Web merchant will have a difficult time competing on the Web in the twenty-first century. Serious merchants, whether online today or not, will have to be prepared to engage in a three-pronged strategy for meeting the demands of their customers, becoming and staying profitable, and doing it all on Internet time:

1. Implement essential technologies

2. Maintain a flexible business model

3. Outsource everything

IMPLEMENT ESSENTIAL TECHNOLOGIES

Business books about technology often cross the line from describing technologies that solve business problems to celebrating technology for its own sake. The same is true of those of us who investigate, recommend, invent, and implement technologies. It's important to keep in mind that technologies don't attract or retain customers. However, sites that fail to provide the services that these technologies can offer will have trouble attracting and retaining customers.

The bar is now so high that few companies have the resources to investigate all the technologies that might be considered essential—to determine which ones are essential, to see how the technologies are implemented, to decide whether the company should build or buy, and if buying, to select which solution to pursue. That's where this book comes in. This book will help your merchant site pole-vault over the bar that's now too high to hurdle by helping you implement the twelve technologies that make up the e-commerce arsenal.

Based on the business needs they meet, the essential technologies can be grouped into three categories: traffic-driving technologies, site-enhancing technologies, and customer-servicing technologies.

DRIVING TRAFFIC. Customer acquisition is one of the most expensive components of most Web sites. Because your site is no closer to your customers' computers than those of your competitors, you have to find ways for your site to be *en route to other destinations* or be on your customers' radar when they're looking for what you're selling. There are five high-value technologies that you'll want to include when planning for cost-effective customer acquisition:

1. Experienced Web users, those most likely to be online shoppers, are even more likely than novices to rely on search engines and directories to find your site.[10] Being found in major *search engines* and directories and in any relevant industry-specific search engines and directories can make the difference between having lots of traffic and having none. Getting traffic that stays and buys is a matter of being found for the right keywords.

2. In a tiny niche between the popular and successful affiliate programs, which allow information sites to get paid for referring buyers to merchant or other information sites, and the viral marketing craze, which rewards senders of e-mail for promoting merchants to their friends, sits an interesting hybrid model called *viral affiliate marketing*. This cost-effective method of motivating your existing customers to return and rewarding them for referring their friends to your site should be part of your marketing plan.

3. The more places your content exists on the Web, the more people will be able to find you. By participating in *listfeed programs* (providing data to get your site listed on comparison shopping sites), making your site spider-friendly (easily traversed and indexed by an electronic agent) using XML (eXtensible markup language), and finding other ways to let other sites harvest your content for display on their own sites, you can benefit from their traffic.

4. Much has been written about *targeted e-mail*, but very few sites are really doing this well. A sound strategy and implementation plan for reaching your customers in their own e-mail in-boxes with information of value to them can, very cost effectively, turn one-time shoppers into regular buyers.

5. Despite the fact that m-commerce (wireless mobile e-commerce) is more hype than reality today, *wireless e-commerce* really is just around the corner. You need to take steps to make sure that shoppers using wireless devices can shop from your site.

ENHANCING YOUR SITE'S FUNCTIONALITY. Once you get customers and potential customers to your site, it's your job to help them find what they need quickly and check out easily and then to remember them and their interests when they return. Five essential technologies can facilitate these business requirements:

1. *Personalization,* so that when your customers return, they feel welcome. There are even technologies you can use to recognize visitors who have never been to your site and make them feel welcome by anticipating their needs.

2. *Shopping wizards* and natural language query handling, so that you can help your customers solve problems rather than just buy products.

3. *Accepting multiple currencies,* so that you can remain competitive as the proportion of nondomestic customers that shop online increases.[11] You also need the infrastructure to deliver products and accept returns from other countries.

4. *Real-time access to inventory and order status,* because no one wants to wonder about the status of an order. Add real-time access to returns-processing information and you've really got a winning recipe for customer loyalty.

5. *An industrial-strength content-management solution,* since you don't have the time or the resources to tinker with a homegrown system. Your customers deserve to see bug-free content, and you need the real-time reporting that only a best-of-breed solution can provide.

SERVICING YOUR CUSTOMERS. Customer service gets a bad rap in both the online and offline worlds. Most organizations see customer service as a necessary cost of doing business. The visionary merchant understands that customers don't want to contact you any more than you want them to. Customers would just as soon find everything they need on your Web site and never need to pick up the phone, send an e-mail inquiry, or click on a live chat button on your site. By implementing two high-value technologies, your site will be on its way to increasing customer satisfaction, while reducing costs:

1. *Real-time presales chat* can help reduce your shopping cart abandonment rate by making real people available *in-stream* to your

shoppers when they're only a click or two away from completing the purchase.

2. *Customer service that is integrated across all channels* is woefully unavailable from almost every company that offers multichannel customer service (e.g., phone plus e-mail support or phone support in conjunction with returns at physical stores). Customer relationship management (CRM) systems receive all the press, but most customers just want to be able to get the same right answer no matter how they contact you.

MAINTAIN A FLEXIBLE BUSINESS MODEL

The Web is full of opportunities—more than most people or sites realize. The Web is a particularly favorable environment for the young, nimble company that's talent-rich and not particularly indebted to any investors or board of directors to stay focused. The problem with typical business focus is that it is on following the plan rather than on following an opportunity that presents itself. Measurements of progress are too often made against some "eight-point plan" concocted by old-school business thinkers and expensive consultants rather than against reality, which is a quickly moving target on the Web.

In the beginning of the Web, there were gaps, therefore opportunities, in existing and available services as big as Mack trucks. Company A offered service A, company C offered service C. Anyone could see that there was a need to provide service B to fill the gap. Today, the opportunities are much narrower and perhaps harder to identify, but they are still present. Company 2.5 is providing service 2.5, and company 2.7 is providing service 2.7, which leaves a very narrow opportunity to provide service 2.6, or even 2.55 or 2.65, for that matter.

The businesses that will thrive online will identify these narrow opportunities and be nimble enough to leap into the gaps to provide the missing products and services. In some cases, the opportunities are geographically based, such as grocery-delivery services. More often, they are narrow vertical opportunities. I refer to these as "crack-in-the-sidewalk" opportunities. There's money to be made online on that tiny sliver of real estate, if it's carefully guarded.

Application Service Providers (ASPs)

Remember the bad old days when every piece of software you needed resided right on your computer? You bought the disks, or they came with your computer. You installed the software, registered it, and eventually upgraded it. Every time you installed a new software package, you did so with the fear that it would conflict with something you had that already worked. Then, if things started acting up even a month later, you couldn't help but have a nagging doubt that you had software conflicts. Even people who knew computers installed software with some trepidation, unsure what the consequences would be.

Times are better for computer owners today. Application service providers (ASPs) provide many of the services that desktop software used to provide. E-mail is an early example. Instead of running Eudora or Outlook Express on your computer and having your e-mail on your local computer, you could use Hotmail or Yahoo! to send and receive mail from any computer connected to the Web. Every now and again, new features would appear on the site, and you, as a user of the site, with nothing installed locally but your Web browser (Internet Explorer or Netscape), would automatically take advantage of the new features without having to migrate data or download anything. Any software application that you use infrequently, such as tax software, is a good candidate for using through an ASP.

Businesses also take advantage of ASPs. Businesses can subscribe to ASPs to get access to data that needs frequent updating, such as shipping costs, taxes, and tariffs. Businesses also use ASPs to administer online advertising, affiliate programs, and customer loyalty programs.

ASPs are one way a business can remain lithe enough to have a flexible business model, keep up with the current trends, and offer the functionality of the twelve technologies discussed in this book without having to write or install every technology in-house.

OUTSOURCE EVERYTHING

In order to implement the dozen technologies that should be in their e-commerce arsenal and retain a flexible business model while doing so, dot-coms should put behind them the days of writing for themselves all the software they need. Smart merchants will acquire best-of-breed technologies either through ASPs or through buying the software and installing and running it on their own servers, which, ideally, would be hosted by a Web presence provider (WPP).[12]

It's easy to see that a dot-com that was originally formed by one business expert and one tech expert might be inclined to the view, based on the fact that it got off the ground on the programming talents of the tech expert, that it should write all its own software. This strategy will, for the vast majority of dot-coms, guarantee that they'll always be small. A company can only grow so fast relying on its own home-grown technologies. If a company is to grow at Internet speed, it must buy or lease (via an ASP) the best products for today, knowing that it can switch gears and migrate into tomorrow's technology when the time comes.

If you've been on the implementation side of this equation, it probably makes you cringe just hearing about "migrating when the time comes." I've been there, too; I know how difficult it is. I've also been, as you probably have as well, on the development side, and I know that developing is slower than migrating. When you select from best-of-breed products, you get features that you could never develop into your phase 1 products. If you buy a mature product, you own a mature product, albeit with the likely pains of installation and configuration. However, if you develop a product, you get a skeletal product to start, and you often outgrow the product before it is mature.

BABY, YOU CAN DRIVE MY CAR

What if you can't afford to implement all these technologies at once, right now? Consider being a service provider. The final part of this book discusses the enormous potential that remains in e-commerce for those who choose not to attract any traffic at all but to serve as part of the infrastructure of e-commerce sites by providing either a technology, an outsourced service, or a prebuilt component.

Opportunities for Those Who Come at the Eleventh Hour

For bricks-and-mortar merchants, manufacturers who have never sold directly to the public, and dot-coms that are still in the back-of-napkin state of development, it's not too late. If you can ante up, you can still compete. The three factors outlined above—implementing the essential technologies, maintaining a flexible business model, and outsourcing development as much as possible—may well mean that as long as you can get a good domain name (and a good one is worth paying for) and have a compelling value proposition, you can come online anytime and compete with the top guns.

Of all the contentions in this book, the idea that it's not too late to be coming online as a merchant is the one that most goes against conventional wisdom. It is too late, everyone insists. If you're not online today, forget it, they say. I disagree. It's inconceivable that no dot-com that isn't already a household name will ever be one. This is like the story of the man who ran the patent office in the late nineteenth century who wanted to close it because he thought everything that would ever be invented had already been invented.

The advantage of coming online late is that a lot of money has already been spent and wasted by e-commerce start-ups, manufacturers, and bricks-and-mortar retailers trying to establish e-commerce sites that can attract and keep satisfied customers. While existing e-commerce sites may have some advantages in attracting and keeping online customers, established merchants who have waited it out also have some advantages—namely, that they haven't yet lost money online and that they can benefit from the lessons and dollars of other merchants. Also, you have this book.

What Are Investors to Do?

Despite the fact that so few dot-com merchants are making money, investor dollars flow freely from one money-losing business model to another. That's an indication investors know there's a lot of money to be made on the Web, but they are uncertain how that money is going to be made and are somewhat overwhelmed by the technology that undergirds these businesses.

The disadvantage for merchants of having waited until now is that the days of easy venture money for dot-coms are at an end. Innovators will still be welcome among the deep pockets of venture capitalists, but duplicators will find the purse strings closed tight. Yes, there's still a lot of money to be made, but there's also a lot of money to be lost and actually being lost daily. Of course, venture capitalists are aware of this.

Investors need no longer be confused by the press-release buzzwords about technology. This book strives to meet the information needs of high-tech investors as much as those of merchants. Unless investors understand what the technologies are and why companies need them, they don't have the information they need to make wise investment decisions. The hot buzzword in 1999 was B2B (business-to-business). Any company that claimed to do that was instantly seen as a good bet.

Investors need to keep up with technology continually, and understand it, to be able to make the right investment decisions. This book puts the technologies into context, through thorough, but concise, explanations. Through those explanations, as well as the information found in resources listed at the end of each of the twelve technology chapters, readers will be able to get the lay of the land in the Internet world without making it a full-time job.

NARROWING THE FIELD

While considerable question remains about the application of Darwin's theory to the animal kingdom, there's no question that Darwin was right about the digital world. The e-commerce field will narrow, and only the strong and customer-savvy companies will survive. There is still room for latecomers, but they need to be ready to ante up right away and invest in the technologies that will provide the services consumers will be demanding. For everyone else, the income-creation opportunities are still fabulous. Entrepreneurs just need to be more creative about where the opportunities are. This book helps explain and expose a wealth of income-producing or overhead-reducing opportunities both for online merchants and for those who choose to serve them.

Success

THE TWELVE technologies in the e-commerce arsenal all fall into one of three categories: driving traffic to the site, the functionality of the site, and facilitating customer service.

DRIVING TRAFFIC

Driving traffic to a Web site is a permanent, ongoing cost of being in business online. Unlike offline business and offline advertising, a Web merchant must make a concerted effort to attract both new and repeat customers all the time. Unlike the bricks-and-mortar world, one merchant's location is no better than another's, so no merchant can count on the fact that a certain percentage of passersby will stop in. Mary Modahl, in *Now or Never: How Companies Must Change to Win the Battle for Internet Consumers*, argues that marketing behaves as a fixed cost, a cost that companies cannot decide to trim.[1]

In my experience with dot-com merchants, when you advertise, you see traffic and sales, and when you don't, you don't. There's a half-life of customer attention. Your message needs to come in often enough that you don't see that half-life affect your business. When Andy Warhol said that everyone gets fifteen minutes of fame, he never knew about the Internet. There, it's more like fifteen seconds. Online, there are simply so many things competing for your prospective customers' attention—other merchants, sports scores, stock prices, pictures of scantily clad women, community groups, and recipe listings, to name a few of the free ones—that your message must appear on your customers' relevancy radar when they need to hear it—and often. Even after you send the message, you need to make it easy for customers to move from reading the message to making the purchase, which is what Part III of this book covers.

Traffic, Schmaffic

In most of the world, traffic is a bad thing, but online, *traffic* is the name used to describe anyone or anything that requests a page on your site from your server. Traffic used to be measured in terms of hits. Do you remember the days when sites had *hit counters* on them? These were usually little boxes that looked like a car's odometer. They dutifully recorded every time a page was requested. Every time the Web master pulled up the page to make sure the site was up, or every time a search engine spider visited the page, the number increased by one. Hit counts never were a very reliable method of measuring traffic. The fact that as many as one-third of all page requests could be coming from spiders or agents rather than real people further undercuts the legitimacy of hit counters as a valid method of measuring site traffic.

A better measurement of traffic on your site is *unique visitors.* There are a variety of ways to arrive at the number of unique visitors to your site. Also relevant are the number of new visitors and the number of return visitors. Most Web servers create *log files,* which record the actions of visitors on the site, along with enough information to determine which visitors are new and which are returning.

Analyzing Log Files

Most Web servers create log files of traffic that record the Internet Protocol (IP) address of the requester, the name and version of the user agent (browser), date, time, and page requested of every click on a Web site. The IP address can be the actual IP address (128.143.7.22) of a computer with a static IP address, or it can be the IP address of the proxy server, which would be the same for every computer behind a firewall. Or, it can be the IP address that's randomly assigned to a dial-up user when that person dials into his ISP. The fact that your Web server is probably already logging all this information, and you've probably never seen any of it, tells you that you (and most other sites out there) have access to far more information than you're using. In the resources section of Chapter 3 you'll find a list of software vendors and ASPs who will analyze your log files for you and turn this mountain of data into information you can use to make intelligent decisions.

Less-Effective Methods of Driving Traffic

There are, of course, various methods of driving traffic. They include banner ads, sweepstakes, loyalty programs, and other hybrids of the technologies I've chosen to focus on in Part II.

There's another method of driving traffic that's very effective but isn't really a technology, so it didn't make my short list. That's advertising in e-mail newsletters. If you've had an e-mail account for more than an hour, chances are you've already subscribed to an online newsletter, also known as an *e-zine*. E-zines tend to reach very highly targeted, self-selecting groups of individuals. They deserve mention as an effective method of advertising that new sites should consider when seeking low-cost alternatives to the glitzier advertising methods. One downside of e-zine advertising is that you often have to dig deep to find the right one for your target market. Not surprisingly, ad agencies make it much easier to advertise with higher-dollar methods.

Banner Ads

Banner ads are the method that most new sites think of first when they're trying to decide how to go about attracting a large customer base. Although banner ads do have some positive effect on your brand—meaning that down the road, people may be more inclined to buy from you because they've seen your banner ads, even if they don't have any other hard data about you—they aren't effective in getting the traffic to your site as a direct result of their being on the browsers of your potential customers. The average *clickthrough rate*—the number of people who click on a banner for every 100 times it's requested from the Web server—is about 0.8. The average cost per thousand (CPM) for a banner ad is around $25, so for each $25 spent, you would expect eight clicks on your banner ad. Because we know that not all those requests come from people (the spider problem mentioned above), the actual number of people who make it to your site is less than eight. Depending on the quality of the ad, and whether it promises a free gift, the clickthrough rate might be higher or lower. However, unless your site makes money simply based on clicks, clickthroughs alone aren't enough.

The instrumental question is: *What's the conversion rate of banner ads?* or in lay terms, "How many of those people who click through on the banner ad stay to make a purchase?" The numbers on that are quite sobering. The industry average is 1.7 percent. That means that there's a pretty slim chance that the $25 in advertising you spent bought you even one customer. The cost of a single new customer, referred to as *cost of acquisition*, via banner ads is around $400.[2] So although people like to see their own banner ads on sites and ad agencies will do their best to convince you that the branding effect is profound, the bottom line is that unless you have reason to believe the value of the customer (over whatever time span you want to use) exceeds the cost of acquistion of that customer, banner ads are a bad deal for your site. Whenever possible, sites should negotiate for marketing deals based on actual sales closed, unique visitors, or new visitors rather than just traffic.

Sweepstakes and Giveaways

Something for nothing is a compelling sales pitch. Sweepstakes and giveaways can be an effective way to get people to your site, to get them to give you personal information about themselves. They can even help get them to buy from you, if the value of the giveaway is equal or nearly equal to the amount they have to spend. However, sweepstakes and giveaways can attract the wrong crowd. There are people whose hobby is entering every sweepstakes. There are sites dedicated to helping them find the best giveaways. And there are mailing lists dedicated to the art of getting something for nothing online. This is not the best crowd on which to base your site's business plan. These shoppers tend to shop only when the price is unbeatable—and who can guarantee that?—and when there's a freebie involved. This same population is part of the "customer base" of every site that's ever offered a giveaway. They tend to be price shoppers rather than value shoppers, and you probably will never recover the cost of acquisition from these customers.

Loyalty Programs

If the amount of e-mail I get from these groups and the number of merchants participating are any indication, loyalty programs, such as Clickrewards, IQ Points, and FreeRide points, seem to be popular. But are they really effective at getting customers to visit your site in the first place and to return to it again later? BizRate.com's research indicates that they're not. According to BizRate's Fourth Quarter Online Consumer Shopping Report for 1999, less than 4 percent of all shoppers indicated that a loyalty program had anything to do with their decision to make a purchase from a site. More important factors included product search tools, discounted shipping, and express ordering.[3] I believe that like sweepstakes and giveaways, these programs appeal primarily to the something-for-nothing crowd. The reason for the ineffectiveness of these programs is that they don't *capitalize on loyalty*, they try to *buy loyalty*. Jupiter Communications reported in 2000 that 22 percent of online shoppers indicated that loyalty points were their preferred buying incentive, but the gap between this survey of shopping intentions and shopping behavior is too vast to dismiss.[4] Much more effective on that front is a permutation of viral marketing—attaching advertisements to the end of e-mail messages—which I discuss in Chapter 4.

SEARCH ENGINES

Being ranked highly in search engines and directories is not as random and beyond your control as you might think. There are some very specific things a site can do to achieve a high ranking. More than half of Web users rely on search engines to find specific products. Although there may appear to be many, many search engines, in fact, only a handful are responsible for most search engine traffic, so it pays for a site to determine the important key words that people ready to purchase are using and figure out how to be ranked highly for those key words. Chapter 3 takes you through the best options for being ranked highly on search engines, along with companies that can help you get and stay ranked.

Lumped in with the discussion of search engines is a discussion of directories. Directory results often appear above search engine results at search engines. You've probably used directories without even realizing it. Getting listed in directories is usually very little work and well worth your time.

VIRAL AFFILIATE NETWORKS

Affiliate programs, in which a merchant rewards Web sites that refer buyers to it by paying them a percentage of sales, have been around for a few years, making them old hat on the Web. Viral marketing, attaching ads to the end of e-mail messages, is relatively new. These are both cost-effective ways of reaching new customers. Even newer than viral marketing is viral affiliate marketing, in which sites ask their members to refer a friend, with the referrer getting some kind of promotional discount in return for making the referral and the recipient of the referral getting some promotional discount for taking advantage of the referral. This variety of viral marketing is more convincing than traditional viral marketing because the sender is a shopper and supporter of the site being referred in the first place. Chapter 4 discusses all of these models, as well as vendors who can help you implement them.

LISTFEED PROGRAMS AND XML

Web sites typically think of their "stores" as being their products and services displayed on their Web sites. This kind of parochial thinking really limits a site's ability to reach customers. Given the cost of getting new customers to go to a Web site, smart sites have come to realize that the more places their products and services can appear and be sold, the better. Instead of forcing customers to come into their own sites to view, evaluate, add to a cart, and purchase their products, sites should put their products out where the customers are. Knowing that on the Web, everything is just one click away, sites should be willing to pay to be where the customers are and do everything within their power to make their own content easily harvestable by other sites.

Chapter 5 discusses how you can get your products into these various shopping sites either by providing your products to these sites in the form of a listfeed file or by making your site friendly to spiders, using XML, so that these sites can harvest your product listings on their own.

TARGETED ELECTRONIC DIRECT MAIL (EDM)

It's much cheaper to get a customer to return to your site and make another purchase than it is to get a random shopper to come to your site and make a purchase. These costs are referred to as the *cost of retention* and the *cost of acquisition*, respectively. Targeted electronic direct mail (EDM) is a highly effective method of getting customers who have shopped with you before to return. The cost of EDM in dollars is very low: an ASP or vendor to do the bulk mailing and the cost of creative talent to put together the promotion you're mailing. However, the cost associated with doing it wrong and antagonizing your customer base is much higher. In Chapter 6, you'll read about sites that offer EDM that get the attention of customers rather than annoy them. The key to success in EDM is to respect your customers' time.

WAP-ENABLING FOR M-COMMERCE

Although e-commerce via wireless device is way behind the wireless hype curve, there's definitely a real market opportunity that you don't want to miss. Just as listfeeds permit you to put your products onto other people's sites so they can be where the traffic is, wireless service providers permit you to put your products onto the valuable real estate represented by the screens of wireless devices. In most cases, you don't even need to make any modifications to your site to have your products listed on the sites of wireless aggregators.

THE SITE

Once you get traffic to your site, you have to keep it there and entice it through your purchase process. There's more to a site than a good interface, clear navigational elements, and cool graphics. You certainly need good site navigation, an intuitive interface, and a site that's fast to load, since even people with 56K modems are actually connecting at closer to 28K than 50K because of overcapacity of ISP phone banks, slow network traffic, and poor phone lines. Most shoppers take these elements for granted these days. What sets apart the sites that are worth recommending to friends? Mostly, the features that enable shoppers easily to find and buy the products they need the first time and every time. Part III of this book takes you through the five technologies that can help set your site apart in a positive way.

PERSONALIZATION

There are two kinds of personalization: overt and covert. Effective sites use both types, whenever possible. Overt personalization ranges from the mildly cloying "Hello, Alexis, Welcome back!" to the invaluable capability to remember billing and shipping information to facilitate a speedy checkout with minimum rekeying. Covert personalization is much more subtle and harder to find. It can be remembering what you purchased on your last visit and showing you complementary products. Or, based on your anonymous profile, it can involve recognizing you before you purchase anything and showing you products you're likely to care about.

If you've ever gone to a search engine and typed "home mortgage" or "auto loan," you've probably noticed that the banner ad at the top of the page is suddenly relevant to what you're looking for. This is a form of covert personalization. The search engine and its advertising partners may not know who you are, but they know what you're interested in based on your previous behavior. Your own site can use similar, more subtle techniques to make sure that the content the visitor sees is always relevant, or at a minimum, inoffensive.

PERSONAL SHOPPERS AND SHOPPING WIZARDS

It's no longer enough simply to give your customers a search box on your home page so they can look for the products they want by keyword. Although

I wouldn't eliminate that search box for the *surgical shopper* just yet, for shoppers who come to your site to *solve a problem*, I would recommend you add a way as well to find the products that solve that problem. Sites that offer problem solving in addition to shopping will stand out above the crowd.

There are three types of shopping assistants that come readily to mind. The first is the wizard, which offers shoppers a number of options, each choice leading to an additional set of options, each selection of which eventually leads to a product. These are great for gift giving. I found a hanging candelabra for my husband's aunt and uncle at Eddie Bauer.com this way. The first question was about the amount I wanted to spend, and subsequent questions asked about the interests of the gift recipients. This wizard helped me find something unique that I would never have thought to look for in the regular Christmas inventory.

The next option is the kind of thing you find at Garden.com. You come to the site with a problem. I, for instance, need something that flowers to put in pots on my patio. The site helps you find an appropriate solution for your environment based on climate, time of year, sun/shade ratio, and so on. Begonias were the answer to my problem. I wasn't even sure what a begonia was when I first went to Garden.com.

The final option combines something I hate, natural language processing, in which the computer looks for keywords in the English query that I type, with something I love, context-sensitive assistance, in which each subsequent query is based on previous results returned or on where I am in the site. This type of guided shopping is ideal when the shopper knows the category of product he wants but doesn't know enough about the differences between products in that category to be able to devise an intelligent solution. The laptop computer is a perfect example of a product well suited to this type of tool because most people don't understand what the tradeoffs are and what all the product specifications mean. It's easier for most shoppers to indicate that they're looking for a good laptop for travel than it is for them to search by weight, not knowing how heavy or light laptops get.

ACCEPT MULTIPLE CURRENCIES AND SHIP GLOBALLY

It really is the World Wide Web. IDC estimates that by 2003, 38 percent of all online shoppers will be outside the United States. The barriers to global shipping and delivery are large, but not insurmountable. Chapter 10 takes you through the technical, operational, and logistical issues you'll need to address to do business worldwide.

REAL-TIME ACCESS TO INVENTORY AND ORDER STATUS

Shopping on the Web should be gratifying, because all the information a shopper needs to make a purchase decision is there when he is in the mood to buy. Too many sites fall down on the job of providing complete information. They may fail to tell customers when the products they're placing into their carts will ship, how long shipment to specific zip codes should be expected to take, where the products customers have ordered are in the shipping process, and even what the status of returned orders is.

Sites that answer all these questions will find that their customer-service costs go down and their repeat business goes up. Most organizations have access to this data somewhere in the bowels of their customer-service or order-management systems. Why not put the data where the customers can use it and save everyone a phone call?

INDUSTRIAL STRENGTH CONTENT-MANAGEMENT SOLUTION

Many sites rely on their own homegrown content-management systems. Some have a staff of technicians and graphic artists who actually make changes to the code (the Hypertext Markup Language, or HTML) that changes what you see when you load that site directly. Others have proprietary software that's administered from a desktop application that permits the content owners of the site—marketing, technology, public relations, or merchandising, depending on the site—to manipulate the contents of the site without having to involve technicians. Both of these solutions to keeping a site's content up-to-date have serious problems.

A forward-thinking site needs to be built around a serious content-management solution, one that's being maintained by an organization that does nothing but keep it up. Very few sites can afford the resources to put into their own content-management solutions to make them comparable to the best third-party solutions available. Sites that want to compete will bite the bullet and spend the serious dollars required to provide this kind of content-management solution.

CUSTOMER SERVICE

Customer service is typically regarded as a necessary evil. Customers demand it, but any improvements made to it come at significant cost. With the customer base on the Web growing so rapidly, few companies can afford to sustain high customer satisfaction ratings. The two most common forms of customer service are e-mail and phone support. The first is inadequate because it takes too long. The second is inappropriate because most U.S. households have only one phone line.

Part IV of this book explores the two key technologies that can turn your site into a place where your customers can see that customer service is paramount. These technologies turn the tables on the traditional customer service equation, in which more service equals more expense, by (1) providing customer-service technologies that scale with the site without incurring additional costs as more customers use them, and (2) offering service at the moment of purchase, when expensive-to-attract customers are most likely to abandon their shopping carts rather than complete their purchases.

REAL-TIME PRESALES CHAT

Real-time chat as a sales and customer support tool has definitely caught on. In September of 1999, real-time chat was almost impossible to find. Sites have realized that this form of customer support, in addition to being timely, is also cost-effective, because support representatives can assist multiple customers at once. It works because it can help you catch customers at that crucial buying moment when they've already taken the time to review your inventory and put the products they want into their shopping carts but are still deciding whether to stay and finish the purchase, whether the shipping charges are fair, and whether they think they can get a better deal elsewhere. Real-time chat is also a great tool for cross-selling customers and thus increasing order totals. Chapter 13 takes you through the technology, the business case for using this technology on your site, and the choices of vendors that can help you provide this kind of support on your site right away.

MULTICHANNEL CUSTOMER-SUPPORT SYSTEM

If you are a bricks-and-mortar store or a catalog store that's been transforming itself into a bricks-and-clicks company, then a multichannel customer-support system is specifically for you. Even if you're strictly online, listen up. Customers expect and should be able to get the same level and detail of customer support, whether it be from your Web site, your phone bank, or your bricks-and-mortar store. Such support could mean anything from accepting returns without a packing slip and knowing what the original purchase price with shipping and handling were, to being able to answer questions about the status of an order that's been placed. Every salesperson at every store needs to have access to the same customer relationship management (CRM) system that the people answering your 800 number have.

It isn't at all surprising that most bricks-and-clicks merchants don't offer this level of integrated multichannel customer support. But it's stunning that even some strictly online merchants often can't answer questions about online orders via their 800 numbers until after some unacceptable time lag. (That time lag could be as much as twenty-four hours—the time it takes for a batch process to be run at night, updating the customer service systems with information from the order-management system.)

TURNKEY GROWTH

This book is about more than just the twelve technologies that your site needs to be implementing to attract and keep customers. It is also about the underlying philosophy that will allow your site to succeed in the volatile environment of e-commerce. As I mentioned in Chapter 1, the three keys to success in e-commerce are to maintain a flexible business model, to implement the twelve technologies explained here, and to rely on third-party vendors as much as possible.

Part V of this book is about how Web sites can remain flexible enough to permit turnkey growth. It's also about the companies that will profit from providing the services that will facilitate the growth. The real money that's being made on the Web is not being made by the big-name dot-coms. It's being made by the anonymous service providers to the Web sites with the brand names and the big dollars to spend. Those much-hyped revenue figures of the major dot-com sites obscure the real problems. Most of them are losing money in any one of the following ways:

→ By spending more to acquire customers than those customers are worth

→ By selling products with too small a margin to cover expenses

→ By expanding product offerings to the point that they're not the "top of mind" providers for any one product category

In the bricks-and-mortar world, the last of these three problems wouldn't necessarily be a disadvantage, since location and convenience play a major role in shopping decisions, but either of the first two could, alone, be the death knell of any merchant.

In order to succeed long term, online merchants need to find sustainable business models through which they can capitalize on the three causes of intense online competition outlined in Chapter 1 rather than fight against them. For companies that simply can't afford the cost of competing, there are still many niches that need to be filled by those who are enterprising and inventive. In Chapter 16, you'll read about lesser-known companies that have found the right niche to remain profitable online, despite all the obstacles.

PART II

TECHNOLOGIES FOR DRIVING TRAFFIC

Acquisition 3

Search Engines FOR Customer

IT COMES as no surprise that search engines are a primary method that online shoppers and buyers alike use to find merchants. What may be surprising is that the most experienced shoppers use search engines to find products online more than others. According to Jupiter Communications, experienced shoppers turn to search engines 54 percent of the time, while other shoppers turn to search engines only 47 percent of the time.[1]

Overall, though, the number of people relying on search engines to find products has fallen from over 80 percent in 1998. It's been hovering around the 50 percent mark for more than a year, but because of the rapid growth of the Web, I would expect it to rise again, not fall, in the future, as long as the search engines do well on three fronts:

1. *Indexing sites.* It would seem that this is the primary function of search engines, but in July 1999, one study showed that no search engine indexed more than 16 percent of the Web and that all search engines

together indexed less than 42 percent of the Web? The Web is growing faster than search engines can index it. Search engines will have to ramp up their indexing efforts to avoid becoming irrelevant.

2. *Keeping search results relevant.* One problem search engines face is that some sites try to fool them. In the hope of getting traffic from errant visitors, they try to get indexed for topics unrelated to the ones they're really about. I once tried to find a listing of area codes at a search engine and found that one of the top five results returned took me to a site with Bill Clinton in bondage attire. Clearly, the site had incorporated mundane key words hoping to get indexed and found by people who weren't looking for pornography but might be pleased to stay once they found it. As long as users of search engines believe the results they get are acceptably accurate, they'll continue to use them.

3. *Keeping their content up to date.* It's often the case that the longer a site has been indexed by a search engine, the higher in the rankings it rises. This results in top listings often being over a year old, which isn't bad if the listing is for a university's home page, but it is absurd when the listing is for a classified ad offering a 386 personal computer for sale or a listing for a conference from 1997.

SEARCH ENGINES VERSUS DIRECTORIES

Search engines and directories are often conflated. In fact, they're two entirely different animals. Search engines make an effort to review, evaluate, and index all the content they come across. Directories are listings of sites by category, similar to a yellow pages directory.

Many search engines, such as Yahoo! and GO, offer both directories and search engines. Figure 3-1 shows the familiar Yahoo! site.

At Yahoo!, the key words a visitor provides search both the directory and the spidered results. The directory listing results are always displayed before the search engine listings. Yahoo! has always used its own directory listing, but has always purchased the search engine results. Now, it gets this data from Google, but it used to get it from Inktomi. If your site is listed in the Google search engine, you're likely to see it listed in Yahoo! as well.

Figure 3-1. Yahoo! offers both a search engine and a directory for finding a site. (Reproduced with permission of Yahoo! Inc. © 2000 by Yahoo! Inc. YAHOO! and the YAHOO! logo are trademarks of Yahoo! Inc.)

SEARCH ENGINES

Search engines find sites to index in two ways. They either find a link from a site and follow it to a new site, which they index, or they receive a link submitted to their site through their link submission system. Then, eventually, they point their spider to that link, index the contents, and make that material available to visitors. An excellent way to have a search engine spider and index more than one page is to submit a Web page comprising only links to your site, rather than submitting the URL of each page individually.

There are variations on search engines. Although most index for content, some also index for popularity. Google, for example, weights search results by the number of links it finds *to a site* elsewhere on the Web. DirectHit weights a site more highly if more people who type a particular keyword click on that result when it appears in the results list.

Because links to your site often can increase the ranking of your site, you will get better rankings if you "inbreed" your site, i.e., put links on all the pages in your site to all the other pages in the site. It is also a good idea

to set up auxiliary domains—other domains you've purchased for the purpose of increasing the link popularity of your site—from which you can
link to your main domains. If you have more than one site, be sure to provide links both ways so that search engines will give you lots of credit for
being popular.

Partnerships Matter

It's particularly true in the search engine space that partnerships
between the search engines and the directories matter to you. The
most comprehensive listing of search engine partnerships that I've
found is available at the Search Engine Watch site (http://www.
searchenginewatch.com/reports/alliances.html). When you're submitting your URL to the search engines and directories for listing, it's
important that you know who's sharing results with whom so you
can submit only either to the main search engine that's doing the
sharing or to the one that spiders most quickly. That's so you can see
results quickly. For example, on America Online, NetFind uses
Inktomi for the search engine results and Open Directory for the
directory listing.

DIRECTORIES

Directories are usually maintained by real people. Every site submitted is
visited and reviewed by an editor who determines whether the site should
be included, and if so, in what category. Directories tend to contain more-
limited collections of sites, but because they're categorized logically, it's
often faster to find a relevant site using a directory than using a search
engine. You can even become a volunteer editor with some directories,
which may be to your advantage, because editors get to decide which sites
get listed.[3] Be aware that editors have been known to discriminate against
their competitors, even though the practice is discouraged by the directory. If you find your site isn't getting listed in a category where it legitimately fits, there may be an appeals process for the directory that you can
pursue. You can also try contacting the editor directly, if the directory provides an e-mail address for the editor. I don't suggest complaining, but it

might not hurt to ask what you need to change about your site to get it listed where it belongs.

The newest major directory project underway is the Open Directory Project (www.dmoz.org), which is the common man's answer to the fact that getting listed in Yahoo!'s directory has not always been easy. In the early days of the Web, getting in a directory was like getting your face in your high school yearbook—only those on the yearbook committee and their friends ever seemed to make it. With the Open Directory Project, a site that submits itself to the appropriate category has an excellent chance of being listed for that category. Then the data is supplied to search engines that have contracted for it, such as AltaVista, InfoSpace, Lycos, Netscape, and others, to use for their directory results.

Regardless of how you decide to handle making sure your site is indexed by search engines, you must make sure you're in the major directories, for example, the Open Directory Project.

NATURAL LANGUAGE DIRECTORIES. In addition to directories that organize material based on the category into which the site falls, there's another type of human-indexed directory. That's the type provided by Ask Jeeves. Ask Jeeves has editors who will visit a site to see if the content of the site is appropriate to answer the types of questions they receive on their site. If so, the content will be indexed in order to be retrieved when visitors to Ask Jeeves ask relevant questions, such as, "Where can I find a recipe for California Wrapples?" Most of the answers provided that end up getting indexed are on sites that have advertising deals with Ask Jeeves, so don't be too discouraged if your site doesn't end up being included.

FREE LISTING VERSUS PAID LISTINGS

When it comes to search engines, there are basically three ways to get listed: on merit, by paying for relevancy (see below), or by buying enough ad space on the search engine. The first two ways are the ones that are most commonly discussed. The third is less well known. Most search engines will formally deny that they do this, until you start discussing million-dollar ad deals with them, at which point they'll start assuring you of superior placement in their search results. Knowing this can help you decide to place more ads with one popular site rather than distributing your money over multiple sites.

PAYING FOR RELEVANCY. GoTo, LookSmart, and Ah-ha all have a great model for a search engine and an easily understood model for a merchant site. Each month, sites bid on keywords. For that month, the sites that bid the most will always be listed above other sites. After all paying sites are listed, nonpaying sites will be listed in order of relevancy (usually with the listings provided by some other source, like Inktomi, Google, or Fast). In my experience, these sites offer very accurate search results for product searches because even if sites are only bidding $.01 or $.05 per clickthrough, they're still investing in certain keywords that they believe people interested in their products will type.

In order for the paid-listing model to work for a site, that site must have good control over its own traffic data, and it must be able to track each visitor who comes through it all the way through the sale. These search engines will provide clickthrough statistics for the merchant, but the merchant will need to know the conversion rate of clickthroughs to sales in order to determine the true acquisition cost of each customer. The only way to know how effective one advertising method is (and that's what a paid listing on a search engine is) compared to another is to calculate the cost of acquisition of customers, and eventually to calculate the value of a customer in terms of the order size and the number of additional purchases the customer makes after the initial visit.

Competitors have been known to click through the same paid link repeatedly, just to drain the account of the site that's bid the highest, or to send spiders to the site repeatedly to click through all the paid links of their competitors. They do this, knowing that each click costs their competitors hard marketing dollars, and hoping to reduce the effectiveness of that search engine for their competitors so they won't bid as much in the subsequent month. This is a difficult problem to track and even more difficult to avoid. People and spiders can come to these paid-relevancy search engines from services like AOL, with dynamically assigned IP addresses or proxy server addresses with their cookies turned off, so you can't trace them. The result is that it's very difficult to prove this kind of misconduct. In the end, all you can do is be smart and monitor your own conversion rates closely to be sure that you're paying for sales and not just for clicks.

TRACKING CLICKS, CUSTOMERS, AND SALES

No matter which technique you use to attract customers to your site, you need steady data about which methods are working and how to make changes to the less productive methods to make them more productive. Two kinds of data will be valuable to you: clickthrough rates and conversion rates. Clickthrough rates tell you how many people were attracted to your listing on another site and came to your site as a result of it. Conversion rates show the ratio between clickthroughs and purchases. You'll also want to measure the average basket size for each type of link (each search engine or directory), so you know where you're finding the best customers. If you're paying more per clickthrough at one site, and the conversion rate is lower but the average basket size is higher, it might be a good trade-off.

You should also measure customer loyalty. Which sites give you customers who will return on their own or in response to targeted mailings that you send them once they're in your customer base?

Submitting Your URL

In the good old days, someone from a site's marketing department or the site owner personally would go to each major search engine and submit his URL as instructed at that site. He wouldn't have taken any great pains to make his site search engine friendly, just visitor friendly. The search engine would, often within a week or two, send a spider to the site to index the text and add it to its own pool of searchable content. Finally, a visitor to the search engine would type in keywords and get a list of sites that happened to match. The results might include the Web site that innocently submitted itself.

SUBMISSION

The submission process was, and usually still is, easy enough. Most search engines and directories have a link on their home page (or on the category pages, when they accept category-specific submissions) to a page that explains the rules for submissions. Usually, you can type in the URL of your site or of all the pages in your site, or you can purchase software or write software that will submit your links in bulk. Most search engine experts believe that submissions by hand, i.e., by a person rather than via bulk submission software, receive priority attention, and some even contend that automated submissions to some engines are ignored or counted against you.

Most search engines restrict the number of pages you can submit for a given URL in any twenty-four-hour period. Directories generally only want to list your home page.

SPIDERS

Spiders are the computer programs that accept a list of URLs as input and collect the material on those sites for indexing. Most spiders follow links around your site and off your site. Spiders can typically be set to index only the page they've been given, to follow all links on a page, or to follow all links for a certain number of levels deep.

After the spiders harvest all the data from Web pages, indexing programs file the material away in a way that's easy to access again later. Because spiders and indexes can't keep up with the pace at which Web sites change and new ones are added, indexes are almost always out of date, containing at least some dead links or links to pages that no longer have keywords for which they're indexed.

Even though there's usually a two- to six-week delay between when you submit your site to a search engine and when the search engine gets around to spidering it, do not submit a URL for a site that doesn't exist yet. Search engines will not return to your site to see whether the site's there yet. Wait until the site is up before you submit the site for indexing.

SHENANIGANS

Not long after the search engines were created, site marketers realized that certain keywords were far more popular than others. They even noticed that certain keywords were more popular than the keywords that were appropriate to their own sites. Some site marketers started to play games with their sites to try to fool the search engines into ranking those sites more highly. Those shenanigans include the following:

→ Listing irrelevant but popular keywords on the site's pages using white-on-white (or black-on-black) text to fool the indexing software into believing that the page is really about that topic. An example would be including the word *sex* as a keyword, thinking that it is one of the most-searched-for keywords, in the hope that the site would get errant traffic that way (as if people who were looking for sex sites want to detour through home electronics sites—or any other sites for that matter).

→ Repeating the same keyword in the keyword list a number of times, because it appears that the search engines rank a site more highly the more times the same word appears in the keyword list.

→ Listing either relevant or irrelevant-but-popular keywords on their pages using white-on-white (or black-on-black) text, either to spoof the indexing software into believing that the page is really about that subject or to receive a higher ranking for those words than the actual contents of the page would merit.

→ Using a search engine spoofing technique such as "fast meta-refresh" to show any spiders one page while showing regular browsers an entirely different page.

Just Enough Tech Background

Without giving you a course in HTML, for which I recommend *The HTML 4 Bible*, by Bryan Pfaffenberger and me, a few HTML-based techniques should be presented so that you understand why other sites outrank yours. All you need to do is look at the HTML source of a competitor's page to see what it has done.

Keywords

Keywords are an optional part of a Web page. By putting keywords in your page, you can tell search engines and intelligent agents what your page is about. Keywords are listed in the META tag, which appears in the HEAD of the HTML document (only content listed in the BODY of HTML document appears on the Web page, with the exception of the contents of the TITLE tag, which appears in the title bar of the browser). The META tag format for keywords is:

```
<META name="keywords" content="keyword1,
keyword2, keyword3, keyword4, keyword5, etc.">
```

Fast Meta-Refresh

A META tag can also be used to force the page to refresh at some certain pace, based on the content parameter. This tag can be used legitimately to redirect visitors from an obsolete page to a current page or to automatically reroute a visitor after seeing an ad or presentation after a certain number of seconds. It can also be used to spoof search engines. Spiders will see and index the contents of the page on which the META tag appears, but visitors will automatically be rerouted to the real page of the site, so what gets indexed won't be the real site pages. The following tag will reroute your page to the Over the Web home page without ever letting visitors see your home page:

```
<META http-equiv="Refresh" content="0;
http://www.overtheweb.com/index.html">
```

White-on-White Text

To produce invisible text, use the following font tag, which will work on almost all browsers even though it doesn't conform to the latest HTML standards. If your background is also set to white, the text will be invisible to your eyes but spiders will find it:

```
<FONT color="white">keyword1, keyword2,
keyword3, etc.</FONT>
```

How It Works Today

As a result of the gimmicks that some Web site marketers have used in the past, most of the tricks outlined above as shenanigans will get a site that uses them banned from the search engines. You might still find indexed sites that use white-on-white text, but any new sites that attempt that technique of spoofing the search engine are likely to be banned.

Today, the search engines are crowded with many merchants competing for what they believe to be the most valuable keywords. Rarely does a site simply create a visitor-friendly page, submit the URL to the search engines, and find itself in the top twenty results for its keywords. There are, however, techniques that Web sites can use to increase their chances of showing up in the right results.

WINNING STRATEGIES

You can do a number of simple things to make your site search engine friendly. You should definitely do as many of these as you can, because they are relatively uninvolved and can result in substantially higher rankings for your pages. There are also some technically sophisticated things that you can do, which can cost you quite a bit in terms of manpower, but in highly competitive keyword categories, taking these steps might be necessary.

The first thing to remember about search engine positioning is that the reason to get a high ranking is *to increase qualified traffic to your site.* This fact is often overlooked. There's no reward for a high ranking if no one clicks on your listing, even when it is in the top fifteen, or if your site is only near the top for keywords so obscure that no one enters them. The name of the game is *qualified traffic.* You want to catch shoppers when they're finally ready to buy. Most people clicking around search engines are still in the information-gathering stage. Although you would prefer that customers visit your site for information rather than your competitors' sites, you definitely want them to visit your site first when they've got their credit cards out and are ready to buy.

SELECTING THE RIGHT KEYWORDS

Who is closer to being ready to buy, a search engine visitor who types "computers" or one who types "Pentium III"? How about a visitor who types "cell phones" or one who types "Samsung 3500" (one model of cell phone)? If the amount the merchant sites are paying to appear at the top of the list of results is any indication, merchants must think that "computers" is more valuable than "Pentium III," because in April of 2000, the highest bidder at GoTo.com was paying $3.00 for "computers" and only $.62 for "Pentium III." The cell phone example is even more telling, with "cell phones" going for $1.38 and "Samsung 3500" going for only $.03. Yet, most salespeople will tell you that the customer with the model number or some of the product specifications is probably closer to buying than the one who only knows the broad name of the product.

By selecting the more precise keywords, you can spend less money on the pay-per-click search engines and less time on the free search engines to be ranked highly. It's more work for you to have keywords appropriate to each of your products (and keeping them current is more work still), but because the name of the game is being found by qualified customers, anything else may be a waste of your time and money.

GoTo.com has a Search Term Suggestions page that helps you find appropriate keyword phrases based on those entered by GoTo.com visitors in the past month. You can find it at http://inventory.go2.com/inventory/ Search_Suggestion.jhtml. The good thing about selecting keyword expressions that have been frequently requested is that you'll see a lot of traffic if you ultimately achieve a high ranking. The bad news is that there will be more competition to be ranked highly and the traffic you see won't necessarily be the most qualified.

MONITORING RESULTS

There are two ways to know how your site is doing in the major search engines: by monitoring rankings, which can tell you what number you are on each engine, or by monitoring traffic, which can tell you how many visitors are coming to your site from each search engine. I recommend you do both. It's a good idea to know how your site ranks at the top dozen or so search engines. The ones that are your top dozen will be different if you expect a substantial portion of your traffic to come from outside the United States, in which case you need to identify the leading search engines or portals for each country or region from which your traffic will be coming. There are a couple of good tools that you can use to ascertain your rankings, but neither one is what I would consider industrial strength. It's surprising that there is a gap in the software currently available for checking rankings. Perhaps one of you readers will evaluate the tools on your own and write industrial-strength search engine–ranking monitoring software. There are also several ASPs that will monitor your rankings for you and notify you daily of how you're doing.

As far as monitoring traffic goes, it's not very difficult to use a commercially available Web log-file analysis package to track the visitors coming in from the various search engines, once you determine the IP addresses of the search engines.

It's important to know both how you rank and how much traffic your rankings are garnering. If, for example, your site is ranked high but the traffic you're getting doesn't result in sales, you might be ranked for the wrong things. If the descriptive paragraph that accompanies your listings isn't catchy enough, you might not be drawing enough traffic, even when your site ranks well on the list of results.

MONITORING RANKINGS. The most popular commercially available software packages for monitoring search engine rankings are WebPosition Gold and TopDog Search Engine Analyzer/Submitter. Both allow you to provide your site URL (or URLs, if you have more than one URL for the same site) and the keywords on which you want to be ranked and select the search engines you want them to check. In the case of TopDog, the list of search engines includes many international search engines, whereas with WebPosition Gold, the list is limited to the top ten U.S. search engines. So choose your software accordingly. Each program checks the search engines to see how your site ranks, and it creates a professional report at whatever interval you specify. With both tools, you can schedule the monitoring tool to run when you're away from your computer, so it won't tie up your Internet connection when you need it. If your list of keywords is long, these processes can run for hours, so being able to schedule the sessions is a valuable feature. Figure 3-2 shows a sample report created by WebPosition Gold.

For some sites it might be useful to hire an ASP to run these reports for you and then e-mail you the results. Disappointingly, most ASPs use either WebPosition Gold or TopDog, so the premium you pay is only for them running the report, not for access to superior results. Before you contract with an ASP, ask which tools it uses to create its reports. (Then compare the sample reports it produces to the one in Figure 3-2 to see if it's the same.) I would pay a premium for something on top of what I can get from these two packages, but no one has yet been enterprising enough to offer such a service.

The packages can track your competitors' sites, and WebPosition Gold will even tell you how you can make changes to your pages to make them more competitive with those that rank better. If used vigilantly, these tools can give you the information you need to keep your site highly ranked on all the major search engines. They can't, however, tell you whether anyone finds your search engine listings compelling enough to click on.

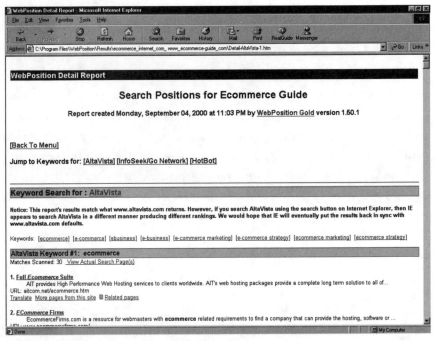

Figure 3-2. A sample report created by WebPosition Gold.

MONITORING TRAFFIC. Perhaps more telling than your search engine rankings is what kind of traffic you're seeing from your listings on search engines. It's true that a site ranked 300 for a particular keyword is unlikely to see much traffic on account of that keyword. (The general rule is that your site must be listed in the first page and a half of results listings for a keyword, which means it must rank between one and fifteen if the search engine lists ten results per page or between one and thirty if the search engine lists twenty results per page.) But a site ranked first for a keyword will not necessarily get more traffic than one ranked fifth for the same keyword. Visitors to search engines read the descriptive paragraphs that accompany the links to determine which sites to visit.

Unfortunately, you often have no control over what text from your pages the search engine chooses to use for that descriptive paragraph. Search engines use different algorithms to select text out of your page. So if you want your page to show up with the right descriptive text on ten different search engines, you might have to write and submit ten different pages, each to the appropriate engine, to achieve the descriptive text you want. Some automatically use the first 100 or so characters of text off your page, even if it includes useless navigational information. If your page contains frames, then the search engine will try to use whatever you put in the <NOFRAMES> tag—even if it's only the copyright statement—as the descriptive text!

Part of the function of the reports produced by the tools mentioned above (and by other tools not mentioned) is to show you how your listing looks on the different search engines on which it's found. So in addition to how well it ranks, look and see how your listing looks.

You should be able to use traffic log files from your Web server, filtered through a traffic analysis tool (see the list of resources at the end of this chapter), to ascertain what percentage of your traffic is coming from search engines. If you're doing your job right, you'll notice that based on modifications you make to your site, traffic from search engines increases as your rankings rise. If you don't see any increase in traffic as you get your rankings to rise into the numbers that visitors review, then consider trying to get ranked for different keywords, or try changing the descriptive text that the search engines are picking up to make your site more compelling.

SUBMITTING YOUR SITE

When you first purchase a new domain name, you'll find that you're bombarded by offers from "Web site visibility" companies that claim to get your site submitted to 700 or more search engines for $49.95 or so. There are a few things you need to know about submitting your site to search engines. The first is that most search engine traffic is going through the top twelve search engines.[4] Although this list changes from time to time, it's been stable for a while:

1. Yahoo!

2. Microsoft Network (MSN)

3. Lycos

4. Netscape

5. Go (Infoseek)

6. Excite

7. AltaVista

8. Snap

9. Looksmart

10. Ask Jeeves

11. GoTo

12. iWon

The second thing to realize about submitting your site is that most search engines have limits on the number of pages from any given domain that can be submitted in a day. Before you submit to a search engine, read the rules. If you submit more than you're allowed in any given day, even if you've never submitted before, you run the risk of having all submissions from your domain discarded. This practice is referred to as "spamming" a search engine, and in the most egregious cases, it can get you banned from the search engine.

The third thing you need to know about submitting your site is that although most sites will accept URLs submitted by automated software or "by hand" (meaning that the URL is typed directly into the "recommend this site" box on the Web site), most experts believe that sites submitted by hand receive better positioning than those that are submitted automatically. Finally, some companies will offer to resubmit your site with great frequency, and some Web site marketers believe that the more frequently they submit their sites, the better. You don't want to submit your site any more often than necessary. How often is that? If your site slips in the rankings and you have to make modifications to it to get it ranked higher, then resubmit your site to the search engines on which it slipped. In the case of some search engines, however, seniority seems to count for something. Some search engines routinely rank older pages above newer pages, which means that resubmitting will guarantee you're always the new kid on the block! Resubmit with caution, and only when you have reason to think you need to.

WHAT ABOUT YAHOO!'S BUSINESS EXPRESS SERVICE?

For $199, you can have your submission to Yahoo! bumped up the list of those in the queue to be reviewed and spidered. The URL is http://docs.

yahoo.com/info/suggest/busexpress.html. Yahoo! guarantees that your site will be visited within seven business days. Is this service worth it? From all the experts I have asked, the answer is a resounding "yes." Use of this service can result in your site being included in the directory when it otherwise might not have been, and having higher rankings than might otherwise be expected. Of course, it's impossible to do a double-blind study, but every reputable search engine placement firm I spoke with told me that they use the service because it achieves superior results.

SHADOW SITES

The best way to have your site ranked highly for your selected keywords is to design it from the outset for search engine appeal. Realistically, however, no one builds a site this way—the first time, at least, because getting customers is the primary concern. Be aware, however, that if your pages aren't specific enough, they're liable to be ranked lower for the keywords you care about. For example, if you want to be found for "teenage drivers," you need to be sure you have a "teenage driver" page and submit it to all the search engines. Your site already has many demands on it to load quickly, have content updated frequently, be easily navigated, and implement most of the other technologies mentioned in this book, so expecting it to be search engine–friendly is probably asking too much.

The obvious answer is to build one site for human visitors and another for spiders. But how? By making use of *agent-detection algorithms,* you can show search engines one site and everyone else a different site. Because your site is probably not static HTML anyway, your servers are probably doing some work creating the material that appears in the browser or to the spider at the time the page is requested. If you're using any kind of personalization on the site (see Chapter 8), the server is definitely creating pages dynamically. As mentioned in Chapter 2, your Web server is already logging the IP address of every visitor, human or otherwise, coming to your site. You can make use of this information to show search engines (at least those whose spiders have known IP addresses) a search engine–friendly site, then let everyone else simply see your regular site. You should base identification of a spider on the *footprint* (the user agent) the spider leaves in your log file, and the IP address, when possible.

If you can't do both, trust the IP address, since the footprint may change. A list of IP addresses and footprints of known search engine spiders can be found at http://www.jafsoft.com/misc/opinion/webbots.html. A database of essentially the same material can be found at http://info.webcrawler.com/mak/projects/robots/active/html/contact.html.

You can also subscribe to services that will provide the spider footprints and IP addresses to you in digital format on a regular basis. It's important that you keep your list up-to-date to ensure that no humans are seeing the search engine version of your site and that no major search engines are seeing the human version.

The important thing about using a shadow site is that you have to use *server-side processing*, meaning that the page the spider sees has to be generated by your server and cannot include a fast meta-refresh (as described above in the sidebar entitled "Just Enough Tech Background") to send either the spider or visitors to a different site. The pages in the shadow site must have the same names as those in the regular site, too. Otherwise, visitors will be sent to nonexistent pages when they click on a link at the search engine.

KEEPING YOUR SHADOW SITE SHALLOW. Most search engines don't spider more than three to four levels deep in your site. If you submit your root URL (e.g., www.overtheweb.com), then you would want every page in your site to be within two or three links of it. If you have a very vertical site or shadow site, with content-rich pages at the end of a chain of several index pages, then you run the risk of not having the "meat" of your site indexed. Figures 3-3 and 3-4 show a typical site map and a flattened shadow site map, respectively. Notice that if a search engine only spiders three levels deep into the typical site, most of the content-rich pages will be left out of the search engine. With the flattened site, the entire site would get indexed.

AVOID CGI PARAMETERS

Even if you don't know what CGI is (common gateway interface) or what CGI parameters are, chances are you've seen them. CGI parameters are those extra characters that are appended to the end of a URL by some sites, ironically, including search engines. CGI parameters are a way of passing data about you from one page on a site to another. If you go to www.yahoo.com,

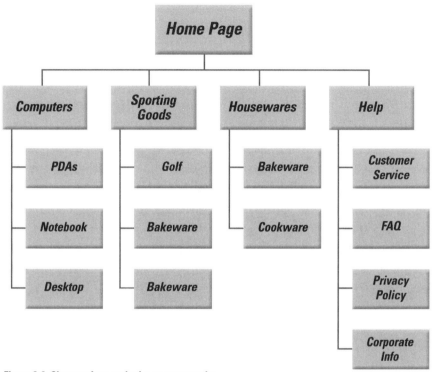

Figure 3-3. Site map for a typical e-commerce site.

for example, and enter "sleep deprivation" as the search term, the URL on the next page will be search.yahoo.com/bin/search?p=sleep+deprivation. Notice the *p=sleep+deprivation* tacked onto the end of the URL. That's a CGI parameter.

On the Web, developers generally have three ways to pass data entered by the visitor or about the visitor from one page to the next:

1. By storing the data in a "cookie," which is ineffective if the visitor has cookies disabled (but only 3 percent of Web visitors have cookies turned off)

2. By sending the data as part of the header of the Web page using a *post*, which means the data is invisible to the visitor

3. By sending the data as part of the URL using a *get*

The third method, which puts the data into the URL, is the most reliable and is easier to use than the second one. The first method is the easiest one to use, but because it doesn't work when visitors have cookies disabled, it's not as reliable.

Search engines (with the notable exception of Lycos) don't spider pages with CGI parameters in the URL. Many e-commerce sites have only one product page, meaning one page of HTML that's produced when a visitor wants to see the details of a product. That page gets populated with the details of each different product in the catalog, depending on what data is passed in the URL. For example, www.overtheweb.com/product.cfm?prod_id=101 might be a toaster oven, but www.overtheweb.com/product.cfm?prod_id=201 might be scented candles. Note that the page name (product.cfm) is the same, but what the visitor sees depends on the value of the CGI parameter *prod_id*. In the case of this e-commerce site, none of the product information would get spidered by most search engines because all links to these pages would include the CGI parameters; thus they would never be followed by the spiders.

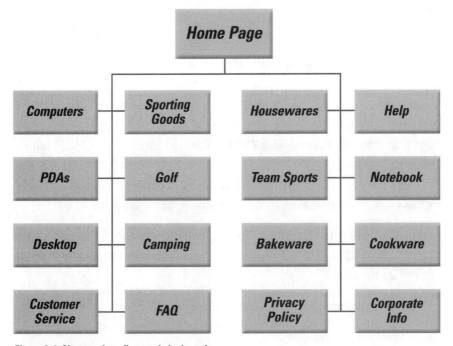

Figure 3-4. Site map for a flattened shadow site.

Because you probably can't revise your site design to eliminate the need to pass data between pages via the URL (using CGI parameters), you can get around this problem by creating a nearly flat shadow site, as shown in Figure 3-4.

KEEP THE SITE LIGHT ON IMAGES AND RICH IN TEXT

Search engines don't see images. What they do see is links to images, which in HTML are conveyed in the IMG tag. For example, in HTML the following code places an image in your page:

```
<IMG src="pics/toaster-oven.gif" alt="DeLonghi
toaster oven" text="DeLonghi toaster oven"
width="300" height="200">
```

The search engine will never see this image, but depending on the search engine's algorithms, the page that contains this code might get weighted more highly for DeLonghi toaster ovens. It would do so because the search engine, reading the file name in the *src* parameter and the description in the *alt* and *text* parameters, believes that this image shows a toaster oven. The *height* and *width* parameters are optional, but they tell the browser how much room to set aside for the image, when it does load.

Search engines give you credit for images they believe to be on your pages. You can use this fact to get your site more heavily weighted for your keywords without actually using any images. This nice little trick—which won't get you into any trouble, by the way—can be accomplished by using *clear GIFs*. Clear GIFs are usually one-pixel by one-pixel images (a pixel being the smallest footprint of real estate on the screen). They don't contain any color; hence the modifier "clear." If you create a one-by-one pixel clear GIF and name it *toaster-oven.gif*, then the following code will lead a search engine to believe that you have an image of a toaster oven or a DeLonghi toaster oven on your page:

```
<IMG src="pics/toaster-oven.gif" alt="DeLonghi
toaster oven" text="DeLonghi toaster oven">
```

Notice that the height and width parameters have been left off. If you include them as 1 and 1, then the search engine will know this isn't a real image of a toaster oven. If you leave them off, it won't know and it won't penalize you, because sites often leave image dimensions out of the code for legitimate reasons.

LINKING FROM CLEAR GIFS

To make your shadow site (or even your regular site) appear to be even more relevant for the keywords you want to be ranked for, consider making each of your images link to other relevant content. Of course, the relevant content to which you link has to exist, or the search engine may grade you down for having broken links, but the following code can turn an image that doesn't exist (to the naked eye) to a link (which also doesn't exist to the naked eye):

```
<A href="delonghi-toaster-ovens.html"
alt="DeLonghi Toaster Ovens" text="DeLonghi
Toaster Ovens"><IMG src="pics/toaster-
oven.gif" alt="DeLonghi toaster oven"
text="DeLonghi toaster oven"></A>
```

These kinds of tactics may appear to be a hassle, but once built into your shadow site, they can do a lot to increase the relevance of your pages for the keywords on which you want to be found. The competition in some categories is very intense and every little bit helps.

MAINTAIN THE SITE

There's an old adage in systems development that development is 10 percent and maintenance is 90 percent of the cost and effort of a project. The same is definitely true in Web site positioning. Putting up a search engine–friendly site or a shadow site is only the tip of the iceberg when it comes to the work that's required to get and keep a good ranking. The three keys to staying on top are monitoring your positions and traffic, modifying your pages as necessary, and resubmitting as required. Search engines aren't static. The rules that they use to decide which pages rank first change. Their partnerships change. You need to plan to invest adequate human resources into staying on top of the game. It's not out of the question for you to do this in house; it's just more of a burden than most companies are willing to bear in the long run.

OUTSOURCING YOUR WEB POSITIONING

Unless you have a significant information technology and marketing staff to monitor both your site's rankings and the changes the search engines are making to their ranking algorithms, it might be worth it for you to consider hiring experts to get and keep you ranked. There are many companies eager to help you achieve success in the competition for search engine rankings. Before you sign up with any of them, review the strategies above to see which are most appropriate for you, then find a company that uses them. Although many legitimate companies offer these services, there are also a number that offer very little value to your site. If you choose to hire someone to get you ranked, be sure that you're spending your money with the right company.

PAYING FOR RANKINGS VERSUS PAYING FOR TRAFFIC

There are three models that are most commonly used by Web positioning companies to determine how you're going to be charged. They are flat fee, paying for rankings, and paying for traffic. In the flat-fee scenario, you promise to pay a set fee to have your site either optimized for search engines and submitted, just optimized, or just submitted. The Web positioning company promises to take certain actions to get you listed, but your payment isn't contingent on their performance. Because making your site search engine–friendly is the real work, if you hire someone just to submit you, make sure that you're getting ongoing submission, then tracking and resubmission of your pages as necessary. Don't pay just to be listed in 700 search engines, because they're not all getting traffic. Make sure your submissions are being made by hand, because that matters. If a company you're talking with won't discuss these issues with you, find a different one. Definitely don't confuse a service in which you enter your URL, pay $50, and click "Submit" with a solution to your needs.

In the paying-for-rankings model, you provide a retainer, and the positioning company makes an effort to get you ranked—usually through some combination of site optimization, doorway pages (pages on your site that are optimized for search engines and discuss individual products, then link to your regular pages), and frequent submission. Any time your listing appears in the top ten (for example), you are billed a set amount. If your listing appears in the top twenty, the amount is lower. In this scenario, the positioning company is motivated to get you ranked, but not necessarily for the right keywords. Also, the positioning company is motivated to check listings with great frequency, because positioning varies from hour to hour on most search engines, and even from one part of the country to another. Be sure you understand what you're getting from this kind of arrangement, how long your site has to remain listed, and how often the Web positioning company will check the search engines for your position. You should also be sure that you're getting frequent reports.

In the paying-for-traffic scenario, the Web positioning company charges you only when a prospective customer clicks on your link in a search engine result. Make sure, however, that you don't pay for traffic from spiders. Usually in this type of arrangement, the Web positioning company builds the shadow site for you and all traffic is routed through that site. The Web-positioning company also does maintenance so that you keep seeing traffic even as the search engine rules and algorithms change. Be sure you're getting good reports from both the Web positioning company and *your own internal sources* to make sure that the traffic the Web positioning company attributes to its listings for your site on the search engines really is coming from its listings. Ideally, you'd also have some reports of the conversion rate of visitors who do click on their links in the search engines to see what your cost of acquisition comes out to based on the conversion rate and the per-click rate you're paying.

RESOURCES

NEWSLETTERS AND SITES WORTH READING AND VISITING

There are many newsletters and sites dedicated to getting found on search engines. The three I list here are the three I've found to be of consistently high quality and felicitously devoid of hype. Also, these three don't spend a lot of energy selling you on any particular solution to your various needs, so they're not long-running ads full of testimonials as some newsletters are. There are almost certainly other valuable sources of information, so don't discount other sources, if you come across them.

> *MarketPosition (www.marketposition.com).* This newsletter is published by the same company that makes WebPosition Gold, the search engine monitoring software. This free monthly newsletter is extremely valuable for keeping you up-to-date with changes to search engine policies and algorithms. This site also has a forum for asking questions of others in this field. It is called MarketPositionTalk. It's a great place to get specific questions answered.

> *SearchEngineWatch (www.searchenginewatch.com).* Danny Sullivan, the renowned expert on search engine positioning runs this site and writes the newsletter. There's a free monthly newsletter and a subscription newsletter that comes out twice monthly. The subscription includes access to the subscription-only resources on the site.

> *SearchEngineWorld (www.searchengineworld.com).* This site publishes a quarterly newsletter and has valuable articles and news about the search engine industry.

FULL-SERVICE WEB SITE PROMOTION COMPANIES

There are more of these types of companies than would fit in this book—even if it were a yellow pages directory devoted exclusively to them. I've selected a handful based on my own personal experiences and contacts. If you need to get started tomorrow, call one of these. Otherwise, ask your own contacts whom they recommend. I will add that my contacts at several of these companies have been valuable resources in reviewing my material for this chapter. To find a relatively comprehensive list of companies that offer these services, go to ***http://dmoz.org/Computers/Internet/ Commercial_Services/Internet_Marketing/Marketing_Services/***.

> *ROIDirect (www.roidirect.com).* Offers search engines positioning as part of a comprehensive suite of tools.

> *WebSiteResults (www.websiteresults.com).* Creates shadow sites and charges for traffic.

SOFTWARE FOR MONITORING YOUR RANKINGS

TopDog Search Engine Analyzer/Submitter (www.topdogg.com). Does not include as many features as WebPosition Gold, but it lets you track your URL at a much greater number of search engines.

WebPosition Gold (www.firstplacesoftware.com). An excellent tool for keeping tabs on where your site is ranked for a variety of keywords. A limited-function trial version is available for download.

ANALYZING TRAFFIC WITH SOFTWARE

The purpose of going to such great lengths in pursuit of search engine rankings is to get many highly qualified visitors. The only way to know whether your efforts are being rewarded is to look at your traffic and see how much you're getting and from where. As with every list in this book, this one is incomplete. Your IT department or Web Presence Provider may well have traffic analysis tools it uses already.

NetTracker Pro (www.sane.com). NetTracker Pro doesn't read the log files, which are plain text; instead, it reads its own database, which is faster to access. The reports can be created and accessed from any Web browser.

WebTrends (www.webtrends.com). WebTrends was one of the first companies offering log analysis software. Its reports are easy to create and easy to read.

LETTING AN ASP ANALYZE YOUR TRAFFIC

Letting an ASP analyze your traffic might be a good move. Two ASPs that offer this service are listed below.

NetAcumen (www.netacumen.com). This ASP relies on log files and other sources of data to compile a complete shopping profile on your customers.

WebSideStory (www.websidestory.com). This ASP merges data from your log files with data it collects elsewhere about your customers to create a multidimensional picture of your customers' shopping habits.

Viral Affiliates Programs 4

AN AFFILIATES program is the online version of "you scratch my back, I'll scratch yours." A viral marketing program is the online version of a personal recommendation for a product or service. Smart sites will take advantage of their existing satisfied customer base to attract new customers by giving their customers some form of on-site currency, coupon, or discount for each new customer they refer. By limiting the compensation to on-site currency, a coupon, or discount, the site is assured of enlisting only actual buyers in their ranks of referrers.

COST OF ACQUISITION

Cost of customer acquisition has been the death knell of many dot-coms. The old marketing adage, "I know that half my marketing dollars are wasted; I just don't know which half," could be expressed more accurately as, "I know that 90 percent of my marketing budget is wasted; I just don't know which 10 percent isn't."

Of course, the cost of acquiring a customer varies by industry, with financial services companies facing the steepest costs and companies selling commodities the lowest. The average cost of acquisition of a new customer is higher for pure play dot-coms, lower for multichannel operators, such as catalog-and-click merchants, bricks-and-clicks merchants, or catalog bricks-and-clicks merchants. According to *The McKinsey Quarterly*, in 2000, customer acquisition costs for online retailers range from $50 to $100.[1]

The same report showed that on average, gross income from a new customer was only $24.50 in the first quarter and $52.50 in each subsequent quarter she remained a customer. Consequently, it takes more than five quarters of customer loyalty to pay for the cost of acquiring a customer. To make matters worse, only 30 percent of customers become repeat customers. The data are grim but clearly expose the only path to profitability: lower acquisition costs and increase customer loyalty.[2]

Viral affiliate programs are the least expensive method of acquiring a new customer. Banner ads are the most expensive method.

AFFILIATE PROGRAMS

Affiliate programs are almost as old as the Web itself. The way an affiliate program works is that affiliates enroll with a merchant and are assigned an identification number. Then the affiliates, all of whom have their own Web sites or Web pages, place links on their pages to the merchant's site. The links can be either text links or graphic links. If the links are graphic links, then the images usually reside on the merchant's server, so the merchant is better able to keep them up to date than if the affiliates were to download the images to their own servers. The links to the merchant site include the affiliate ID tacked onto the end of the URL as a CGI parameter. (See Chapter 3 for more information about CGI parameters.)

When a customer clicks through an affiliate link to a merchant site, the customer is tagged with the affiliate ID, so the merchant can track how many customers clicked on the links of that affiliate, how many purchases were made, and specifically, what was purchased. On a regular basis, the merchant reports back to its affiliates how many clickthroughs they had, how many products were ordered, what was ordered, and so on. Commission is paid to the affiliate for the customer referrals based on this data.

WHY THEY WORK

Affiliate programs work for the merchant because the merchant only pays for buyers, not for lookers. Affiliates bear the cost of attracting traffic to their own sites. If done properly, an affiliate program doesn't cost the merchant much more if it has 10,000 affiliates than if it has only one.

Affiliate programs also work for the merchant because unlike in the world of atoms, in the world of bits it's possible to display a product in thousands or millions of places concurrently without ever losing possession of the product. It's in a merchant's interest to have his wares on display as many places as possible. No matter where customers see a product displayed, they're always just one click from purchasing it. With an affiliate program, the merchant doesn't care if the conversion rate is half that of a banner ad, or even a tenth, because he's only paying for the sales. The pay-on-performance model of advertising is the least risky for merchants.

News and information sites like affiliate programs because they allow them to use spare page space and existing traffic to generate revenue with very little time or money required to get set up. Affiliates join affiliate programs by completing a simple application. All they really have to do is put up links to merchant sites, making sure to include their affiliate IDs in the links. They then receive checks from the merchants when purchases are made and the commission amount exceeds some total (most merchants won't write checks for under $25). Because the images used in the links actually reside on the merchant's servers, it's up to the merchants to keep the products being advertised up-to-date.

Most sites that participate in affiliate programs don't see enough traffic to attract banner ads. They're often specialty sites that cater to very narrow vertical audiences, which can be perfect for a merchant. The most successful affiliate sites are those that keep their content current so that visitors return frequently and those that write product reviews about affiliate products they then link to, such as About.com, which reviews books and then links to bookstores so that visitors can make the purchase.

COMPENSATION MODEL

In *Now or Never*, Mary Modahl writes that the value of getting the customer to the site is worth 5 percent of the purchase price, on average. For higher-margin items, like jewelry and flowers, the amount may be higher. For lower-margin items, such as computers and consumer electronics, the amount may be lower. Affiliate programs generally use one of two methods to determine compensation: They either pay a percentage of the value of the products sold or they pay a flat fee per product. In either case, there may be a sliding scale, with the percentage going down as the product price goes up, or a flat fee, which increases as the total value of products sold by that affiliate increases. Whichever model the merchant uses, it needs to be high enough to compete with other merchants selling comparable products, without being so high that all products sold will be at a loss.

VARIANTS ON THE AFFILIATE MODEL

Most sites that participate in affiliate programs do so for the affiliate revenue. But some sites, such as ebates, dash, and Schoolpop, offer the affiliate commission as a rebate back to the customer or to a charity of the customer's choosing. As a merchant, you may find that these affiliates bring a lot of traffic to your site, and a lot of revenue as well. However, the goal of an affiliates program is to pay the affiliate for a customer once—that being the cost of acquisition—and to attract the customer on subsequent occasions through less expensive methods, such as electronic direct mail. If the merchant is in a low-margin industry and the margin is less than the commission revenue that the merchant has to pay to attract affiliates, then accepting affiliates that bring the same customers back—with the concomitant affiliate commission—may be a bad deal for merchants in the long run.

With dash, the customers install the dashBar into their browsers. Any time they click on a link to a merchant or type the merchant's URL, the dashBar pops up a dialog box reminding them that they can purchase from this merchant through the dash network and get a rebate. This is great for absent-minded consumers, who might forget that they can "get paid for every purchase," but terrible for merchants who want returning customers to return on their own accord, without bringing an affiliate ID with them.

Ebates pays customers any time they make a purchase with a merchant in their network and provide an ebates.com e-mail address. In both cases, the merchant pays the acquisition cost every time a customer returns, so the value of these customers is much less than the value of customers who come through more traditional affiliates.

LEGAL ISSUES
The U.S. Patent and Trademark Office, in its zeal to grant overly broad patents for every offline activity that's translated to the digital arena, has granted Amazon, one of the most aggressive pursuers of Internet patents, a patent for its affiliate program. Amazon's site says nothing about this patent, and BeFree.com, one of the major affiliate networks, insists that its system doesn't conflict with the Amazon patent. Amazon did not respond to my requests to discuss its patent, but the fact that it hasn't sued anyone yet over patent infringement for this patent suggests that it won't be overzealous in keeping others out of the affiliate business. If, however, you're planning to create your own affiliate program rather than relying on an affiliate network, have your lawyers check the patent to make sure the system you're planning to use won't put you in violation of the Amazon patent.

VIRAL MARKETING
Viral marketing is the Web equivalent of two neighbors talking over the fence, with one recommending a good product to the other. If you've ever received an ad for a site from a friend with a note saying, "Thought you might be interested in this," then you've participated in viral marketing. The Web makes viral marketing easy. Much of the buzz about new sites on the Web still relies on informal viral marketing. Sites can become overnight sensations, strictly by word of mouth, via e-mail.

WHY IT WORKS
Viral marketing works when we trust the person sending us the message. I'm much more likely to click on a link in a direct marketing message forwarded to me by my sister that advertises a sale on sweater sets than I am

to click on that same link in the same message when it comes directly from the merchant. I know that my sister has already been to the merchant site, prescreened the merchandise for me, and that she—who knows me and my tastes—thinks it'll be to my liking. I know it was at least a little bit of trouble for her to forward the message to me, rather than just deleting it, and I appreciate it. Even if I don't buy a sweater, I will probably visit the site, let her know what I think, and thank her for thinking of me. Viral marketing creates a buzz.

OPTIMIZING VIRAL MARKETING

In the example above, viral marketing works because my sister knows me and my tastes, and because I have no reason to suspect her motives. If I knew she were making a commission on any of my purchases, I would be less inclined to click on a link, not because I wouldn't want her to get a cut, but because I would assume that my interest in the sweater might be secondary to her interest in making a sale. When a merchant site sets up a viral marketing program, it has to be careful to balance its interests in getting its customers to forward ads or attach ads to their own e-mail messages with the interests of those who receive the ads in believing the content is relevant.

Viral marketing programs tend to rely on e-mail. There are two basic variants: commercially run and merchant-run. The commercially run viral marketing programs, such as that available from Epidemic.com, attach an ad to the end of each e-mail message sent by the participant in the network. Participants enroll at the vendor's site and select the merchant program in which they want to participate. The merchant-run viral marketing programs often rely on a simple statement like "forward this to a friend" somewhere in the ad that the existing customer receives. The merchant may offer an incentive to customers who forward the message, such as enrollment in a sweepstakes (for simply forwarding the message), or a discount (if the forwarding results in a purchase), or it may not offer any incentive at all.

In the ideal viral marketing program, customers are given an incentive to send ads only to their friends and associates who might be interested in making a purchase. Good viral programs should see high conversion rates—much higher than those of banner ads or typical affiliates programs—because the marketing should be better targeted to the audience, as in the example I gave above of my sister telling me about a sale on sweaters.

CASE STUDY: OurHouse.com

Gary Briggs , Chief Marketing Officer

"In March of 2000 we decided we could no longer ignore the click-through and conversion rates associated with viral marketing, so we made plans to run our own viral marketing campaign. Since we wanted to run the program in the very near future, we didn't want to

Figure 4-1: Refer-a-friend e-mail sent from OurHouse.com.

develop the tracking software in-house. We generally do send targeted e-mail ourselves.

"We evaluated the vendors who were providing viral marketing solutions, and selected Digital Impact on the basis of their client list. Together we decided to target our OurHouse.com members who had opted in for promotional updates via e-mail. We believed our customers would respond to a viral promotion because of the attractive offers to both themselves and their family members.

"The viral campaign consisted of an offer letter to existing OurHouse.com members. The initial letter, shown in Figure 4-1, explained the promotion to members: Refer a friend, get 20 percent off your next product purchase, and OurHouse.com would send the friend a $10-off coupon as well. In addition, there was an opportunity for the initial e-mail recipient to earn gifts based upon the purchasing behavior of those to whom they forwarded the e-mail. The more friends that actually purchased, the bigger the gift they were eligible for, ranging from a snake light for two to four friends shopping to a $150 gift certificate for twenty or more friends shopping.

"Each friend referred received e-mail with the $10 coupon and the name of the friend who made the referral. When the member made the referral, he received a thank-you note with the 20 percent–off coupon. We tracked how many of our members opened our offer— even though the list we mailed to is opt-in, a certain percentage of people don't read promotional offers at all—5.8 percent referred friends, and up to five friends on average were referred. We also tracked how many referred friends purchased with their $10 coupons, how many members purchased with their 20 percent–off coupons, and what the average basket sizes were for both categories."

This promotion is a good example of a successful viral marketing campaign because of the high rate of participation by existing customers. Online merchants guard their data pretty closely, but both OurHouse.com and Digital Impact conceded that they were very pleased with the results of the viral marketing campaign and the cost of customer acquisition through this promotion.

COMPENSATION MODEL

There are a few ways to compensate members of your viral network who refer customers to you. The two most common ways are by giving them a coupon good for a percentage off a future purchase and by giving them a coupon for a dollar amount off a future purchase. Some programs pay cash, but this provides the wrong type of motivation. None of the members of your viral network—which is drawn from your customer base—should be making a living or attempting to make a living by viral marketing your site. Paying cash motivates people to spam e-mail lists, which reflects negatively on you, even if you're not aware it's going on.

Viral marketing works best when those doing the referring are users of the product or service. If they're already buying from your site, then a coupon toward a future purchase is almost as good as cash, and it has the double benefit of rewarding them and encouraging them to purchase again soon.

LOYALTY PROGRAMS

Loyalty programs are intended to attract your former customers back to your site. In theory, your customers remember that there's some reward for shopping with you every time, instead of, say, buying the replacement cartridge for their printer with you one month and then with your competitor next month. Loyalty programs can take a variety of forms. The simplest kind works like the buy-twelve-get-one-free card at your local frozen yogurt shop. The currency is only good at that merchant.

The most popular credit card in the United States is the Citibank AAdvantage card, which earns miles in the American Airlines AAdvantage Frequent Flyer Program. Shoppers who use this credit card (and others like it) earn frequent flyer miles with American Airlines that can also be used toward other purchases. The popularity of this card shows that some types of loyalty programs can cause shoppers to behave differently.

On the Web there are dozens of companies that offer a variety of types of loyalty programs. The programs range from network loyalty programs, such as e-centives, Clickrewards, and FreeRide, to private-labeled solutions that provide promotions and tracking of an on-site currency that can only be used on your site, such as iGain. Merchants can also administer their own loyalty programs if their volume and membership base warrant the investment.

HOW LOYALTY PROGRAMS WORK BEST

Loyalty programs work best when they're already familiar to the shopper. Few shoppers will make a purchase just because they are promised they will be given fifty points if they enroll in a program they have never heard of. The obvious question by the shopper would be: How many points does it take to get a reward?

In-house or private-label loyalty programs are effective at sites where shoppers are likely to make frequent purchases, the products are basically commodities, and there's not much to distinguish the merchants, such as with books, music, videos, and office supplies. Shoppers who return to a merchant often can be reminded why they should shop from that merchant rather than click over to a competitor to comparison shop. For example, the customer can be reminded that he is about to run out of contact lens solution and by purchasing at your site, where he's part of a loyalty program, he's earning points toward a free gift or trip with every purchase.

For most merchants, network loyalty programs are probably a better bet than private-label loyalty programs. With network loyalty programs, the reward earned is fungible among the merchants in the network, but the merchant who joins such a network automatically benefits from the thousands of shoppers who have accounts and receive promotional e-mail from the network. This type of loyalty program works best for merchants who sell infrequently purchased items that are less homogenous, such as flowers, cookware, furniture, clothing, and gifts. Figure 4-2 shows a promotional e-mail from Clickrewards, one of the larger loyalty networks. You can see that multiple merchants and types of merchants are included in this promotion. And because they are not direct competitors, it's no problem for them to share a promotional e-mail.

THE DEBATE OVER LOYALTY PROGRAMS' EFFICACY

Many merchants participate in loyalty programs, but whether they really work is still a matter for debate. Jupiter Communications reported that

22 percent of shoppers surveyed said they'd be more likely to return to a merchant if a loyalty program were present.[3] However, BizRate's research of buyers immediately after making purchases indicated that fewer than 4 percent attributed their decision to purchase at that time to a loyalty program.[4] The disparity may be between those who shop and those who buy, with Jupiter interviewing the first group and BizRate interviewing the second. Alternatively, the difference may simply be between intent and

Figure 4-2: E-mail from the network introduces the customers to multiple merchants.

action, with shoppers intending to make a purchase based on being able to get a reward but actually making a purchase on other criteria.

 HOW VIRAL AFFILIATE NETWORKS SHOULD WORK

The optimal model of a viral affiliate network is one that combines the best of the affiliates program with the best of a viral marketing program with the best of a loyalty program. In this model, merchants reward their own customers for referring their friends with in-house currency or promotions. Mainspring, an e-business strategic consulting firm, reported that based on their research, "on average, each apparel shopper referred three people to an online retailer's site after her first purchase. After ten purchases, that same shopper had referred seven people to the site. For consumer electronics, the average customer had referred thirteen people after ten purchases."[5]

By offering special promotions to customers for forwarding the company's e-mail promotions to their friends, practical merchants, such as OurHouse.com, are already capitalizing on the natural proclivity of satisfied shoppers to share their newfound satisfaction. This is the optimal arrangement all around. The cost of acquisition is very low—just the cost of the discount—and the value of the newly acquired customers is likely to be high, because people aren't going to annoy their friends with promotions those friends aren't likely to appreciate.

RESOURCES

NEWSLETTERS

Viral Marketer (www.viralmarketer.com)

VIRAL NETWORKS

Many of the commercial e-mail services now offer viral e-mail services as part of their suite of services. If you already use an e-mail marketing service, check with them to see what they offer.

Digital Impact (www.digitalimpact.com). Offers complete e-mail services as well as targeted viral campaigns to a merchant's membership.

Epidemic (www.epidemic.com). Was the first major viral network provider on the scene. It has a large network of merchants. Its network relies on initiative by the customers rather than viral campaigns by the merchants.

GreetPage (www.greetpage.com). Sponsors the *Viral Marketer* newsletter and offers a viral marketing network.

AFFILIATE NETWORKS

BeFree (www.befree.com). Runs one of the larger affiliate networks.

Commission Junction (www.commissionjunction.com). Runs one of the larger affiliate networks.

LinkShare (www.linkshare.com). Runs another large affiliate network.

AFFILIATE RESOURCE WEB SITES

These sites review merchant affiliate programs for the information sites that are considering joining. They usually charge the merchant a fee to have a program reviewed. The affiliate business is strictly a "pay to play" business, so expect to pay for every mention of your program and company. It's worth it to be listed on these sites, though, since active affiliate sites rely on the information contained herein. They are:

AssociatePrograms.com (www.associateprograms.com)

Associate-it (www.associate-it.com)

CashPile (www.cashpile.com)

Refer-It (www.refer-it.com)

ReveNews (www.revenews.com)

2-Tier (www.2-tier.com)

LOYALTY PROGRAMS

There are quite a few out there. Here are but a few (the Web sites match the company names): Clickrewards, MyPoints, iGain, e-centives.

Listfeed Programs AND XML

IN THE BRICKS-and-mortar world, it's been said that the three principal factors in the success of a business are location, location, and location. In the digital world, it's possible to be located at every intersection and have your products on display at every intersection without giving up much. Because the distance between any two points on the Web is a click, it redounds to your benefit to have your products as many places as possible.

KNOWING WHEN TO BRING THEM TO YOU AND WHEN TO GO TO THEM

There was a time when online merchants believed that the name of the game was getting traffic to their own sites. Many dot-coms still labor under this misconception. Megastores went online to satisfy the perceived need for "one-stop shopping" online. Merchants assumed that the dynamic on the Web was the same as the dynamic in the real world: Customers would prefer to satisfy their shopping needs at a single site rather than purchase office and school supplies from one merchant, consumer electronics from another, and books and CDs from yet a third. Between privacy concerns (how many times did shoppers want to divulge their personal information?), security concerns, and shipping and handling charges, many shoppers had reservations about trying out a new merchant or about making small purchases from any merchants.

The dynamic of the Web has changed. Although average order totals have gone down and then come back up since 1998 for just about every industry, consumers are generally more favorably disposed to spending small sums on online orders rather than trying to find everything they need at one site to save on shipping and handling charges. Many sites do offer free shipping for orders over a set dollar amount, but those amounts are usually pretty modest, averaging around $50.

Today's smart merchants not only don't worry about selling everything to everyone, they also don't worry about displaying and selling merchandise in their own stores. The smart merchants make their products available to every product-comparison site where the traffic merits it and, when possible, participate in universal shopping carts—where orders are actually taken at another site. Bringing the customer to the merchant is almost as quaint a concept as selling vacuum cleaners door to door. Instead, you take the product to the customer. Retailing has indeed come full circle!

AGGREGATORS

Once you realize the value of taking your products to your customers and the relative cost effectiveness of making your inventory available to aggregators, such as price comparison engines, product review sites, and buying clubs, you need to decide in which programs you want to participate. There are far too many programs for every merchant to participate in every one. Some of the better known aggregator sites include PriceSCAN.com, BizRate, AltaVista, Excite, Yahoo!, priceWonders.com, Deja.com, and PricePulse.com. There are far too many to list here, so don't assume that anything left off this list isn't a major player.

The three factors to consider when deciding where to participate are cost of participation, effort needed to comply with their system, and traffic coming through their site.

COST OF PARTICIPATION

Usually, there's no cost for getting started with an aggregator. Payment is generally on a per-click or combination of per-click and per-impression basis. Depending on the site, there may be a per-impression charge for having your logo appear next to your products. Optimally, you can negotiate for an affiliate type of arrangement when you first sign up (for the first ninety days or so) until you see that the traffic coming through the aggregator does, in fact, yield the conversion rate that it claims. The higher the conversion rate, the higher you can expect the clickthrough rate to be. Figure 5-1 shows real data with which you might have to work and how to determine the best deal for your site.

Clickthrough rate: *$.50 (the aggregator wants)*

Conversion rate: *5 percent (the aggregator says)*

Affiliate commission: *3 percent (you offer)*

Average cost of a product you're displaying on the aggregator's site: *$700*

If, in fact, the conversion rate is 5 percent, then one in twenty clickthroughs generates a sale. That sale (or the cost of customer acquisition) would cost you $10 (calculated as $.50/click for 20 clickthroughs). If the arrangement were for the standard affiliate commission, instead of the clickthrough charge, the same sale would cost you $21 (calculated as $700 x .03). Consequently, you could negotiate for the standard affiliate commission on purchases, which should be more profitable for the aggregator for thirty to ninety days until you have your own data about conversion rates. Then, if the conversion rate really is 5 percent or is anything more than 2.38 percent (one in forty-two), a per-click arrangement would be cheaper for you.

If the conversion rate is worse than that for a $700 product, then either negotiate a more favorable clickthrough rate or negotiate for an affiliate arrangement whereby the aggregator gets paid only for sales, not for clicks. You need good data about the average product price so you can do calculations based on that figure.

If, instead, the average product price were $250, to calculate the clickthrough rate you'd need to break even with an affiliate commission, you would multiply your average product price times the commission and the average number of clicks required to make one sale or the conversion rate. In this case, that calculation would be:

$250 average product cost x 3% commission
x 5% clicks = a cost of $.375 per click.

I suggest you negotiate initially for a strictly pay-on-performance deal, even though the data from the aggregator might suggest that pay-per-click is more attractive to you, as in the example above. If you can take the numbers to the aggregator, showing how it will make more money on an affiliate deal based on their clickthrough and conversion data, then you're in a stronger negotiating position. Once you have your own clickthrough and conversion data from traffic through that site, you can see whether you should renegotiate for a pay-per-click arrangement and what a reasonable amount per click would be. You can also see whether the numbers you were provided were inflated enough to make the affiliate arrangement more attractive to you after all.

So in this case, if your clickthrough rate is more than $.375 for a click, you're paying in excess of your affiliate commission model. You need to have good numbers and the ability to work with them in order to negotiate the best deal with the aggregators.

Figure 5-1: An example of getting the best terms when negotiating with an aggregator.

Whose Customers Are They, Anyway?

When you rely on other sites to bring you traffic, or more accurately, to bring you sales—you may or may not ever see the actual traffic—then you have to negotiate carefully with those sites so that you know whether people who buy from you on someone else's site are yours or theirs. Most privacy policies spell out how much of a customer's data a site will share with third parties like you, and consumers are justifiably concerned about having their data shared between sites. Of course, when you're the one billing the credit card, shipping the order, handling customer service and returns, and bearing the cost of fraud, it's difficult to accept that this activity is what most customers think of as *sharing data*. If you didn't have the customer's data, you couldn't fulfill the order. This is a real catch-22 for many listfeed, universal shopping cart, and merchant sites.

Usually, the aggregator site will want you to send order confirmation and shipping status e-mail messages to the customer, but whether you're permitted to market directly to these customers again is what you're negotiating for. The more of a relationship you can develop directly with the customer, the better. If the customer remains the property of the aggregator, then you have to pay for subsequent sales every time.

EFFORT NEEDED TO COMPLY WITH AN AGGREGATOR

Every aggregator has its own unique rules for inclusion in its site. For the most part, an aggregator wants as many paying merchants as possible to be listed on its site. The cost to the aggregator is setting up the site and processing the data. Once the software has been written for that, there is very little cost to the aggregator for adding new merchants. Aggregators also want high conversion rates. They generally don't care where the customer clicks, as long as that customer eventually purchases from one of the listed merchants.

In general, I've found that smaller aggregators who don't yet see much traffic and don't have many merchants are less flexible about how they receive your data and what the compensation model is. It's counterintuitive, but larger aggregator sites are often more willing to work with whatever data you can send them, massage it into their own format, and give you thirty days at no cost to prove that their sites will be moneymakers for you. Smaller aggregators seem not to have caught onto the fact that without merchants, they're sunk.

The human cost of complying with every different standard that every aggregator wants to impose can be high. Once you've decided on a system for sending your data to the aggregators, stick with aggregators who can work with your system. Unless you have people sitting around on your side, it's frequently not worth it to provide data in multiple custom formats for every aggregator who requests it. Let the aggregator know what you have, and that that's all you can offer before you do cartwheels trying to meet its standards. Don't assume it's "their way or the highway." You'll be pleasantly surprised at how flexible many sites can be.

TRAFFIC

Traffic is one of the major considerations that will affect your decision to participate with an aggregator. Typically, more traffic is better, but lots of traffic with a high conversion rate is best. Since you're probably, eventually, going to end up paying for clickthroughs, you need not just traffic but traffic that's ready to buy. Visit the sites of aggregators that you're considering using to see whether they truly give a shopper enough information to make a purchase or just spew products, merchants, and prices sorted by price. To avoid wasting money, make sure you have a thirty-day out on your contract so that you can cancel your relationship with sites that don't perform or that show inordinately high clickthrough rates without many sales.

Without a Wire

The fastest way to make your site accessible to shoppers on wireless devices is to participate with a wireless aggregator. Chapter 7 discusses WAP-enabling your site—making it accessible and legible from wireless devices that support the Wireless Application Protocol—but when all you really want to do is to WAP-enable your products, making them accessible to shoppers, then a wireless aggregator is just what you need.

Wireless aggregators come in many flavors. They also have very active business development teams. Take your time to pick the right one (there are plenty out there) rather than just the one that comes to you. Some of the differentiating features between wireless aggregators include:

+ How they get your product listings: by spidering your site, by accessing your database directly with application protocol interfaces (APIs), or by receiving a product listing from you.

+ How they are compensated.

+ Their visibility on various wireless providers' networks (an aggregator on the menu of multiple carriers will command a higher price than an aggregator that's not on the menu of any wireless provider). Even if they're not on a menu, it can still be worth it to be included with that aggregator, but you should be able to negotiate for a lower rate.

+ Who takes the order—you or them.

The issue of customer ownership is also paramount when negotiating a deal with a wireless aggregator. Some aggregators provide a turnkey service for merchants and other content providers without charging, but then they own the customer profile. Although the customers' information is no longer valued as highly as it once was—because of the customer loyalty issues discussed in Chapter 1—a merchant still doesn't want to sign away rights to contact wireless customers by e-mail on an opt-in basis.

LISTFEEDS

A listfeed is a file of your inventory that you make available to aggregators so that they can display your products on their sites. Not all aggregators will accept listfeed files, but most will. It's less work for aggregators to take a daily listfeed file from a number of merchants, process the data, and format it into their own sites on a scheduled basis than it is for them either to spider merchants' sites, pulling relevant data, or to visit the merchants' sites in real time to pull pricing and availability data.

Different aggregators will request that you include different fields in your listfeed file and make it available different ways. The skeletal data that almost all aggregators will want include the following:

→ Merchant SKU (or unique ID number for product)

→ Manufacturer's SKU

→ Manufacturer

→ Product name

→ Price

→ Availability

→ Shipping cost

→ Product description (short)

Most aggregators will simply want you to put your entire inventory, or inventory for the categories of products the aggregators handle, into a text file with a delimiter between fields. The tab character is a common delimiter. Figure 5-2 shows an example of a listfeed file with these fields:

17123	SON-123	SONY DVD Player	249.00	In stock	Free	Get the best picture…
17124	TOS-599	Toshiba CD Player	49.00	In stock	Free	Holds 5 disks…
17125	DEL5719	DeLonghi Alfredo Toaster/Oven	79.99	Ships in 1-2 days	Free	

Figure 5-2. A sample text-only listfeed file with tab delimiters.

The columns won't line up exactly because not all fields are the same width. The computer receiving the file doesn't care, though, and will see the tabs where they're supposed to be.

Listfeed files are usually transmitted daily from merchants to aggregators. The choices of transmission include having the aggregator pull the file off the merchant's server using standard communications protocols such as HTTP, secure HTTP (HTTPS), FTP, or SCP, or having the merchant deliver the listfeed file to the aggregator by means of FTP or SCP.

The What and Why of XML

The other way to make your content available to aggregators and to others who are willing to display your products on their sites as part of their own content is to mark up your site with XML. That way, aggregators or wireless aggregators, since they generally prefer to come looking for your products in real time, can find the essential product fields, including price, without having to guess.

XML (extensible markup language) is an architecture for defining languages. Each industry can define its own languages using its own terminology as long as it complies with the XML architecture. Unfortunately, merchants have not been anxious to create a standard for use across merchant sites. For one thing, it makes spidering by competitors easier. For another, most aggregators prefer to receive a listfeed file.

There's not really any XML standard for product markup, as there is for payment transmission, so you're going to have to work with the aggregator to find a standard that it can use. Inktomi has its own proprietary Product Markup Language (PML), but the point of XML is that it's not proprietary. It's an open standard. If you stick with some fairly standard labels for your fields, most aggregators who choose to spider your site can probably work with you.

```
<MERCHANT_SKU>18193</MERCHANT_SKU>

<MFR_SKU>KRI-107</MFR_SKU>

<MFR>Kringle Company</MFR>

<PRODUCT_NAME>Personalized Letter from
Santa</PRODUCT_NAME>

<PRICE>7.50</PRICE>

<AVAILABILITY>In Stock</AVAILABILITY>

<SHIPPING>Included</SHIPPING>

<DESCRIPTION>This personalized letter from
Santa, postmarked from the North Pole, will
make any child's Christmas that much mer-
rier.</DESCRIPTION>
```

CATEGORIZING PRODUCTS

The most difficult part about complying with listfeed requirements of aggregators is that no standard product categorization scheme exists for products on the Web. Most product comparison sites want to be able to group products in a logical fashion so that their customers can "drill down" and find what they want. If a shopper knows he wants a Pentium III laptop computer with 128 megabytes of RAM and a DVD player, he can start by clicking on Computers, then on Notebooks, in most shopping sites to arrive at some subset of products from which to choose.

The problem for most merchants is that they've already devised their own categorization scheme, and to recategorize all products in the store for every aggregator would not be a trivial undertaking. Fortunately, most good-sized aggregators have come to recognize the problem and have chosen one of three ways to address it:

1. Map products by manufacturer into the aggregator's own categorization scheme

2. Map categories in each merchant site into the aggregator's own categories

3. Request a category hierarchy as part of the daily listfeed, then map dynamically as well as possible

MAPPING BY MANUFACTURER SKU

This technique is generally easiest for the merchants. The aggregator works directly with the manufacturer to get the complete SKU list with product names, then sorts all merchant data based on the manufacturer SKUs. The merchant doesn't have to provide any categorization data because the aggregator maps the SKUs ahead of time. The downside for the merchant is that any products to which the merchant has exclusive access probably won't be listed, nor will any bundles, because bundles usually have distributor or merchant SKUs, not manufacturer SKUs, since multiple manufacturers are usually involved.

MAPPING CATEGORIES

Category mapping involves deciding which of your categories align with which of the aggregator's categories. It can be an effective way to make sure your products appear in the appropriate categories on the aggregator's site. If you have to do the mapping, category mapping can be very time consuming. Most aggregators that want you to do the mapping will provide you with their master category list. If you ask, some aggregators (even some of the biggest) will map for you. The problem with category mappings is that categories on both sides can change, and someone has to stay on top of the categories to make sure that new products, or products in new categories, get mapped properly.

SENDING CATEGORY HIERARCHY

Yet another approach to getting your products into the right categories is to send the aggregator the equivalent of your own category map with each product, showing how a customer would drill down to find a product in your site. This would be one of the fields in your listfeed. As an example, the notebook computer mentioned above might have a field that looked like this:

Computers | Notebooks | Pentium III

It's not uncommon for aggregators to request a category hierarchy as part of the listfeed file.

UNIVERSAL SHOPPING CARTS

Another way to make sure your products are everywhere a shopper happens to be is to participate in sites that offer universal shopping carts. A universal shopping cart is the logical extension of an aggregator. With an aggregator, the customer selects a product and clicks into your site to complete the purchase. With a universal shopping cart site, the customer collects all the products he wants into his cart on that site—even if they're from different merchants—and makes the purchase on that site. You, the merchant, get notification of the purchase, and you fulfill the order as if it were taken on your own site.

Why would you want the purchase to be made elsewhere? Generally, you wouldn't. But you might not have access to the customers in any other way, so you'd be willing to work in this environment to make the sales. Two examples of this situation are buying clubs not letting the customers leave their sites to complete purchases, and government purchases in which the aggregator has to complete copious paperwork to be permitted to sell to the customers.

CASE STUDY: NIC Commerce
David Fishman, Vice President of Marketing

"NIC Commerce is a leader in government procurement, and a division of NIC [Nasdaq:EGOV]. Our organization was recently selected by the Air Force Standard Systems Group (SSG) to provide the e-procurement engine for the Air Force's Information Technology Superstore. The Air Force Superstore, operated by CIT-PAD (Commercial Information Technology, Product Area Directorate), offers buyers access to an extensive product list from more than thirty different hardware, software, networking, and service contracts and blanket purchase agreements (BPAs). Under our agreement, NIC Commerce will partner with the Air Force to customize and make advancements in its software solution to allow buyers enhanced product comparison of similar products across multiple manufacturers.

"Located at Maxwell Air Force Base-Gunter Annex, Alabama, SSG manages information technology contracts and standard information system programs universally used at all active and reserve Air Force bases and many other Department of Defense agencies. Responsible for obtaining competitive pricing, SSG chose the NIC Commerce solution for the Superstore to provide an enhanced and efficient procurement tool that allows customers to locate, compare, customize, and purchase products online at competitive price points. In addition, our industry-leading XML-based solution provides vendors with an easy-to-use mechanism to update their product line and pricing.

"Air Force buyers will now be able to compare similar products on a side-by-side basis across multiple vendors. All features are viewable for the buyer so that they can determine which product is the best fit for them. Once a buyer selects the product he would like to purchase, he can then place the order online.

"In addition, through Document Type Definition (DTD), vendors use a standard spreadsheet format to update their product offerings and price lists as necessary. An XML file is created with the new information and then uploaded into the system. Once the Air Force program manager and contracting officer approve the modification, the information is then uploaded into the CIT-PAD database of record."

There are a few ways to participate in a universal shopping cart. Usually, if you want to participate, you need to comply with the guidelines of the site hosting the cart. The host site may request you support electronic commerce markup language (ECML) (www.ecml.org), which is the e-commerce flavor of XML; that you permit an application programming interface (API) so that the site can update your database securely via the Web in real time; or that you accept the orders after they've been placed via either e-mail or a batch file transmitted to you at the end of the day. Another way for the host site to communicate the order is via electronic data interchange (EDI). Any site that has long-term plans for any order-transmission method that's not real time is one you want to avoid. You should know about the order the moment it's been placed and have the privilege of running the fraud check on the payment information, since you'll be stuck with the loss if there is any attributable to fraud, and with denying the order, if necessary.

RESOURCES

There are many, many sites that offer aggregation, price comparisons, product reviews, and the other features that help shoppers decide which product to purchase. The best place to look for these sites is in directories, such as the Open Directory Project (www.dmoz.org) and Yahoo! (www.yahoo.com).

Direct Mail 6

E-MAIL, AS as a method of bringing customers back to your site, is more cost-effective than any other method. A merchant should be using targeted electronic direct mail (EDM) to make relevant appeals to its existing customer base, relying on information it already has about its shopping and buying behavior. There are other types of e-mail a merchant can send, but they can't achieve the same goals as targeted EDM.

Additionally, e-mail should be based on both the frequency with which the customer has requested (or agreed) to receive it and the behavior of the customer vis-à-vis the site. Customers who click through e-mail promotions often should be targeted more narrowly and promoted to more aggressively.

CUSTOMER LOYALTY

Targeted EDM can help you overcome the competitive problem on the Internet of lack of customer loyalty. You can't create loyal customers with targeted EDM alone. Customer service and good value creates loyal customers, but targeted EDM reminds your existing customers that you're out there willing to help them solve their problems.

Your site needs to be in front of the customer as often as possible so that it's on the customer's radar when the customer is ready to make a purchase. Because the Web is so instantaneous, a targeted message from you can remind the customer that he *did* need to purchase a new printer cartridge and he'd simply forgotten until now. He can click through your ad, use your expedited checkout process, and have the print cartridge on its way to him in five or six clicks. And you've done him a favor by jogging his memory so that when he gets home from work at 7 P.M., he doesn't kick himself for forgetting to stop at the office supply superstore to pick up the printer cartridge.

Before you can send targeted EDM, however, you need to have a list of e-mail addresses. You also need to have some knowledge of the purchase history or profile of these customers so that you can target your messages effectively. Finally, you need to decide how you are going to target these customers—by their own indicated preferences, by some purchased profile information, or by a recommendations engine. In any case, the narrower you can focus the message, the better the results will be.

There are brokers who will sell you "opt-in" lists (lists of e-mail addresses of people who have agreed to receive e-mail on certain topics) of e-mail addresses, which you can then use to market your site. However, since you have no relationship with the recipients and they haven't expressed any desire to receive mail from you or about your products, the success rate of these lists is roughly comparable to that of direct marketing by mail. Even people on these opt-in lists may consider unsolicited e-mail offers to be spam, which devalues your company and your brand. Although there are "reputable places" from which to purchase opt-in lists, since marketing to strangers falls under the category of customer acquisition, not customer retention, it isn't the focus of this chapter.

GETTING THE LIST

There are only two legitimate ways to get a list for purposes of direct mail: cultivate it yourself or purchase it from a business partner. To the degree possible, EDM should be used on your existing customer base. These people are already familiar with your company, your site, and your products, and they're less likely to delete your message, add your address to their *blocked senders list* (so that your messages go into the deleted folder before they even see them), or send you hostile mail threatening you with legal action if you don't stop sending them mail.

If you've been selling primarily through channel partners and you'd like to communicate directly with your customers, who happen to be their customers, then you might be able to acquire the lists of customers of your channel partners who have purchased your products. Many technology sites, in addition to asking whether the customer would like to receive occasional updates from the site, ask whether the customer would like to receive relevant updates from related business partners. These lists are fair game from a customer loyalty perspective because the customers have *opted into* the list.

Any other list you can get your hands on is probably not one with which you want to be associated. EDM is often classified as *opt-in* or *opt-out*. Be aware though, that opt-out lists are universally viewed as spam by potential customers. Opt-out lists take e-mail addresses from wherever they can find them, such as my address on my columns at Internet.com, then inform the recipients of messages how to be removed from subsequent mailings. Legitimate opt-out lists will remove recipients who request to be removed from them. But some unscrupulous lists may only use removal requests to confirm that the e-mail address is in fact still valid. They have no intention of removing the e-mail from the list. Spam has such a bad name that it tarnishes any site that is perceived to be utilizing it.

OPTING IN VERSUS BEING OPTED IN

There's some debate as to whether a Web site should have the checkbox checked when a customer is setting his preferences, to indicate that he'd like to receive occasional mailings, or whether it should default to unchecked, in which case customers have to take action to participate. I don't think the debate is worth much ink. I'd rather see sites putting effort into sending out quality, targeted EDM. If the site were mine, I'd leave the box checked by default, and let those customers who don't want mail—and they're used to doing this everywhere they leave their e-mail addresses—uncheck the box.

COMPILING CUSTOMER PROFILES

Once you've acquired a list of e-mail addresses from people who have agreed to receive your messages, you've still got to take some action to prevent having your messages miss the mark entirely. You need more than e-mail addresses; you need information about these people and their interests. There are three ways to get this coveted information: from the people themselves, from comparing the purchases and demographics of the people to those of others to determine what are good cross-marketing opportunities, or from an agency that compiles shopping profiles. I recommend the first.

ASK AND YE SHALL RECEIVE

Perhaps saying that online shoppers are willing to give you their personal information for the asking is a bit cavalier, but the bottom line is that no one knows a shopper's interests like that shopper. When you purchase shopping history, you risk getting dated or inaccurate information about shoppers.

Rather than just asking whether customers would be willing to receive occasional updates and special offers, sites should ask all of the following—and respect customers' answers:

- *About which of the following categories of products/services [as appropriate for that merchant] are you interested in receiving e-mail updates and offers?* If nothing is checked, then don't send any EDM.

- *Would you prefer to receive e-mail as plain text or HTML-enriched?* Alternatively, you can ask what e-mail software customers use and then send what works with that software. For example, Pine and Elm—Unix-based e-mail software—don't support HTML. AOL also has unique formatting requirements for e-mail.

- *How frequently would you like to receive updates?* Offer options ranging from daily, if changing inventory warrants it, to quarterly.

Figure 6-1 shows the Overstock.com opt-in page, which both shows a customer that Overstock.com respects his mailbox and gives the customer control over how often he chooses to hear from Overstock.com. Overstock.com is unique in that its inventory changes often enough to make daily mailings legitimate. A bookstore, on the other hand, would have more difficulty justifying a daily mailing, unless it were just a list of new books published that day.

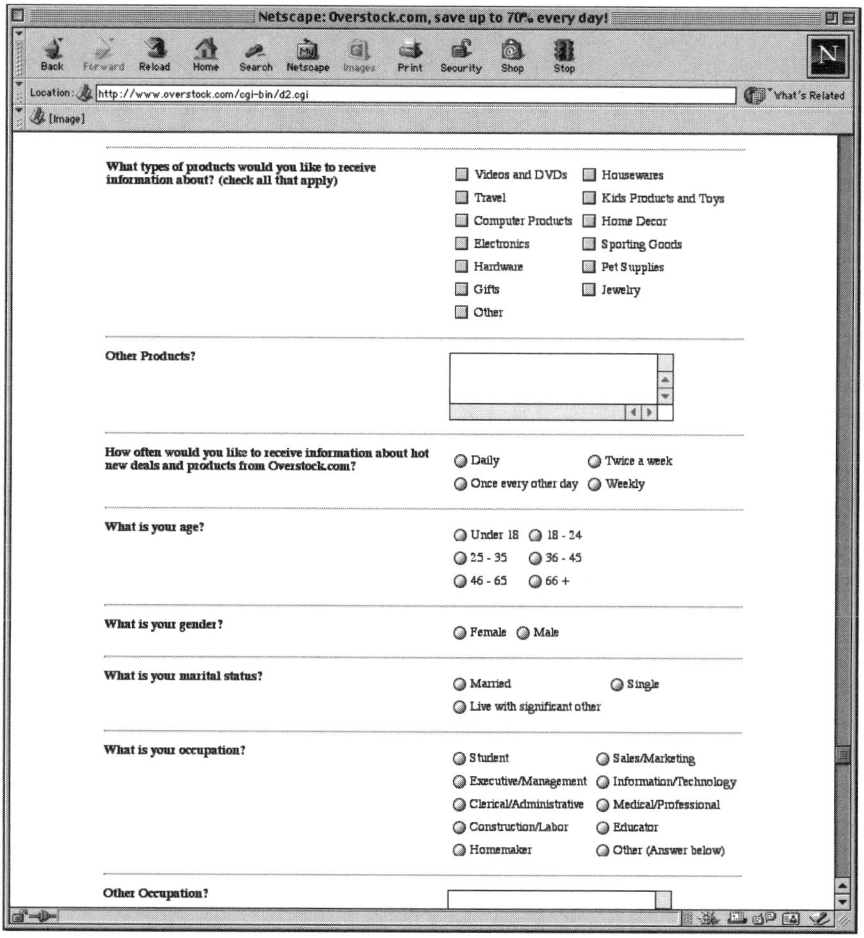

Figure 6-1: Overstock.com's opt-in page.

SHOPPING PREDICTIONS

If you can't ask shoppers what they care about, you can compare their purchases and known demographic information—frequently based on their zip codes—to others who have made purchases on your site, to arrive at reasonable predictions of what they want. Recommendation engines like

Net Perceptions and ShopTok's TokAdvisor—the first of which is installed directly on your server, and the second of which is an ASP—watch and learn about shopping behavior, and can do this for you. Several of the high-end content management solutions (discussed in Chapter 12) can also mine your customer base, recommend targeted e-mail campaigns by groups of shoppers, and send the mail for you.

It can take time to develop shopping predictions based on purchases made in your store, up to two to six months, but the results can be very powerful. Wouldn't it be useful to know that shoppers who purchased barbecue grills one month often purchased patio furniture the next, or that shoppers who purchased washers and dryers in the fall often purchased lawn mowers the following March? These are the kinds of specific recommendations you can get from shopping behavior engines.

SHOPPER PROFILING

The third way to determine what shoppers care about is to compare the profile information you have about them to the information that profiling companies like Cogit.com and Angara have collected, based on monitoring shopping behavior at many sites and monitoring traffic using cookies. Shoppers can be aggregated by products purchased or by demographic data for purposes of targeting. You may find success by sending the same ad to all shoppers who are married, make $100,000 per year, own their own homes, and have three children between six and fifteen years of age. Certainly, you can target your message better to these narrower demographic groups than you can to one shopper described by that demographic information and a single twenty-three-year-old shopper who makes $25,000 and rents.

HONING THE MESSAGE

Once you've gotten as much information as you can get about the people who are going to be receiving your EDM, you need to determine what you're going to tell them to make them come and buy from your site. Clearly, the better you understand who they are, the better you can target the message. Don't assume that because a buyer purchased a computer, he wants targeted mailings about computers. Find complementary products to sell him, instead.

Even if a customer explicitly tells you he's interested in home and garden products, you need to offer something more compelling than "here are our home and garden products" in your mailings. Some sites use EDM as an opportunity to unload overstocks. I would discourage that approach, unless that's part of the stated message, which can be done with tact. Scott Moehler, President of MobileShift, a wireless solution provider, suggested that EDM should be like "whispering a special secret in the customer's ear." More often, it reads like the digital equivalent of the hot dog vendor at the ballpark.

The first thing your EDM has to do is not annoy your customers. Here are my top five ways not to annoy the customer:

1. Don't send mail any more often than the customer has agreed to receive it, and if you don't let the customer choose, assume the pact is for once a month. Opt-in is not carte blanche.

2. Don't send mail simply showing the products that are already listed as specials on the site.

3. Don't send ads for products the customer has already purchased. This is particularly true for computers, where the prices fall, and customers resent being told how much more computer they could have purchased by waiting another month to buy.

4. If you send HTML-enriched mail, which I recommend, make sure people who can't read it see something they can read.

5. Make sure all the links work. Test. Test. Test.

The second thing your EDM has to do is have a reason for existence. In May 2000, I received e-mail from a travel site I hadn't visited in over a year. The mail began, "I know you haven't heard from us in a while…." And that was as interesting as it got. The fact that you haven't written to your customers is not necessarily of interest to them. The fact that you're finally getting around to making use of your huge database of addresses is not of interest to them. You're intruding on their time and space by sending them e-mail. Don't forget that. Make sure you have something interesting to tell them, make it fast, and don't forget to make it relevant to their lives. If you have some specials that you're only making available to recipients of your e-mail promotions, then that's something worth noting. The message, "you won't find this on our site unless you click here," should get their attention. Then make sure the specials really are noteworthy. Proflowers.com has a page of specials that are only available to frequent shoppers. With so tantalizing an offer, I had to click through the ad to see what I was privy to that others weren't.

The third thing your message must do is prompt action. If you've just instituted a free-shipping-for-orders-over-$35 policy, that's probably worth a message, but only if you go on to show what you have that's worth ordering that will qualify for free shipping. Your EDM should not read like a press release. You have less than five seconds to make the cut and stay out of the deleted folder in your customers' mail clients. Make a compelling case for clicking on a link to your site, and make it right from the beginning.

Finally, your EDM campaign must generate data for you. Unless you can look at what worked and what didn't, you don't know what appeal to make to which group the next time you send them mail. The sidebar entitled "Tracking Clicks" explains how to track each of the links in each of your messages to arrive at data about what tactics are successful.

CASE STUDY: Garden.com
Anne Dooley, Retention Marketing Manager

"Garden.com began working with Digital Impact in 1999 when we decided to outsource our e-mail marketing program. We were looking for an e-marketer that could provide us with the targeting capability and capacity needed for our e-mail campaigns. Digital Impact currently works with us to provide our customers with personalized e-mails. Our goal is to provide the consumer with information that is needed to be a better gardener—e-mail has been an effective tool in doing just this.

"Garden.com evaluated vendors based on their targeted marketing solutions and selected Digital Impact because of the mass personalization engine (MPE) technology and the optimized media delivery capabilities of plain, clickable AOL text and HTML e-mails. Garden.com currently uses Digital Impact to target their customer base on a veriety of attributes and elements, including the type of communication the customer prefers, the origins of the customer's relationship, and the customer's geographical location. Garden.com utilizes their knowledge from customers' past purchases, level of gardening expertise, and gardening seasonality to send timely and relevant content and product and promotions directly to those customers who have registered for e-mail marketing programs.

"Garden.com is an Internet-based company that uses information technology to bring the consumer a wide variety of products, gardening information and services to make the consumer's experience as valuable as possible. Along with these tools, they have designed e-mail programs to educate, inform, and advance the consumer's gardening abilities. These e-mail programs include Shopper's Preview, Bloom Times, GardenMinder,™ and New and Noteworthy.

"Communication is one of the keys to building a relationship with the consumer. Through Garden.com's weekly Shopper's Preview Program the customer receives, via e-mail, a sneak preview of new products and promotions available at Garden.com. The data collected from this marketing campaign is analyzed to determine product preferences and promotion efficiency. Sales generally increase on the days the e-mail is delivered, and most sales can be directly linked to the promoted items.

"Other customer retention tools that Garden.com uses through Digital Impact are the monthly newsletters Bloom Times and New and Noteworthy. With Bloom Times, the customers receive timely garden tips customized to their geographic region; monthly, gardening trends and techniques; and upcoming online magazine features. The New and Noteworthy e-mail campaign provides customers with information on new plants for the season, as well as 'Test Garden Tested' varieties. Garden.com e-mails are written by expert gardeners and leaders in the industry.

"The GardenMinder™ program is a one-to-one e-mail, where customers can receive a unique e-mail twice a month containing gardening lessons they have registered for with step-by-step instructions on particular topics tailored to the customer's region. Topics include flower gardening, herb gardening, salad gardening, fruits, vegetables, bulbs, and lawn care. Digital Impact's one-to-one technology enables Garden.com to send customized e-mails to consumers detailing information specific to their garden.

"Garden.com has worked with Digital Impact to provide customers with an experience that is targeted and pertinent to their regional location, maximizing the role of customer conversion from browser to repeat buyer. The e-mails uniformly represent the Garden.com brand and are reviewed and analyzed to ensure that the frequency and timing of the e-mail communications are appropriate."

Tracking Clicks

In addition to writing targeted e-mail that's effective, you need to be able to write e-mail that's trackable. This means that every time you include a link to your site from within the text of your e-mail you include a CGI parameter in the link that you later track on the site. Both text and images should link to pages on your site. The CGI parameter, which can be as simple as the link=1 in the following example:

```
<A href="http://www.overtheweb.com/track.cfm?
link=1">See our selection!</a>
```

In the link above, the question mark (?) separates the URL from the CGI parameter. There's only one CGI parameter, and we've numbered that 1. If we had five links in a single message, which is normal, we might number them 1 through 5.

Once you've assigned an identifier to each link, you need to make sure that the visitor who arrives with this link identifier doesn't lose it. The easiest way to do that is to send all visitors from e-mail links to a tracking or landing page, where the link identifier is stored in a cookie and associated with the visitor permanently, or at least for the duration of the visit to the store. Visitors don't actually stop at the tracking or landing page but just pass through on the way to the page that's relevant for the link on which they clicked. Figure 6-2 shows a data flow diagram with the visitor coming through a tracking page.

By tracking the link identifiers, you can get very specific data for each of your targeted messages (and you will be sending different messages to different groups), which tells you:

→ Which types of links have the highest clickthrough rates;

→ **Which types of promotions result in the most clickthroughs;**

→ **Which types of promotions result in the highest conversion rates; and**

→ **Which types of promotions are most frequently mailed to friends.**

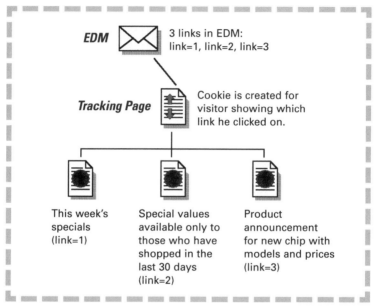

Figure 6-2: How the tracking page works in a typical EDM.

The important thing is to track the effectiveness of the types of messages, the specific messages, and the promotions—down to the product level—for each message you send. You also want to be able to monitor whether products you promote through e-mail end up selling better after you send a message, even if the buyers don't come through the tracking page. Customers may forward your messages to friends, or they may delete the messages, then return to your store through the home page a week later, when they realize they really are interested in what you are offering.

Without data, every e-mail message you send is purely guesswork. Although it's good to look at what the rest of the industry is doing, and what your competitors are doing, there's nothing like having your own hard data about what's working for your site with your customers. If you work with an ASP to send your targeted EDM, it will probably have a way of tracking the statistics I suggest you collect above, whether it's using a tracking page or another technique.

Cost Effectiveness

Whether you manage your own EDM campaigns using homegrown software, manage your campaigns using commercially available software, or outsource the task to a full-service mailing company such as Flonet or Digital Impact, targeted EDM is the most cost-effective way to reach your customers and to get them to return and make a purchase. The clickthrough rate for targeted EDM—around 7 percent with a conversion rate at around 0.5 percent—is much higher than for banner ads, and the cost of producing and sending the e-mail is nearly zero. There's simply no question that the math supports putting your marketing budget squarely behind your e-mail efforts. Since you shouldn't be paying for your list, anyway, you can see that the cost of e-mail is a tiny fraction of the cost of getting customers any other way.

Testing the Messages

It may seem that all targeted EDM uses one standard format. True, when you've signed up to receive e-mail from several different merchants, they all do begin to look the same. But it's still the case that you can improve your own success rates—both clickthrough and conversion rates—by testing your messages before you send them out. Commercial e-mail providers often make test messages part of the package you're paying for because they understand the difference that testing can make. If you're negotiating with a commercial e-mail provider—particularly with a full-service company— make sure that testing is part of the package. With EDM you can't go back and do it over. If you're irrelevant to your customers for too long, you'll cease to be read and noticed.

What part of your message should you be testing? Ultimately, everything, but you can't test everything at once. Testing should include both overall features and demographic market testing. Overall features include the number of images, the sizes of images (the overall download size and time, assuming you have an actual connection speed of 28K), the length of the message, the amount of text, and the type of promotion (e.g., seasonal sale, dollars off, rebate offer, co-marketing with another site). Demographic market testing involves testing types of messages against different audiences in your database. The reason you carefully collect information about click-through rates and conversion rates, by using the information in the Tracking Clicks sidebar above, is to use that information to cultivate ever-more-effective messages.

The exciting part about testing EDM is that you get nearly instantaneous feedback from the recipients—or not. You can conduct a test in a day to see how clickthrough rates compare for two different offers or for two different lengths of offers, or for whatever you're testing. Don't think that testing needs to slow you down. Most e-mail recipients read their mail daily, so if you design the test well, you'll know quickly which offer works best to send to your entire list or to a specific demographic.

EVENT-DRIVEN E-MAIL

What if you had a system that could automatically send e-mail to customers when you knew that something they'd purchased from you was about to run out? That would be a huge service to the customers as well as a great marketing technique. The days of refrigerators that automatically reorder milk when it's getting low are still a way off, but you can use event-driven e-mail to stay in touch with your customers and provide a valuable service as well.

You might use event-driven e-mail to cross-sell a customer immediately after your order management system has received notification that the product has shipped, so that the mail arrives just before his previous order does—or just as it does. Alternatively, you might use it to offer an extended warranty on a product shortly after the product has been received. If you have any information about previous purchases that were sent as gifts—even if you don't know the occasion—why not promote products that appeal to the same demographic three weeks before the occasion arrives in the subsequent year?

I have a teenage goddaughter. I never know what to purchase for her and frequently find that her birthday is upon me before I've had time to make a decision or place an order. What a great service it would be if Gap.com would send me a promotion based on the following information it has about me:

→ I ordered something from its site last year during the last week of January.

→ The product was to be packaged as a gift (wrapped, with a gift receipt).

→ It was sent to an address other than my own.

I wouldn't ever have to "sign up" for their gift reminder service, which I probably wouldn't ever do. They could just help me remember her birthday. They even know—and I don't—whether she liked and kept the sweater I sent or returned it to the mall for something else. They also know how much I spent. What a great service it would be if they would send me a timely message showing products that are in the right price range and in the style similar to what I sent or what she exchanged it for! They could even use a subject line of "Need a Gift for Anastasia?" to grab my attention, since they have her name. This is the future of personalized, event-driven e-mail, and I can't wait until it arrives in my mailbox.

CASE STUDY: Musicland
Steve Danker, Chief Information Officer
"We have an extremely high SKU base and a very broad demographic base of users—everything from the teenage fanatic to the middle-aged deep jazz and blues customer. With a large number of SKUs and a high customer base we had the data available to produce accurate recommendation, but didn't have the solution that would do this for us.

"We went out to the market to see what we could do. We had already selected LikeMinds for recommendations because of its ability to scale to support our multiple channels of distribution. Customers could buy anything from any channel, a physical store, the Web site, or by special order from stores.

"The reason we picked Macromedia LikeMinds Personalization was its ability to scale to bricks-and-mortar stores with a Web presence where we service 100 million customers a year and have a customer loyalty program with 1.2 million current customers enrolled. We sell the customer loyalty program (called 'Replay') and customers receive discounts in return.

"The customer now has built a history with us. If he's a Replay customer, we can track his purchases across channels; otherwise, we're considering using 'cookie on a card.' This is a card with an identification number that will be used either in customer interactive devices or at point of sale. It will track a customer's buying history without the demographics. At the point of sale it will be used to provide 'bounce back' coupons for products based on a customer's buying history.

"It will be anonymous and trackable. We'll offer discounts for people to use the card, and there will be no forms to fill out. If the customer elects to receive pertinent information via e-mail, then LikeMinds can analyze across both offline and online customer data to create personalized e-mail campaigns. In this way, we are able to garner information about customer purchase history and can use LikeMinds to make recommendations based on both online and offline customer behavioral data. The customer wins because s/he receives information perfectly tailored to his/her individual taste, and Musicland is able to gain an understanding of our customers across multiple channels, something that has been difficult or impossible to accomplish in the past.

"We're currently sending out about half-a-million e-mail messages per month. In the future, we hope to increase that by four times. We will be able to deliver very tight product recommendations to our customers, fostering a sense of trust and keeping them coming back for more. Currently, we outsource the e-mail campaign management, relying on Macromedia LikeMinds for the most accurate recommendations, but have plans to bring the whole operation in house soon."

By using event-driven e-mail and a recommendations engine, Musicland can mine the rich data it has on customers and products and do customers a service by contacting them with relevant product offers, while increasing customer loyalty and sales.

WHY NOT SEND THE E-MAIL YOURSELF?

Even if your technology department assures you that you have the technology resources to send e-mail to your membership—or even to send targeted e-mail with multiple messages going to different demographic groups—I strongly encourage you to consider using a commercial provider of bulk e-mail services. Why? As you've read above, sending the e-mail is exactly half of the work involved in running a successful targeted e-mail campaign. The other half is evaluating the results of the campaign and making changes based on those results. In my experience, technology departments are very good at creating the solution that you request—though not usually as fast as you'd like. Technical folks thrive on clear definitions. E-mail seems like a perfect candidate. It's easy to understand the requirement: build me a system that can send out 2 million e-mail messages in a twelve-hour window to multiple groups of users without bringing our systems to their knee. The part of the requirement that you can't possibly enunciate and they couldn't meet, even if you could explain it, is the need for analysis and reporting. Until you've seen really great, useful reports from commercial providers of bulk e-mail services, you don't know that you're working with only half or less of the information you need. Marketing can't take advantage of the great customer list you've developed if it can't continuously tweak the message, the message style, and the audience based on measurable results. When you do interview and select a bulk e-mail provider, ask to see the interface you'll see when you create reports. Be sure the reports you can create from your data on its system provide you with all the information you'll need to improve your campaigns.

The trends in e-mail marketing will continually change. E-mail marketing is a relatively new medium. The question of sending HTML-enriched e-mail versus plain text has been pretty solidly answered: ask and send what the visitor requests. The initial backlash against HTML-enriched e-mail passed, and the vast majority of Web users today can handle HTML e-mail. In order to be aware of the latest trends in e-mail marketing, I encourage you to subscribe to at least one of the newsletters in the resources section below. In order to take advantage of the trends, however, you're going to need flexibility you're not likely to get from a homegrown solution.

 RESOURCES

WEB SITES AND NEWSLETTERS

ClickZ (www.clickz.com). Newsletter and Web site that includes at least one column on e-mail on most days. Experienced professionals share their accumulated wisdom.

ECommerce Guide (ecommerce.internet.com). Newsletter and Web site that covers many topics related to e-commerce, including news and technology. Excellent source of wide-ranging information with frequent coverage of marketing issues, including e-mail. You can subscribe to my columns here.

WorkZ (www.workz.com). Newsletter and Web site aimed at solving e-commerce problems for small businesses.

FULL-SERVICE COMPANIES

Digital Impact (www.digitalimpact.com). Provides e-marketing strategic consulting as well as technology resources to deliver integrated, targeted e-mail campaigns.

Flonet (www.flonet.com). Full-service e-mail direct marketing company.

COMMERCIALLY AVAILABLE SOFTWARE FOR SENDING BULK MAIL

DesktopServer 2000 (www.desktopserver2000.com)

WAP-Enabling FOR M-Commerce 7

ESTIMATES OF the number of digital wireless users who will be surfing the Web continue to eclipse each other at an exponential rate, so I hesitate to begin this chapter with startling statistics about how widespread wireless Web access will be by any particular year. Regardless of whose mind-boggling number you believe, there is little doubt this increase results from the proliferation of WAP-enabled cell phones worldwide and the nigh-universal desire to get at information and products on the Web anywhere, anytime. In fact, within the next five years, more Web visitors might come from wireless devices than from wired devices.

You need to get your site up and running on wireless so shoppers who want to purchase your products can do it wherever they are. As with putting up a Web site and taking your Web site global, going wireless has advantages for those who are early to market.

WIRELESS APPLICATION PROTOCOL (WAP)

The wireless Web relies on the Wireless Application Protocol (WAP), a set of protocols and languages that, once implemented, will allow any WAP-enabled device to communicate with any service provider. Using WAP, a content provider can ensure that its site can be viewed by anyone with a WAP-enabled device, regardless of who the carrier is. The protocol was developed by a consortium of wireless device manufacturers, service providers, content providers, and application developers. The goal of the WAP Forum, the standards body that developed the WAP, was to create a standard that would allow its members to develop solutions that are inter-face-independent, device-independent, and fully interoperable.

The Wireless Lingo and Landscape

In order to understand the players in the wireless world, it's useful to see where the responsibilities of one end and those of another begin. Figure 7-1 shows graphically the players involved.

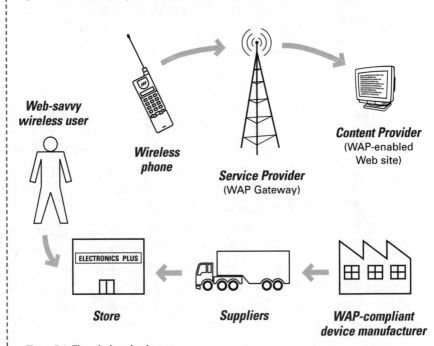

Figure 7-1. The wireless landscape.

> The wireless user contracts with the *service provider* (e.g., AT&T or Sprint PCS or GTE) to receive wireless services. He purchases a wireless phone or PDA that works with that provider's nondigital networks. All WAP-compliant devices work with all WAP gateways, so digital compatibility is assured. Using his wireless device, the wireless user can access WAP-enabled Web sites, which are hosted by *content providers*. Any Web site can be a content provider; however, having a WAP-compliant Web site requires more than just translating your site into wireless markup language (WML) or handheld device markup language (HDML).

Before the WAP, device manufacturers were working on their own proprietary standards that required service providers to build customized content delivery systems so that the content would display properly. The situation was even more complicated for content providers and application developers, who had to develop to the proprietary standard for every type of device on which they wanted their content and applications to work. Customers were the big losers. By virtue of the fact that each of their different wireless devices was likely to work with only one service provider, they were bound to a service provider as long as they owned the wireless device.

AFTER THE WAP: IMT-2000 (AKA 3G)

In Europe, the International Telecommunication Union (ITU) is already working on the successor to WAP. It's called IMT-2000, or 3G (for Third Generation Mobile Systems). IMT-2000 relies on radio waves (specifically 230 megahertz) to carry wireless communications. It has many advantages over the current systems, including the fact that the bandwidth is much greater, communications can travel farther and faster, and outside of the United States, access to wireless communication is less expensive than wired communication. For now, however, WAP is the place to be. WAP-compatible devices are flooding the market at affordable prices. More and more service providers are offering digital, WAP-enabled networks. And WAP is the only standard in place that handles secure transmission of data for financial transactions.

WIRELESS FOR MESSAGING

Wireless commerce (also called *m-commerce,* or *mobile commerce*) is a very small percentage of Internet commerce in the United States as of the year 2000. Will wireless access to the Web ever be the dominant means of "going online" in the United States? Given that the U.S. is one of the few countries in the world in which local phone service is not billed by the minute and the largely inferior online experience of a digital phone or a personal digital assistant (PDA), compared to a desktop, I would say no. However, the United States continues to shrink as a percentage of the worldwide consumer market. In most other countries, local phone service is billed by the minute, landlines to homes are expensive, and there are often multiyear waiting lists to get new landlines installed. In those countries, wireless Web access will probably outpace wired access in the not-too-distant future.

In the United States, wireless devices will continue to be the domain of luxury users, status users, and business users. Already, we see that U.S. wireless phone penetration is a fraction of what it is in Western Europe and in Japan. Because of prohibitive per-minute landline charges for local calls outside the United States, a large proportion of wireless phone users consists of teenagers on allowances. They're neither surfing the Web nor talking; they're sending text messages to one another. Text messaging using short message service (SMS) is the most cost-effective method of communicating in their economic world, and teenagers can be very resourceful when it comes to stretching their allowances.

Text messaging isn't limited to use by teenagers. Business users frequently want access to up-to-the-minute information about stock quotes, news updates, school closings, and even sports scores. There are quite a few companies that offer this kind of content delivered to handheld devices. The better services, like SmartRay (owned by LifeMinders), use very narrowly defined filters to select out just the material from a content site that would be of interest to the device owner. For example, a mother might not get everything about education, but she might be provided everything about the district or school her children attend.

Corporate uses of wireless devices also are many. Business-to-business (B2B) exchanges often rely on a quote being accepted in a very narrow window of time. Real-time messaging to a wireless device with the ability to use WAP to respond can solve that problem.

How Web Surfing Differs from Wireless Web Surfing

Look at a wireless device, either a digital phone or a PDA, then look at your computer monitor. You can see that the experience a visitor to your site is going to have is going be very different, depending on what device is used. After you get past the tiny screen size of most wireless devices—as small as 14 x 7 characters on some—there's the input mechanism to deal with. Most wireless devices have neither mouse nor keyboard. The keypad of a digital phone and, to a lesser extent, the handwriting recognition capabilities of a PDA are a poor substitute for a QWERTY keyboard and modest typing skills.

Navigation on a wireless device can't include image maps (clickable images), and on many devices you get no images at all! Navigation must rely on simple lists with drill-down capability, because all that most wireless devices can do is scroll and select one option from a list.

Because the Web viewed with wireless devices has so little of the eye appeal of the Web viewed with a color monitor, and because the interface with wireless devices is so much more awkward, Web visitors via wireless devices have different goals when they're online. They are more likely to have a very specific task they want to perform. They're unlikely to appreciate any extra clicks. So you should give them the most direct route to their destination, and there are three ways to do this:

1. Have strong search capabilities for your site, with results listed in order of relevancy (or another order that they specify) and results delivered as a list with drill-down capability.

2. Show site contents by category as a list with drill-down capability.

3. If you have a list of special purchases, make it a separate category on par with other categories, also with drill-down capability.

The only logical way to display products in a wireless Web environment is hierarchically. Product names should be as terse as possible, with descriptive text provided only after a visitor has drilled down through the hierarchy to that particular product.

BEING FOUND

One of the important and often overlooked aspects of going mobile is being found by shoppers. The myth of the strong online brand has been exposed in a number of ways, recently with the Forrester Research report, *Demise of the Dot-Com Retailers* (April 2000), which claims that differentiation is the most pressing challenge for online retailers. Although most sites believe they have a strong brand, in reality, many customers don't make the distinction between, say, PriceSCAN.com and PriceGrabber.com, both of which offer similar services.

So then the question becomes how to stand out in this crowded space of online retailers and aggregators. In the wireless environment, there's one easy (and expensive) way, and that's to be a menu item on the service provider's main menu. All wireless users have the home page of the service provider, which simply consists of a numbered list. Positions on that list are auctioned off to the highest bidder. For a wireless user, the alternative to selecting from a merchant on that list is having to type the URL of the WAP-compliant Web page of a merchant into a limited keypad. And that URL isn't just http://www.overtheweb.com. It's more like http://www.over theweb.com/index.wml (or something like that). That's a lot of typing. Of course, the smart wireless user will quickly bookmark his most frequently used addresses, but there are many, many people in the world who, even after years of Web use, never figure out that they can choose their own home page on their desktop computers. They just continue to load the Microsoft Internet Explorer or Netscape Navigator home pages. The average user is far more likely to select from the home page of the service provider, hence the high price tag for that real estate.

PROFILE: Internet2Anywhere (In2a)
Gary LaFever, President and CEO
"Pacific Internet, recent recipient of top honors at Telecom Asia's annual Readers' Choice Awards 2000 as the 'Best Asian Internet

Service Provider (ISP),' has elected to use Internet2Anywhere's WebRinger technology to extend Internet applications to reach friends, family and co-workers when they're offline.

"In2a's technology offers a new way to use the wireless Internet that is better suited to the inherent limitations of mobile devices and wireless services. Rather than today's conventional method of sending information that only alerts by SMS or text paging, In2a's intelligent signaling technology utilizes telephony signals to reach offline devices and automatically launch embedded applications. In2a's solution enables wired and wireless service providers and device manufacturers to do away with time-consuming and costly Web browsing by allowing users to predefine what they're interested in and then reaching out to them offline and automatically launching applications that connect them to previously requested content, e-commerce opportunities, etc.

"It's clear that the wireless Internet will not be the same as the wired Internet. The wireless Internet will not be all about content, but more about real-time communications, personalization, and localization. Since you can't get a lot of information on a mobile device, the real value will come from the timeliness and personalized nature of the information.

"Pacific Internet is initially launching WebRinger to extend instant messaging, chats, and Internet telephony to users on offline desktops, laptops, and wireless devices. Subsequent wireless e-commerce applications will go beyond mere notification of time-sensitive events to put users one click away from completing transactions with their mobile devices (for example, auctions, closeout sales, flight cancellations)."

This is almost magic. They literally phone the computer's modem and send information in the ring without ever connecting the computer to the Web. The computer, which isn't connected to the Web, launches an application (pop-up box) alerting the user that there's a reason to go online. A single click by the user connects him to the time-critical information/action site he needed to know about. For example, say he's been outbid at an auction, or he's been asked to quote a price on a B2B exchange.

GOING MOBILE THE EASY WAY

It is imperative that you make your site mobile. The method you use is secondary. There are two ways you might do it. The first, the easy way, is signing on with a wireless aggregator, also known as a *wireless shopping portal.* Through one of a number of methods—listfeed, XML file, direct access to your database, or harvesting from your site in real time—this company will take your current inventory and integrate it into its own hierarchy for search and comparison by the wireless visitor. The downside to participating in this kind of arrangement is that usually, you're competing largely on price against other merchants who sell the same products you do. The upside, however, far outweighs the downside. You do get traffic.

The wireless aggregator only makes money when you or your competitors sell products through its site, so it is interested in attracting traffic. It is the responsibility of the aggregator to try to get onto the menu of as many carriers as possible so that shoppers will find the aggregator easily. Alternatively, shoppers would have to type in the URL of the aggregator.

If you decide to pursue a wireless aggregator, be sure to evaluate your options on the following criteria:

→ *Cost of participating.* Are there any fees to have your merchandise included? Do you pay an affiliate fee only when a purchase is made, or are there costs for keeping your inventory in sync on its system?

→ *Access to inventory.* How will the aggregator get your products and prices into its own system? Will it be through XML, in which case your site has to be tagged properly, via a listfeed that you provide, or via an API directly into your database, which has security consequences for you?

→ *Product categorization.* Do you have to recategorize or map your products into the aggregator's categories? Because there are no "standard" categories, every system is proprietary. The best option is for the aggregator to match your products with the customer's requests based on manufacturer SKUs, which can be categorized ahead of time by the aggregator.

→ *Visibility in the carrier's system.* Has the aggregator negotiated for menu space on any of the major wireless carriers' networks? If not, then you have to rely on the aggregator advertising enough to get customers to find it and type in its URL. Does the aggregator have any other methods of being found?

→ *Shopping cart.* Will you receive the order in real time directly from the customer, or will the order come to you after the fact, the aggregator having taken all the payment details (or having them on file in a customer profile)?

→ *Customer service.* Can the customer take advantage of click-to-voice (see below) or any other voice-related customer service option on the wireless phone? Does the aggregator provide anything in the way of customer service?

→ *Display of information.* How do your products get displayed on the wireless device? Is it strictly by price? How good do your products and prices look compared to those of your competitors?

→ *Exclusivity in categories.* Will the aggregator negotiate contracts with your competitors to have their prices listed alongside yours, or will you be the only supplier in your product categories?

→ *Exclusivity of wireless arrangement.* Are you permitted to participate with other wireless aggregators, or do you have to put all your eggs in this one basket?

→ *Ownership of the customer.* Will you be able to contact the customer on an opt-in basis in the future, or are you strictly the fulfillment house for the aggregator? Profiles of wireless customers are particularly valuable in the United States because of the unique demographic of wireless shoppers, who tend to be upper income, urban, educated, and convenience-driven.

Most CMSs store the content in XML, making it easily ported across platforms. Then they use XSL (extended stylesheet language) to format the XML content into the proper markup language for the device requesting the "page." If the browser requesting the page is a microbrowser, it might deliver WML or HDML. If it's a PC browser, it would deliver HTML. Chapter 2 discusses CMSs at length.

WAP-Enabled Content Management Systems

There's actually another easy way to WAP-enable your site. That's by making sure that your content-management system (CMS), the software that manages the content on your site, can deliver to WAP devices. Typically, the commercial solutions require you to develop templates for different platforms: PCs, wireless devices, other non-PC devices. Once your content is in the CMS and the templates have been created, a visitor from any platform sees the appropriate content for that platform.

DO-IT-YOURSELF MOBILE

If you decide that you don't want to participate with an aggregator, or that even if you participate, you want to WAP-enable your site, then you're going to need to convert your site into one that's wireless. The first thing you need to know is that despite the hype associated with XHTML (extended hypertext markup language), the XML version of HTML, simply converting your HTML code into XHTML is not adequate. The difference between HTML and XHTML is very small. In theory, XHTML will parse properly in a WAP device, but in practice, it's not how the XHTML parses that matters, it's the structure of the site.

Other than XHTML, developers or consultants who know technology but don't know the wireless interface may tell you that writing the site in XML, then using XSL to convert the site into HTML for wired browsers and into WML for wireless microbrowsers is the way to go. Technically, it's an elegant solution, but practically, unless you want your wired site to be based on a hierarchical structure, which would reduce navigation options on your wired site, it's not the way to go. The XSL translators available today do not address navigation issues well. Using XSL to build your Web site is like using a translation tool to translate Shakespeare. The results are sure to disappoint.

WML

The way to build your site from the ground up to look good on a wireless device is to develop in WML. It's very similar to HTML, but more limited and more appropriate for wireless devices. Using WML in conjunction with whatever server-side processing you're already using—for example, ColdFusion, Active Server Pages, Java servlets, or Perl—you can create dynamically generated pages that render appropriately on wireless devices. In other words, you end up having two different sites or two different templates to display the data appropriately for the relevant device.

CLICK-TO-VOICE

There are many who believe that the "killer app" (most valuable application) in the wireless arena is voice. This belief ignores the number of wireless devices that aren't phones, but that's okay for now because phones still dominate the wireless arena. Surfing the Web on a digital phone isn't a very satisfying experience. Customers frequently cannot get enough information to answer all their questions when shopping online, so they don't complete a purchase. The result is a very high shopping cart abandonment rate—estimated by BizRate to be 75 percent. More disturbing is that according to the same research, 42 percent of shoppers who abandon carts do not return to the merchant's site where they abandoned the cart.

Wireless phones are ideally suited to closing the sale by voice. Shopping on the Web is great for finding the one or several products a customer thinks he wants to purchase, but when it comes time to buy, if the customer has a lingering question, he should be able to connect seamlessly to a customer service representative at the merchant. Given the limited keypad of a wireless phone—or any wireless device, for that matter—real-time chat probably isn't an option. It would be an incredibly tedious option at best. A merchant has two options for letting the customer close the sale by phone. One is to publish the phone number of customer service on the site—which the merchant is probably already doing. However, because the customer will probably have to wait on hold to talk to a person, then explain to the customer service rep what he was looking at—now without the assistance of product information on his phone's display—the odds increase that he will just give up.

The other option for offering shoppers the ability to close the sale on the phone is click-to-voice. Using this technology, the merchant provides a button on one (or every) page of the WAP-enabled Web site. The customer who wants to talk to customer service simply clicks on the button to be called back by the merchant. When the phone rings, the customer knows that a real person will be at the other end of the line, so there won't be any waiting on hold, and that that person will have information about what he was looking at, so he doesn't need to explain what he was doing. One provider of click-to-voice services is RealCall.com, which began by providing click-to-voice for wired Web sites.

CASE STUDY: GiantBear.com
Deepak Mahbubani, Senior Vice President,
Strategic Alliances

"In May of 2000 we were approached by a regional cellular carrier who was interested in accessing our personalized WAP portal software for their small but growing wireless Web-enabled subscriber base. They were interested in offering more value to WAP phone customers, and wondered if there was anyone who could give them more customized functionality than was being offered by Phone.com and others in this new field.

"The strength of our offering versus competitors is that we aggregate WAP-enabled content and deliver it through a portal that can be private labeled for each carrier and that can be further personalized to meet the needs of each individual user. We looked at the competitive landscape and concluded that our superior position would be cemented if we could offer the carrier a way to extend the value of our portal using voice delivery combined with WAP. After evaluating build versus buy, we chose to partner with RealCall for voice-enablement of our content.

"The pilot we conducted allowed users who received GiantBear.com's service to access a wealth of information via their WAP phones (including email, news/weather/sports/horoscopes/

local movie locations/times, etc.). Our users could also request that long messages, such as movie reviews, be read to them via their phone—delivered by passing our content through the RealXChange server. The feedback: In the short span of the pilot, two users of the competing service who became acquainted with the GiantBear offering brought their phones back to the carrier and requested to be given our service!

"The bottom line: The carrier's users were pleased to be able to personalize the content and its delivery to meet their needs. The carrier was glad to have the extra minutes of usage, and [they] are now talking with us about extending the availability of our portal to all their users, not just those with **WAP** or digital phones, but to everyone, since our content alerts are voice-enabled."

One example of when click-to-voice would be handy is when an air traveler is in transit. Before leaving for the airport, he uses his wireless phone to confirm on the airline's WAP-enabled Web site that his flight is on time. If the flight is on time, he heads for the airport. If he finds that the flight is canceled, he can click directly through to the airline's customer service center. When a representative at the center receives the click, she already has his phone number, the flight he was looking at, and possibly his name as well. Good click-to-voice systems let both the merchant and the customer have some say in how much data is sent with the click. In this case, the airline representative is prepared to tell the traveler what other options are available because she knows that the traveler's flight was canceled. What a fabulous personal service to the traveler!

RESOURCES

WEB SITES

WAP Forum (www.wapforum.org). The source for WAP specifications.

WAP.com (www.wap.com). An information site for WAP developers.

Phone.com Developers' Site (www.phone.com). An excellent source of documents and resources for developers, including a forum where developers can post and respond to questions about implementing WAP.

WIRELESS AGGREGATORS

MobileShift (www.mobileshift.com). Offers e-commerce ordering with very few clicks for wireless shoppers who create accounts with it.

RealCall (www.realcall.com). Click-to-voice e-commerce capabilities from wireless devices.

WIRELESS CONTENT DELIVERY

SmartRay (www.smartray.com). Offers content from information sites in exchange for owning the customer profiles.

I3Mobile (www.i3mobile.com). Offers content delivered to wireless devices from content providers at a fee to the content provider.

PART III

TECHNOLOGIES FOR MAKING BUYING EASIER

Personalization for Customer

IN THE REAL world, you expect that if you make frequent visits to a bookstore (other than a megastore) or restaurant (other than fast food), the employees will acknowledge your familiarity with a smile or a nod and perhaps even make recommendations based on what you've demonstrated you already like. There's nothing like visiting a restaurant and having the waiter intimate to you, "We have your favorite soup as a special today." Overall, Web sites have been slow to catch on to the phenomenon of personalization.

Sure, many sites will ask for your name, then refer to you by it later, but in the personalization game, that's not much more than reading the nametag a person wears when attending a conference. If I facetiously tell you my name is "Gorgeous Brunette" when you make me identify myself, and you refer to me later as "Gorgeous Brunette," you haven't exactly enriched my shopping experience—or made me more prone to buy any particular product on your site.

Personalization is about more than reading the "cookie" you've planted on my computer. The cookie you've planted is my ID card. What are you going to do with the data you have about me that doesn't fit on that ID card? How are you going to make me feel welcome and incline me to purchase something else?

OVERT VERSUS COVERT PERSONALIZATION

Overt personalization is the scenario discussed above: You ask for my name, then use it when I return. Overt personalization is extremely valuable, and although it's easy enough to do, it shouldn't be dismissed for being too hokey. A site that's asked permission to keep a customer's credit card on file, and then permits the customer to make a purchase without rekeying the credit card number is making use of overt personalization. Customers love that kind of convenience. According to BizRate's Q1 2000 Consumer Online Report, 36 percent of buyers indicated that express ordering played an influential role in their decision to make a purchase then and there.

I shop online often enough to have my credit card number memorized, but I still resent having to retype it every time I want to make a purchase at sites I purchase from often. Book sellers, such as Amazon and Barnes & Noble, and travel sites, such as Travelocity, understand how much I'd rather just select the card I want to use for today's purchase from a list of those I've given them permission to store. I couldn't find any statistics on the difference in shopping cart abandonment rates between sites that offer expedited checkout and those that don't. It would be interesting, though, to see if having all of a customer's shipping and billing information already on file, and thereby making the checkout process much less arduous (especially for those who aren't speedy typists and don't know that Web forms permit you to tab between fields), makes customers less likely to click away, rather than click through to purchase.

Covert personalization is the future of the Web. As computers get faster, disk space gets cheaper, bandwidth gets more available, and online shoppers get savvier, merchants and service providers will come together to provide value-added personalization to customers. A working pregnant woman will arrive at Gap Online (www.gap.com) and find that the featured item on the home page is a maternity business ensemble. A thirty-five-year-old mother of two small children will arrive at Gap Online, and the same space will hold BabyGap and GapKids outfits. A teenager who arrives at Gap Online will see two teens decked out in today's trendy clothes (the ones on display at the mall), with midriffs exposed. A professional man who arrives at Gap Online will see khakis in the same space. Sure, without personalization any of these items are only one click from the home page, but how much more compelling is the site to the visitor when the items he's most likely to be looking for are the featured items? He doesn't need to know that they're only featured for him.

One of the few types of sites that's doing a good job with covert personalization today is bookstores. My husband, who spends a lot of time at the online bookstores, called me over to the computer one day when he saw that all the books shown on Amazon's home page were either about history or about computers. He couldn't believe that that was what was selling. I told him that Amazon simply had our number and knew what was selling in our house. There was simply no point in advertising romance novels or science fiction or anything other than the very few categories of books that we were buying over and over again.

OVERT PERSONALIZATION

Overt personalization is undeniably of enormous value to shoppers. They'll say so themselves when asked. Any kind of personalization requires tradeoffs, however. In order for a merchant to personalize a site for a shopper, the shopper has to give up some personal information. Privacy has always been a hot topic on the Web. Surveys consistently show that shoppers are reluctant to share their personal information for fear it will be disseminated more widely than they'd consented.

PRIVACY

Although many merchants have privacy policies, few of them commit to much in them. Worse still, despite the fact that online shoppers consistently report that they are concerned about their online privacy, Web server log files consistently show that these same shoppers don't read the privacy policies that are published to inform and appease them.

As a merchant, there are several things you can do to avoid falling out of favor with your customers, the privacy industry, and the FTC, with respect to privacy:

1. Publish a thorough, accurate privacy policy. Unfortunately, the more thorough it is, the longer it is going to be, and the less likely it is to be read. Try not to make it sound like it was written by lawyers for lawyers. TrustE.org has a privacy wizard that can help you create an incredibly comprehensive privacy policy. The policies this wizard produces are very off-putting, but in order to be thorough, it has to mention things about which most shoppers have no knowledge, such as Web server log files. Telling shoppers that their IP addresses—if they even know what that means—are being recorded isn't very instructive, since every Web server with which I'm familiar captures this data by default.

Amazon made modifications to its privacy policy in September of 2000 in which it "clarified" its policy by explaining that customer data was a corporate asset and could be transferred or sold if the company desired. It was strongly criticized by privacy groups for this change, but it was a wise move on Amazon's part to clarify this before it was in discussions with purchasers or in receivership, like ToySmart.com. Part of the reason Amazon received so much criticism is that it mailed its revised privacy policy to everyone in its database, and its privacy policy was written in such a way that regular folks could understand it. To keep its policy to a reasonable length (three pages printed), Amazon makes extensive use of links to definitions and examples, such as explaining what a customer will miss if he visits the site with cookies turned off, then providing a link to a page with a list of anonymous surfing software. By all means, read its privacy policies and those on other sites to get a feel for the good, the bad, and the ugly.

2. Make sure your marketing department and your merchandisers get a chance to review the privacy policy before you post it. That way, they know what you've promised to customers and they have a chance to say whether there's some way they might be sharing the data of which you are not aware. Toysrus.com could have avoided being caught by Interhack

with an inaccurate privacy policy if its marketing department had reviewed the privacy policy and informed the legal department that it was, in fact, using a third party to analyze customer information. Marketing may be out making deals to give customer data at something other than an aggregate level to manufacturers. Also, if any of your products are shipped directly from distributors, then you are already sharing customer data, since your distributors can't ship without customer names and addresses. If you apply for manufacturers' rebates for any products or supply sales information to manufacturers for purposes of warranties, there again, you are sharing customer information. Both these types of "sharing" redound to customers' benefit, but you still need to be straight with them on this front.

3. Put an executive summary of the privacy policy on all your checkout pages, something as simple as "we never share your personal data" or "we take your privacy seriously, which is why we never sell any personal information or e-mail addresses." Linking to the thorough privacy policy is all you need. Make sure the complete privacy policy pops up in a new window so that you don't help your customers abandon their carts. The truly concerned will be able to get at the entire story, and the rest of your shoppers will feel a bit more confidence giving away their personal details.

4. Join a branded organization such as BBBOnLine.org or TrustE.org and show the logo on every checkout page and on the home page. BBBOnLine has the less rigorous standards of the two organizations, but both of them convey to shoppers that you're a good corporate citizen.

5. Everywhere that you request information from your shopper or visitor that you'd like to keep to make subsequent shopping experiences better, ask specifically whether you have his permission to keep it. If there's anything that's more of a selling point than privacy, it's choice.

6. Before you save shipping or billing information, make sure it's okay. No one likes to be surprised by seeing that a site that one doesn't visit often remembers so much. Although you may intend this customer to be a regular shopper, he may intend to shop at your site just this once. Let it be his choice whether you keep his profile on file or not.

DATA COLLECTION

What kinds of data should you be collecting or trying to collect overtly about your customers? That depends on how you plan to use it. A good rule of thumb is: Don't ask for anything you're not going to use. Visitors will be annoyed when you ask them what they're interested in, they respond with, say, "gardening information," and you then show them a broad range of information unrelated to gardening, including NASCAR driver profiles.

There are basically two categories of overt profiling information: that which relates to expediting checkout and that which relates to purchasing interests.

OVERT PERSONALIZATION FOR EXPEDITED CHECKOUT. The checkout portion of the data you request from customers would probably include the information shown in Table 8-1. The field descriptions, field names, and minimum suggested field lengths are taken from the electronic commerce markup language (ECML) Version 1.1 Field Specification. To save time and to build systems that can later talk to other systems, as much as possible you should try to rely on definitions and standards provided by industry standards groups, such as the ECML (www.ecml.org). If digital wallets ever catch on, using the ECML standards would permit a visitor to auto-populate all your shipping and billing fields by permitting your site to read his digital wallet, saving him typing and you the inconvenience of incorrect data.

My only complaint with the fields and field lengths provided in the ECML is that there's a clear U.S. bias, two-character state/province codes, for example. The ECML standards will work with the digital wallets if your minimum field lengths are at least those recommended in the specification (shown in Table 8-1), so if you must extend field lengths international payments, you won't be precluded from participating and complying.

Field Description	Field Name	Minimum Length
Ship to title	Ecom_ShipTo_Postal_Name_Prefix	4
Ship to first name	Ecom_ShipTo_Postal_Name_First	15
Ship to middle name	Ecom_ShipTo_Postal_Name_Middle	15

Ship to last name	Ecom_ShipTo_Postal_Name_Last	15
Ship to name suffix	Ecom_ShipTo_Postal_Name_Suffix	4
Ship to company name	Ecom_ShipTo_Postal_Company	20
Ship to street line1	Ecom_ShipTo_Postal_Street_Line1	20
Ship to street line2	Ecom_ShipTo_Postal_Street_Line2	20
Ship to street line3	Ecom_ShipTo_Postal_Street_Line3	20
Ship to city	Ecom_ShipTo_Postal_City	22
Ship to state/province	Ecom_ShipTo_Postal_StateProv	2
Ship to zip/postal code	Ecom_ShipTo_Postal_PostalCode	14
Ship to country	Ecom_ShipTo_Postal_CountryCode	2
Ship to phone	Ecom_ShipTo_Telecom_Phone_Number	10
Ship to e-mail	Ecom_ShipTo_Online_Email	40
Bill to title	Ecom_BillTo_Postal_Name_Prefix	4
Bill to first name	Ecom_BillTo_Postal_Name_First	15
Bill to middle name	Ecom_BillTo_Postal_Name_Middle	15
Bill to last name	Ecom_BillTo_Postal_Name_Last	15
Bill to name suffix	Ecom_BillTo_Postal_Name_Suffix	4
Bill to company name	Ecom_BillTo_Postal_Company	20
Bill to street line1	Ecom_BillTo_Postal_Street_Line1	20
Bill to street line2	Ecom_BillTo_Postal_Street_Line2	20
Bill to street line3	Ecom_BillTo_Postal_Street_Line3	20

Bill to city	Ecom_BillTo_Postal_City	22
Bill to state/province	Ecom_BillTo_Postal_StateProv	2
Bill to zip/postal code	Ecom_BillTo_Postal_PostalCode	14
Bill to country	Ecom_BillTo_Postal_CountryCode	2
Bill to phone	Ecom_BillTo_Telecom_Phone_Number	10
Bill to e-mail	Ecom_BillTo_Online_Email	40
ReceiptTo title	Ecom_ReceiptTo_Postal_Name_Prefix	4
ReceiptTo first name	Ecom_ReceiptTo_Postal_Name_First	15
ReceiptTo middle name	Ecom_ReceiptTo_Postal_Name_Middle	15
ReceiptTo last name	Ecom_ReceiptTo_Postal_Name_Last	15
ReceiptTo name suffix	Ecom_ReceiptTo_Postal_Name_Suffix	4
ReceiptTo company name	Ecom_ReceiptTo_Postal_Company	20
ReceiptTo street line1	Ecom_ReceiptTo_Postal_Street_Line1	20
ReceiptTo street line2	Ecom_ReceiptTo_Postal_Street_Line2	20
ReceiptTo street line3	Ecom_ReceiptTo_Postal_Street_Line3	20
ReceiptTo city	Ecom_ReceiptTo_Postal_City	22
ReceiptTo state/province	Ecom_ReceiptTo_Postal_StateProv	2
ReceiptTo postal code	Ecom_ReceiptTo_Postal_PostalCode	14
ReceiptTo country	Ecom_ReceiptTo_Postal_CountryCode	2
ReceiptTo phone	Ecom_ReceiptTo_Telecom_Phone_Number	10
ReceiptTo e-mail	Ecom_ReceiptTo_Online_Email	40

Name on card	Ecom_Payment_Card_Name	30
Card type	Ecom_Payment_Card_Type	4
Card number	Ecom_Payment_Card_Number	19
Card verification value	Ecom_Payment_Card_Verification	4
Card expire date day	Ecom_Payment_Card_ExpDate_Day	2
Card expire date month	Ecom_Payment_Card_ExpDate_Month	2
Card expire date year	Ecom_Payment_Card_ExpDate_Year	4

Table 8-1: Fields to store to expedite checkout as part of overt personalization.

OVERT PERSONALIZATION OF SHOPPING INTERESTS. As with targeted e-mail, the best way to find out what people care about is to ask them. You may have a shopper pegged as a late-thirties, high-income career type, when in reality, she may be about to get married and be planning to put her career on the back burner and start a family immediately. She knows; you don't. Although using her zip code and other demographic data you can scrape together will get you part of the way, asking her directly will get you all of the way. The key is to couch your questions in terms of her convenience.

MOTIVATING SHOPPERS TO GIVE YOU THEIR PREFERENCES

Again, the two prerequisites to collecting this type of information are to disclose your privacy policy and give the visitor a choice. Even though I'm generally opposed to extravagant giveaways, if you can find a modest raffle item that appeals to the demographic of your site, say, a Palm VII for a career site, you will have greater success getting most visitors to provide information that will permit you to personalize the site. Don't give away anything too extravagant or you'll attract "raffle sluts," as the VP of one major research firm calls them. They're not likely to make a purchase in the first place, let alone return to shop again. Your database space will be wasted storing personalization information about visitors who will surely never return, and you'll be disappointed when you realize how many visitors never return.

Another reason not to be too generous in giving things away is that you encourage people to clutter up your database by signing in to the promotion hundreds of times. I had a client who gave away a very spiffy new laptop computer, and one (not particularly clever) individual entered the sweepstakes for the laptop 653 times in one week, all from the same e-mail address. It is possible to monitor for these things (in this case, the rules specified that multiple entrants would be disqualified) and clean out the database after the fact, but you have better things to do. It's better not to give your visitors incentive to enter multiple times.

COVERT PERSONALIZATION

Covert personalization, when done well, is beautiful to behold. Unfortunately, very few sites are doing this well right now. Personalization should be so transparent that a visitor to the site quickly reaches the conclusion that the site sells exactly what he's interested in. There may be other inventory items filed neatly away under the proper categories, but all the featured specials and graphics on the home page are exactly what he cares about.

There's a site I like to shop at that's missing a golden opportunity to market to me. They've asked me and I've told them what I care about among their product lines, and they continue to show me specials for golf clubs—something I don't need in a category of products in which I've never expressed an interest—every time I arrive at their home page. This happens regardless of whether I type their URL directly into my browser or whether I click through one of their e-mail solicitations. They know me when I arrive and identify me by name, so they could make an effort to gear their home page specials to me. At any given visit, there are a dozen things I consider buying. If they were to perform click-stream analysis (see Click-Stream Analysis section later in this chapter) on me during any given visit, they'd see me peruse their housewares selection, their lighting fixtures selection, and their garden tools and furniture. Yet they either don't analyze this data, which should be in their server log files, or they don't have the capability to apply it when they see me request a page.

Actually, there is another possibility. Many sites sell home page space to the manufacturers of the products displayed there. They know that the manufacturer of the golf clubs has paid for a given number of impressions of its clubs on the home page, and they believe that the golf club maker is their customer. They're wrong. I am their customer, just as I am the prospective customer of the golf club maker. If they were to analyze their visitors and show targeted ads to visitors based on one of the techniques discussed below, not only would they have a better chance of selling me something, they'd be able to charge more to the golf club maker for showing its specials to an audience that's interested.

CASE STUDY: G.U.S. Home Shopping Limited

GUS Home Shopping is a major player in home shopping in the U.K. It is the second biggest general retailer in the U.K. and is a division of The Great Universal Stores plc Group. GUS is also Britain's largest catalog retailer, with a market share of around 24 percent. The GUS Home Shopping telephone service takes in a total of more than 70 million calls per year and between 15,500 and 23,400 calls per hour.

GUS Home Shopping, whose business lines include the Great Universal, Choice, and Kays catalogs, applied the Net Perceptions personalization technology offline in its call centers to increase both up-sell rates and overall basket sizes. In a pilot study it was able to increase the up-sell acceptance rate—additional items recommended to a customer who has already phoned in to purchase a specific merchandise item—by 50 percent, and it boosted the average value of each up-sell item by 60 percent. Moreover, GUS found that orders that included a personalized recommendation were 23 percent larger than those without such recommendations.

"The results are a clear hat trick," says David Main, Commercial Director of the GUS Home Shopping Division. "We increased our up-sell acceptance rate, boosted the average value of each up-sell item, and showed that personalization technology, when properly applied, is significantly more efficient and effective than a more manually intensive approach. In addition, we found that our sales advisers were enthusiastic about discussing personalized recommendations with their customers."

USING A RECOMMENDATIONS ENGINE

One very effective way of covert profiling is to use some sort of engine that analyzes what customers buy, then gives you direction to show customers who have already purchased other things in which they might be interested, based on the fact that other customers have purchased that combination of products. For example, analysis of purchase patterns may show that people who buy five-quart Calphalon Dutch ovens (that's a medium-sized pot, for those of you who don't cook) also purchase imported clay garden pots, and that people who purchase microwaves also purchase resin garden pots. Knowing which to show a visitor may make the difference between a sale and a lost sale.

PROFILE: Net Perceptions

One company that provides an intelligent engine that can review purchases in your database and make recommendations in real time is Net Perceptions. The Net Perceptions recommendation engine has two components: analytics and collaborative filtering. The analytics piece evaluates your data as a batch process, clustering customers on the basis of order history and detailed transaction data. Demographics such as age, sex, and income can, but don't need to, factor in. It also clusters products on the basis of what's purchased either at the same time by these clusters of shoppers or on subsequent visits—such as batteries with an inexpensive flashlight, for instance, or batteries and a sleeping bag with an expensive flashlight. The analytics engine also tells you which clusters are long-term value customers and which are bottom-feeders (customers who only shop when the price is unbeatable or when there's something free involved), as well as which products are associated with which types of customers. The collaborative filtering engine (see Figure 8-1) uses the data sets created from your database by the analytics engine to make recommendations.

The collaborative filtering and rules manager operates in real time, using the data sets created by the analytics component about customers, products, and content, and also making use of click-stream analysis to show the right products and promotions even to new visitors, based on what they choose to look at. The collaborative filtering and rules manager recommends products for each cluster. When the collaborative filtering engine makes recommendations, it also provides a confidence level so that the merchandiser can see how much more likely one product is to sell with one cluster than another. The merchandiser can then make decisions based on both confidence and profitability.

The collaborative filtering and rules manager does more than provide a graphical user interface to the merchandiser to indicate which cluster of shoppers will see which promotion. The merchandiser can also model the shopping behavior of the existing customer base against various promotions he might be considering, to see which promotion will be most profitable. Of course, the Net Perceptions engine provides after-the-fact profitability reporting for its recommendations as well, but it's the only tool in this category that projects behavior and profitability before you run a promotion.

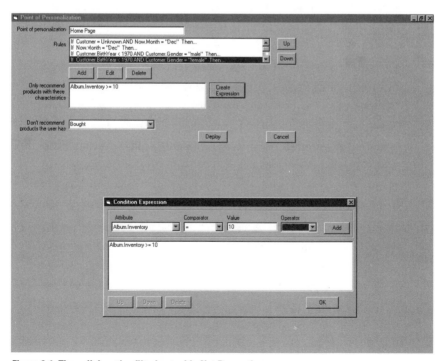

Figure 8-1. The collaborative filtering tool in Net Perceptions.

The analytics tool can also analyze your log file to see where your most and least valuable customers are coming from, and evaluate the value of the referring IP addresses (the site from which they're linking into your site) for each cluster. This gives you valuable information you can use when a new visitor comes from the same IP addresses. Your content management system will instantly know what products to display, and you will know whether you can expect this to be a long-term value customer. You can also use this information to place cost-effective advertising on sites that have traditionally referred you long-term value customers.

PROFILE: ShopTok's TokAdvisor

A relatively new product offers a recommendations engine comparable to Net Perceptions via an ASP business model. No software needs to be installed on the merchant's site. ShopTok hosts a variety of applications—TokBoards, TokAdvisor, TokClubs, and TokSupport—all of which are linked to a powerful data-mining engine and knowledge base called TokEngine. TokAdvisor is a product merchandising application that uses a recommendation engine to link user queries to specific products and services on a merchant's Web site. But the really interesting part, and the part that merits its inclusion here, is that the TokAdvisor can be easily integrated with a customer support application called TokSupport Instant Communication (IC).

TokSupport IC offers a real-time chat interface to enable sales representatives to effectively cross-sell and up-sell customers who contact them with customer support queries. Figure 8-2 shows the chat tool that the sales representative sees.

Unlike Net Perceptions, the TokAdvisor doesn't permit advance modeling of profitability of different recommendations against the customer database. The TokEngine catalogs all user questions that come in via chat, along with the answers that the sales reps use, so that when similar questions come in later, the sales reps can select from a preformatted list of appropriate responses. All conversation about products is stored as meta-data (data about the data) and linked with a rich object-oriented database of product information. In other words, the conversations and queries about products become part of the product database, rather than residing elsewhere.

Because all the software resides on the ShopTok's servers, implementation is very fast—averaging two days for a typical configuration. ShopTok's products are all XML-based, so they integrate smoothly with any platform. ShopTok receives real-time updates

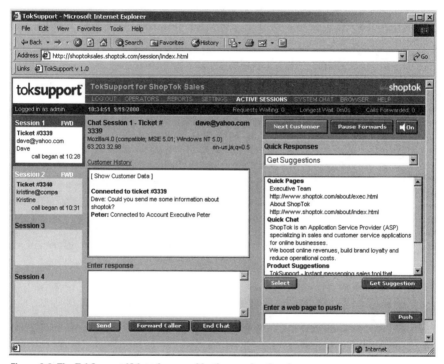

Figure 8-2: The TokSupport IC interface used by the merchant's sales reps.

from merchants' servers when purchases are made, and it maintains product and order databases on its own site, so the real-time clickstream analysis of customer conversations doesn't slow down the merchants' servers.

ANONYMOUS PROFILING

One way to deliver relevant content to visitors, which can be used with the method described above, is to use anonymous profiling of visitors. This has the disadvantage of not being as accurate, but the advantage of being applicable even to visitors who have not been to your site before or have never purchased from you. In this scenario, you can show targeted, relevant content even to new visitors.

PROFILE: Angara Converter

One company that can provide anonymous profiling for your site is Angara. Using its Angara Converter, the company can help you customize your home page with content that's relevant to each visitor's demographic data (e.g., age, income, location, sex). This means that the first time a visitor comes to your home page, you already know something about what you should be pushing in the way of content—even if it's only golf clubs or no golf clubs (e.g., high-income man versus middle-income woman).

Using Angara Converter, you can tailor your message by the location of the visitor, telling international visitors, on your home page, what your international shipment policies are rather than burying the policies in your frequently asked questions (FAQ) section. Or you can offer promotions based on regional concerns such as weather (e.g., ceiling fans in Texas), hobbies (e.g., canoes in Oregon), or fashion trends (e.g., black leather jackets in New York City). Angara compiles its anonymous data from online data suppliers like Naviant and PrivaSeek. It owns more than 100 million anonymous, cookie-based profiles of users around the world, which means that if any of those 100 million visitors comes to your site, you will already "recognize" them and know what content would be most relevant to them. Best of all, when your content management system is talking to its databases, you can pull the information that you need from its databases in the split second that it takes your visitors to request the page and then send a customized home page. Your visitor never needs to know that everyone who visits that site doesn't see the same thing. And that is the beauty of great personalization.

Angara is also a big hit from a privacy perspective. While your system is serving targeted content based on age, income, sex, race, and location, neither you nor Angara has access to any personally identifiable information about the visitor. All Angara knows (and realize, this data never sits in your own database) is that the demographics are associated with the cookies on the visitors' computers. Sure, you're going to risk guessing wrong when visitors come to your site from libraries, coffee shops, and university computer labs, but even then the demographic data will be largely the same across visitors (excluding race and sex).

CLICK-STREAM ANALYSIS

Click-stream analysis is one of the more sophisticated things you can do to your Web server log files to find out about who's shopping on your site (see Chapter 3). Most sites only use their Web server logs after the fact to see which sites are referring them visitors, what browsers their visitors are using, and how many unique visitors or page requests they've had. Real-time click-stream analysis permits you to see where visitors have been on the visits in progress and show them relevant content while they are still on your site.

PROFILE: Blue Martini Software

Blue Martini Software unquestionably offers one of the best-of-breed products in the CMS space. Its solution comprises eight components: a Web store interface, a call center component, a customer-collaboration tool, a merchandise management component, a customer management component, a content management component, tools enabling business users to change and update the system and related content, and a data-mining module for micromarketing (personalization). All in all, it's a very impressive suite of products for serious contenders in many industries, including the retail space, financial services, and manufacturing.

The two main selling points of the Blue Martini solution are the extensive personalization of the site that it permits, based on business rules, and the real-time click-stream analysis that can be used to apply the business rules. The Blue Martini solution facilitates interaction with customers across Web sites, call centers, in store systems, WAP devices, and handles multiple currencies and languages.

Corporate users, including product managers and merchandisers, define the business rules, which can tell the system to show content based on a number of criteria. The tools provided permit real-time measurement of the effectiveness of marketing campaigns in increasing average sale size, increasing closure rate, and ultimately increasing the value of a customer. More than just measurement, however, the analysis or measurement of this information is turned back into actionable changes to the system to improve the user's experience. While Blue Martini has its roots in enabling Web-based retailers, companies in other industries are also rapidly finding that the integrated personalization and content management offered by Blue Martini helps them to attract and retain customers both online and offline.

RESOURCES

The personalization space is crowded on the lower tiers, but less so on the upper rungs of the ladder. I suggest you start with:

Net Perceptions (www.netperceptions.com). The top-of-the-line personalization and recommendation engine. Most other solutions mentioned in other chapters in this book can work with Net Perceptions. This is the personalization technology with which all others are compared.

ShopTok (www.shoptok.com). An ASP providing a full e-commerce support platform, from personalization and recommendations right through real-time chat where customer service representatives can make cross-selling suggestions based on the recommendations engine.

Blue Martini (www.bluemartini.com). Personalization is part of its suite of software. It works with its content-management solution.

WinWin (www.winwin.com). This company offers opt-in personalization based on information it collects from the many sites in its network. Customers must opt-into the WinWin system in order to benefit from personalization, which makes it less of a target for the privacy industry.

For click-stream or log analysis software, visit *http://dmoz.org/ Computers/Software/Internet/Site_Management/Log_Analysis/* for a variety of vendors of log analysis software in all price ranges.

WebTrends Live (www.webtrendslive.com). An ASP offering Web server log analysis and reporting in real time.

Coremetrics (www.coremetrics.com). An ASP offering very sophisticated click-stream and marketing campaign analysis and reporting. The reports offered here are unequaled by any other company in this space.

Keylime (www.keylime.com). An ASP offering click-stream analysis and real-time reporting. In addition to the reports, you get access to a consultant who can help you determine what data you need to see and provide reports that are appropriate.

As far as anonymous profiling goes, there's no inexpensive way to get at that data. It's a relatively new field, and it's not yet crowded.

Angara (www.angara.com). Unique anonymous profiling to help customize the visitor's experience on the very first visit.

Cogit (www.cogit.com). Anonymous profiling for visitors in its extensive database. It actually combines online data with offline data to compile a comprehensive lifestyle profile, then strips out personal information to make the profile anonymous. The lifestyle profile can help you deliver a personalized experience even to first-time visitors.

You may find that the content management solution you select has personalization built into it, using one of the models mentioned above or some other. If you're using a commercial content management solution, check to see what it offers in the way of personalization.

Search

Shopping Wizards AND In-Context

SEARCH BOXES on Web sites and shopping by category don't begin to address the needs of shoppers. Is that how anyone shops in person at Home Depot or Circuit City? Perhaps when shopping is a social event—with lunch at Nordstrom's café—shoppers want to meander through the store and see what's in style and on sale. But when the inventory of products is large, they can only see a handful at a time, and they don't necessarily know the exact specifications of what they are looking for or even what the options are. They are then more likely to hunt down a salesperson. For most shoppers looking for stereo equipment, computers, cameras, lawn and garden equipment, and hardware, some assistance is required, if only to find the page or rack that displays the handful of products from which they're to choose. Hardware is probably the most extreme example, where shoppers can frequently only describe in vague terms what they're looking for—that *thingy* that connects the hose for the washer to the wall—being completely unfamiliar with the vocabulary of professional craftsmen. What they do know is that they're looking to *solve a problem*, not to *purchase a product.*

Successful sites will begin by offering to solve the problems that shoppers have when they come to their sites and let them buy as a consequence of having their problems solved. This chapter takes you through the four technologies that address the problem-solving needs of Web shoppers: shopping wizards, in-context search tools, natural language search tools, and knowledgebases. In theory, there are two kinds of shoppers: the surgical shopper, who knows just what he wants, and the casual browser, who is just looking around to see what you have available, what's on sale, and so on. The surgical shopper is the one who is relatively underserved by most online merchants. That type of shopper is also the one who's closer to being ready to make a purchase.

WHO'S SHOPPING ONLINE?

The very best source of information on who's shopping online today and who will be in the near future is Mary Modahl's book, *Now or Never: How Companies Must Change to Win the Battle for Internet Consumers*, which is based on Forrester's Technographics™ Study. The first third of the book goes through the demographics and motivations of today's and tomorrow's online shoppers. If you can't imagine a book published in 1999 could have anything relevant to say about online demographics, then subscribe to Forrester's Technographics Service and get the updated version; there's a few thousand dollars difference in the prices between the book and the subscription, though.

Now or Never explains that in surveys with over 200,000 Americans, Forrester was unable to find any demographic quality (age, sex, income, race) that explained why some people were buying online and some weren't—until they started to probe for attitudes about technology and motivation to use technology. At that point, Forrester saw clearly that technology optimists were more likely to shop online than technology pessimists—regardless of income, age, sex, race, and other factors. Also, motivation to be online fell clearly into one of three categories: career enhancement, community and communications, or entertainment. Finally, they found that the third most important factor was, indeed, income. With this information at hand, they proceeded to break the world of Web shoppers into ten groups. Each group was assigned a catchy name (such as "fast forwards" for high-income technology optimists who went online to advance their careers, and "gadget grabbers" for low-income technology optimists who went online primarily for entertainment).

Although the demographics of the high-income technology optimists and the high-income technology pessimists weren't that different, Forrester noted differences in cell phone penetration, number of phone lines, number of computers, whether computers were connected to the Internet, and number of hours spent online. Their findings confirmed what most merchants knew by the end of 1999: most online shoppers before the Christmas season were Web veterans with high incomes. The really remarkable part of *Now or Never* is that Forrester believes that the rest of the population that's interested in going online or shopping online won't take as long as Web veterans did to become comfortable with the process. Forrester fully expects everyone but low-income technology pessimists to be online and shopping by the end of 2002. According to *Who's Not Online*, published by the Pew Internet & American Life Project in September 2000, 57 percent of those without Internet access say they do not plan to log on.

All of this also means, however, that merchants have to meet the needs of the not-as-savvy, new-to-the-Web crowd. Merchants can no longer take for granted that their shoppers are experienced enough to figure out confusing interfaces or unintuitive search boxes. More than ever before, merchants have to be prepared to guide the shoppers directly to the merchandise that meets their needs, with a minimum of clicks, and a maximum of understanding that the shopper may be a bit uncomfortable with the experience. Sophisticated search tools and shopping wizards can insulate shoppers from the confusion of navigating through a store by product category or using a search box when they don't even know what the product they want is called.

What Did I Do Wrong?

The online shoppers of 1998 were technically savvy Web veterans who understood how to navigate the Web. Shoppers knew that if a site had an error when they clicked, it was the site that was at fault. These early Web shoppers hailed from the "wild west" days of the Web, when there were more broken links and malfunctioning sites than working links and faultless sites. When early Web shoppers encountered a site error, they were as likely to screen-capture the page and send the error to the Web master as not.

Today's Web shoppers are a different breed altogether. They're more like my dad. If they click on a link that gives them an error message, they assume that they did something wrong. They're used to software applications that work. They've never recognized the difference between when they're doing it wrong and when the software isn't working. These are smart, educated, affluent people who just don't spend all day at the computer and tend to blame themselves for any computer problems.

How does the difference in computer competence and comfort levels of shoppers affect a merchant? To build the confidence of these new-to-the-Web shoppers, a merchant needs to make a shopping experience completely without incident. In fact, every merchant benefits when other merchants have seamless sites, because Web shoppers then have the confidence to become Web buyers. One bad shopping experience can sour a new-to-the-Web shopper from buying for six months. Every merchant suffers as a consequence.

SHOPPING WIZARDS

Shopping wizards are a terrific way to help solve the problem of the gift buyer. EddieBauer.com has a very useful Gift Finder. They've identified three criteria that factor into the gift-finding decision: recipient information (sex, relationship to you, age, individual or couple, etc.), occasion for giving the gift (with all the usual American gift-giving occasions listed), and price range (from under $25 to over $100). Based on the shopper's selections, a set of products is displayed. Each of those products represents a product category where multiple products that meet the criteria are displayed. By clicking on a product that they display, you can see other products in that category that also match your criteria. For example, if you indicated you wanted a birthday gift for a woman in the price range between $50 and $75, far too many products would be returned to be displayed on one page. The Gift Finder would show one sweater, one pair of pants, one handbag, and other things that matched your criteria. The sweater, pants, and handbag would each link to pages with more items of that type that matched your criteria.

BUILDING A SHOPPING WIZARD

The concept of a shopping wizard is very simple. It's basically just a decision tree, as shown in Figure 9-1. Unlike the gift wizard above, where the answer to all the questions are known up front, in most shopping wizards,

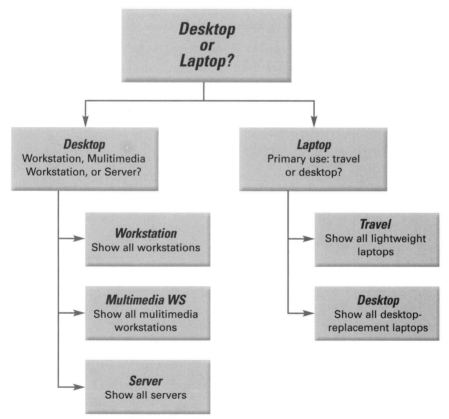

Figure 9-1. A simple decision tree that could be used to narrow down computer choices for a computer shopper.

it's the job of the wizard to ask progressively more specific questions until the product selection is eventually narrowed down to a small handful of products or even a single product. The shopping wizard in Figure 9-1 only goes a small part of the way. In fact, most sites selling computers would still have dozens, if not hundreds, of computers to display as matches for the second question. This wizard would probably need two or three more questions (decisions) on any of the branches to achieve a reasonable number of matches. Certainly, price range would probably be one of the wizard questions. If the audience were sophisticated, chip speed and memory would be another wizard question. If not, that might only obscure the results. For an unsophisticated audience, it might be better to ask something like: "Will you be using this computer primarily for surfing the Web, listening to music, playing games, running spreadsheets, or checking e-mail and typing documents?" The right proportion of memory to chip speed to modem could reasonably be ascertained from the answer.

POPULATING A SHOPPING WIZARD

The important thing about a shopping wizard is that the products that result from answering all the questions must be kept up-to-date. There are two ways to populate a shopping wizard. The first way is simply to make sure that whoever enters products into categories for your site also enters (and removes) products from the shopping wizard. This is the riskier route to take, because if someone isn't paying attention, the wizard is likely eventually to be populated with products that are out-of-date or no longer available.

The better way to populate a shopping wizard is to have variables associated with all products that are set when the products are entered into the database (typically by the merchandisers). These variables should match up with the questions asked in the wizard. Some products may match for more than one set of answers, depending on the questions, and using variables is the best way to ensure that all products that match always end up on the results page. Table 9-1 shows fictitious products with variable values for desktop computers.

There's no magic to the variable values I've selected. Because of the way these questions are asked, it is possible for one path through the questions to lead to no values. If you want to avoid that, make sure the third question about price range doesn't include any price range that won't contain products such as under-$700 desktop-replacement notebooks. The questions asked in this shopping wizard—which are associated with the variable values in parentheses—are:

1. Desktop or notebook? (D, N)

2. If desktop, what's most important: speed, having multiple applications open at once, great graphics, great sound, Internet connection (S, M, V, A, I). If notebook, will you be using this primarily for travel, for presentations, or to replace a desktop computer (T, P, D)?

3. Regardless of question, price range under $700, $700-999, $1000–1199, $1200–1499, $1500 or more (1, 2, 3, 4, 5).

	Desktop or Laptop	Most Important Feature	Price Level
Big Connected Desktop	D	SMVA	4
Zippy Desktop	D	S	2
Memorable Desktop	D	M	2
Flashy Desktop	D	V	2
Super-Audio Desktop	D	A	3
Multimedia Desktop	D	VA	3
Internet-Ready Desktop	D	I	2

Table 9-1: Fictitious computers and values for results of the desktop path through the shopping wizard.

IN-CONTEXT SEARCH CAPABILITIES

Another form of shopping wizard is an in-context search tool. An in-context search tool allows the shopper to begin to define his needs, usually using natural language. The user could say "I need a computer for college" rather than "computer and college" or some other search engine syntax. The in-context search tool then produces increasingly narrow searches based on the context provided by previously defined needs. For example, returning to the example of a consumer interested in purchasing a computer, the dialog would proceed as follows:

> *Shopper:* I need a fast laptop.

> *Search tool:* 72 computers match your specifications. Please specify price range, speed, memory, or weight to narrow down the choices.

> *Shopper:* Lightweight.

> *Search tool:* 23 computers match your specifications. Please specify price range, speed, or memory.

> *Shopper:* Enough memory and good enough graphics to run online games.

> *Search tool:* 7 computers match your specification. Please click on one below.

Even if the shopper didn't know a lot about computers when he started this dialog, he would probably be able to get something out of the "conversation." Compare this to the experience the same shopper would have if trying to find a computer that matched his specifications by hunting through categories of products. Many sites don't list products within a category across manufacturers but expect shoppers to look into each manufacturer's products separately, giving shoppers no good way to compare apples to apples.

Figure 9-2 shows a very nice in-context help system at CNet Computers.com. The vendor providing this solution is Soliloquy. Notice the friendly language and helpful suggestions. Also, under the text box for entering questions, example questions appear below the text-entry box, helping the shopper understand how to phrase a question.

PROFILE: Soliloquy

At the forefront of the next generation of Web infrastructure technology is Soliloquy, a company that creates natural-language interfaces that humanize e-commerce by making online shopping conversational and interactive. There are two components to Soliloquy's cutting-edge technology: Soliloquy Experts and Dialogue Mining.

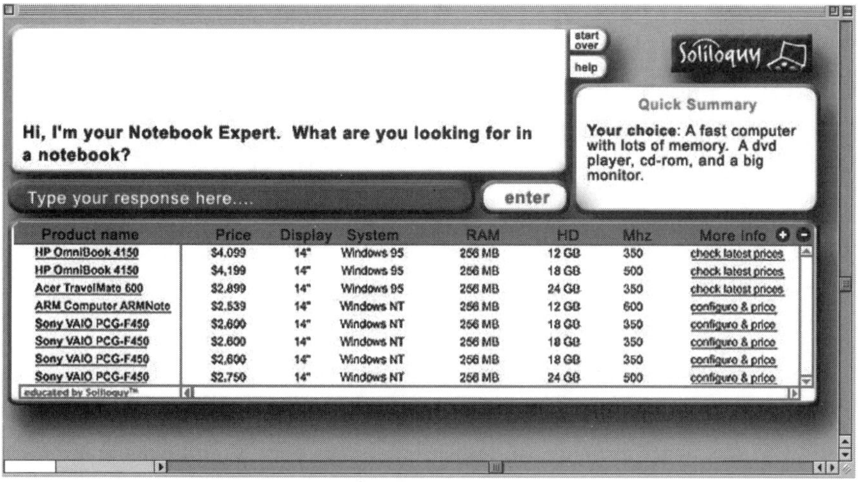

Figure 9-2. In-context product location assistance at CNet.com.

Soliloquy Experts enable shoppers to come onto your site and hold intelligent, two-way conversations with the site as if they were speaking with a real person. The Experts allow shoppers to type (or speak) in their own words, moving them smoothly through the buying process to a buying decision. The product is based on an advanced linguistic technology that transforms words into their functional representation, allowing the system to understand the actual meaning of a person's conversation. The system infers the shopper's goals and preferences in order to carry on a truly intelligent dialogue and take advantage of cross-selling and up-selling opportunities.

Soliloquy's Dialogue Mining Technology offers your company the ability to gain valuable insights into your shopper's buying psychology. Soliloquy captures and logs all of the customer interactions and then mines the data to provide you with real-time online tools that help you better understand your shoppers. Unlike basic click-stream analysis, Dialogue Mining digests the actual words and context built up during each exchange to determine what shoppers are asking during the online buying process, why they are buying a given model, and what they are not finding that causes them to leave your site.

Merchandising and marketing can use the reports generated by Soliloquy about what customers are asking about and for to redesign the site or portions of the site and to feature relevant products. For example, if a lot shoppers are asking about computers for their children leaving for college in May, perhaps to give as high school graduation gifts, then the site should have a promotion responding to that on the home page, rather than assuming that people shop for back-to-school items in August. The reports produced by Soliloquy give marketing the ability to satisfy customer desires better by thinking in terms of solving the customers' problems, rather than thinking in terms of what products they want to "unload."

Soliloquy also offers the benefit of being a turnkey solution that makes implementation quick and easy. Products are delivered through an ASP model, thereby placing the burden of development and synchronization on Soliloquy rather than on you. Soliloquy scalable products are database agnostic, which means they are not wedded to any particular vendor, and they support various types of input/output, including text, speech, gestures, and animated characters (which show expressions and do things on the screen).

NATURAL LANGUAGE SEARCH TOOLS

In addition to making products accessible, you need to make information accessible. Customers will have questions about products, fulfillment, policies, and especially about services. Your customers will probably have the most questions if they are signing up for a service. The problem that many Internet customers, even experienced Web users, have is that they're not familiar with your particular vocabulary. A standard search tool might expect customers to type the word "membership" when they think they're buying a "subscription." When keyword searches on what seems like the right vocabulary to them fail to return appropriate results, the customers get frustrated and leave.

I once went to a site to find a stroller. I typed "stroller" and was told there were no matches on products. Then I found jogging strollers under athletic equipment. Just to test out the search tool, I typed "stroller" again and found no matches, then "strollers" and was shown the jogging strollers. Clearly, no merchant can expect the average customer to display that much tenacity (or curiosity).

Natural language search tools actually seem unnatural to those of us who live in the world of the Web. We're so used to having to condense our search questions into keywords—as you have to do on most search engines if you want to see meaningful results—that when we're told to ask questions in plain English, we don't know what to type. However, to those who don't know that to get the best results on, say, Yahoo!, typing a plus (+) before each keyword will limit the search results to sites that match on every word, natural language search tools can be a dream come true. The best natural language search tools also display sample questions on the page to help users phrase their questions.

Ask Jeeves, of search engine fame, offers a natural language search tool for merchants and content sites. Financial services is one area where everyone in need of the products might not be familiar with the vocabulary to search for products and information about the products. Datek, the financial services company, implemented the Ask Jeeves solution on their site. Their user base comes to them at all different levels of financial savvy. With a natural language search tool, visitors to the site can have their plain-English questions either answered by the search tool or refined into the proper question, which can then be answered. Ask Jeeves, the natural language search tool, has been an excellent choice for Datek. It not only permits the visitors to find the right products and information on the site, it also reports back to Datek what visitors are asking for and about so that Datek can feature these things prominently. Figure 9-3 shows both a query asked in English of the search tool and the results.

PROFILE: Ask Jeeves E-Commerce and E-Support Services

Ask Jeeves' e-Commerce and e-Support Services provide customers with an easy-to-use intuitive search experience. There are many useful features central to this experience. First, there's what the visitor sees: a friendly, familiar interface with natural language questions appearing in the peak box beneath the search box, suggesting both questions and formatting of questions to the visitor. Once the visitor poses a question, the Ask Jeeves service does what most help desks do, which is to ask for clarification. Ask Jeeves does this by offering multiple possible paths for the visitor to follow to find the results she's seeking.

Behind the scenes, however, much more is going on. The peak box that's displaying sample questions is also suggesting questions to the visitor—questions the merchant would want the visitor to be asking. Additionally, every question that comes into the system is being logged. This means that you can see what your visitors are asking about, and what they're having trouble finding on your site. Perhaps they're looking for material you're not even publishing. Before they click away to a competitor's site in frustration, they leave you with invaluable information as to what they wanted.

Ask Jeeves works with your merchandising department to formulate questions and answers that will highlight the products and services you want highlighted. They can help you cross-sell and up-sell products as part of answering questions. For example, if the

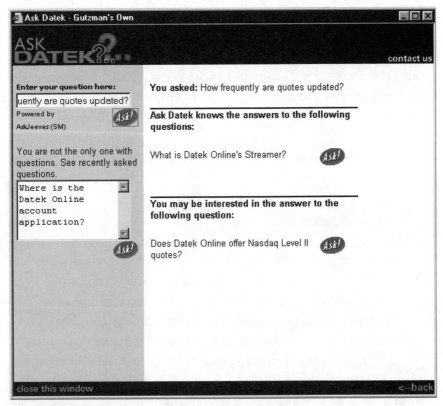

Figure 9-3. Searching for answers to questions at Network Solutions.

visitor uses the word *printer* in the question, one of the answers returned might be a link to a page showing how to find the right printer cartridge for each printer.

If you've never used Ask Jeeves' technology and services, you should go to Ask.com or one of its many client sites to see it in action. It's user-friendly and very responsive, and it can help your customers find answers to their problems.

KNOWLEDGEBASE

If your site visitors are reasonably technically savvy, then a straight knowledgebase may be the way to go. A knowledgebase is a collection of questions and answers about products and services on your site. The days of the FAQ (frequently asked question list) sufficing for a customer service page are long gone. A knowledgebase can be built by hand, with writers from your site creating likely questions and answers, or it can be generated dynamically from actual questions that come into the customer service center via e-mail, chat, or by phone. The latter approach generally makes more sense.

The best example of a thriving knowledgebase of which I'm aware is 3Com's knowledgebase (Figure 9-4). 3Com sells a wide range of networking products to a wide range of users. For a technically competent user, the knowledgebase is generally the fastest way to get a specific technical answer. In addition to answering general technical questions about 3Com's products, the knowledgebase has answers to very specific, arcane questions about conflicts between drivers, operating system issues, and other factoids of which it would be impossible to keep every member of their technical support staff apprised. In fact, the technical support staff, which is also available via an 800 number, uses the same knowledgebase that the company makes available to its Web visitors to answer technical questions.

RESOURCES

Generally speaking, you don't want to go out and build your own tools for enhancing the accessibility of your site—with the exception of shopping wizards, for which I am not familiar with any commercial solutions. There

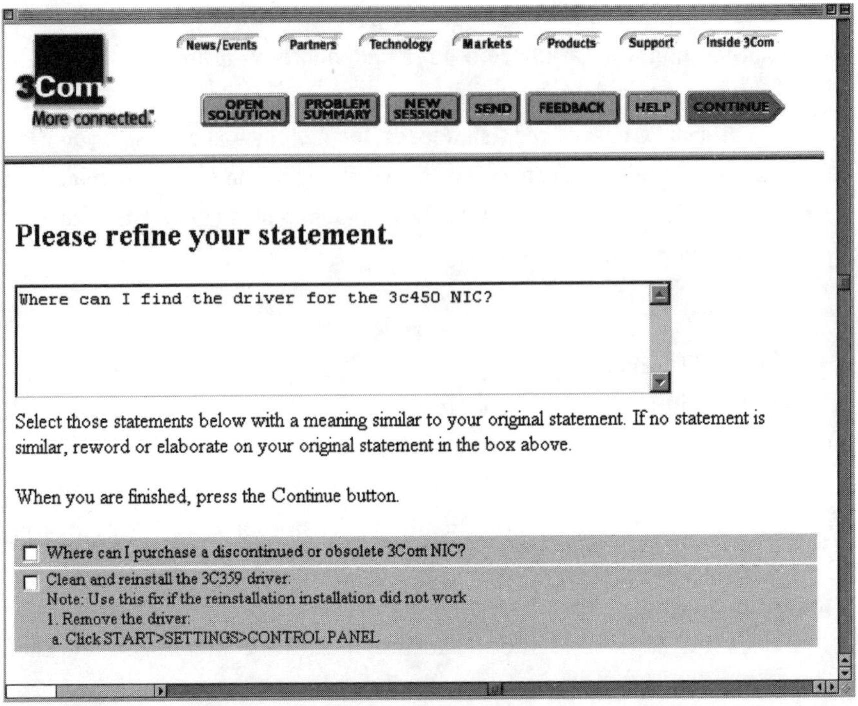

Figure 9-4. Using the 3Com knowledgebase to find a driver for a network interface card.

are many vendors providing corporate search tools. The ones to avoid are those that require any special syntax on the part of the shoppers. If the shopper is expected to know to type a plus (+) or "AND" or quotes (" "), or anything else other than the search information, run away.

Ask Jeeves (www.askjeeves.com). Natural language search tool that suggests questions and helps visitors find the right path to find what they're looking for. Also provides extensive reporting to you on what customers are looking for.

Soliloquy (www.soliloquy.com). Its in-context search tool is very impressive, but only works on a limited set of products for which it's been populated.

eGain (www.egain.com). Provides a "virtual assistant" to handle real-time customer service inquiries from customers with scripted answers. Can be very hokey or well done, depending on the degree of detail of the scripted responses.

Vendors who provide tools to build knowledge bases on the fly include:

RightNow (www.rightnow.com). Provides automated customer service solutions, including in-stream knowledge base building based on questions that come into customer service and answers your representatives provide.

BrightWare (www.brightware.com). Essentially the same solutions as RightNow with more emphasis on automated replies by e-mail using previously created responses.

ShopTok (www.shoptok.com). Allows your site to create a knowledge base as you go using incoming mail queries and outgoing customer service responses. This tool is offered as part of their complete customer-service suite, which they provide as an ASP.

Capability   10

THE YEAR 2000 represents the last year that U.S. shoppers will constitute a majority of online shoppers, according to IDC. The question then becomes, what percentage of your revenues can you reasonably expect to see coming from overseas markets? This depends to a large degree on what you sell. Some items, such as blow dryers, toaster ovens, and blenders, won't sell well outside the United States because the United States uses a different electrical standard than the rest of the world. Other items, such as computers, cell phones, and PDAs, won't sell well in non-English-speaking markets because the operating systems are in English. Shoppers in other countries want operating systems for their local languages. Still other products, such as wireless digital devices, won't necessarily work in other countries because wireless services overseas use standards with which U.S. wireless devices usually don't comply.

Personal-care products, clothing, and shoes will generally find themselves in demand globally. Making your site friendly to visitors from every country with a significant potential for Web shoppers is essential. There are several levels of commitment to selling globally that a merchant can demonstrate. At a very minimum—and depending on the types of products you sell, this may be all you need—you need to offer shoppers the ability to buy in their local currencies and the ability to provide shipping and billing information to their own countries. On the operations side, you need to have systems in place to handle shipping overseas, collecting and paying for tariffs, handling customer service, handling returns, and fraud checking and resolution. This is not a trivial undertaking, but the alternative is being left behind.

If you really want to compete globally, and be the first-choice merchant in every country in which you wish to have a presence, you need to localize your site for each country. The second half of this chapter discusses this approach

Minimum Requirements to Compete Globally

Ask your network administrator to tell you what percentage of traffic that's already on your site is coming from overseas. If you're like most U.S.-based merchants, it is 30 to 40 percent. This is true even if you're not currently shipping overseas. Some of this traffic is clicking around your site to find the tiny little statement you've buried on the page in the checkout tunnel that asks for shipping and billing address, that notes in passing that you only ship to the United States.

With the help of third-party solutions, the complexities of selling and shipping worldwide can be mitigated to some degree.

PUBLISH SHIPPING POLICIES UP FRONT

Make sure that on your home page, or within one click of your home page, you indicate where you ship. Better yet, use IP-based geographic identification to identify where a visitor is coming from—at least by continent or region—so that the first news to greet customers is a friendly message telling them that you do, in fact, ship to their locations. This saves aggravation on the part of the international shopper, who's accustomed to wasting time, often at slow download speeds, trying to find your international shipments policy. By greeting visitors with geography-specific shipment information, you save traffic on your server and create good-will with your customers.

MODIFY SITE TO HANDLE INTERNATIONAL BILLING AND SHIPPING ADDRESSES

Most U.S.-based merchant sites use very standard forms to restrict the information—thus the room for error—provided by shoppers during checkout. These forms often restrict the states to which to ship, filled in by shoppers, to the fifty U.S. states or to two-character state abbreviations. They also restrict telephone number formatting. Usually, they only accept numeric data as zip codes. Sites that want to ship internationally need to make sure their form fields are flexible enough to handle the following information:

→ States and provinces outside the United States and Canada. The ideal situation is to ask for the country up front in the form, then use dynamic HTML to provide error checking based on the state/province codes of that country.

→ Postal or zip code formatting that includes alphabetic characters, in addition to numbers, formatted as 3+3, in addition to 5+4, since many countries format the postal (zip) code as three characters followed by three characters.

→ Phone number formats that accommodate a variety of formats with country codes, unless you specify otherwise.

MAKE CUSTOMER SERVICE ACCESSIBLE GLOBALLY

U.S.-based merchants rely too heavily on the telephone for customer service. When you're serving customers outside the United States, the telephone is not a particularly effective communications tool. Be sure you have customer service that does not require an 800 phone call. An 800 number doesn't work outside the United States or the United States and Canada. Click-to-voice (see Chapter 7) or real-time chat (see Chapter 13) are good customer service alternatives. E-mail alone is not an adequate substitute for instant human interaction.

Even if you post a non-800 number on your site for international calls (and pick up the charges), any phone system that requires the user to press numbers for the appropriate department probably won't work. European phone tones don't work in U.S. phone systems.

REDUCE DOWNLOAD TIMES BY REDUCING GRAPHICS

Unless you're selling graphics, you should make a version of your site that's text intensive (or make the primary version of your site graphics light and spare all your visitors the graphics smorgasbord). Overseas customers, who don't always have access to high-speed connections, and often pay for access time and phone time by the minute, can then get to the products and checkout quickly.

MODIFY SITE TO ACCEPT CURRENCIES

Another step you need to take is to express the price of each product on your site in a choice of currencies. There are several ways to go about this. One is to ask visitors early in the shopping process in what currency they'd like to see the prices. You can do this in conjunction with the IP-address identification mentioned above by stating something like "Our South African visitors may now shop in Rands. Would you like to see prices in Rands?" Then give the visitor a chance to indicate U.S. dollars, S.A. Rands, or any of the other currencies in which you price goods. Another way to handle currencies is to show all currencies at all times in a select list (also called a drop-down window). Make note of which currency the visitor selects on the first screen, then default to that on subsequent screens. It's much better to have all the prices converted when the page loads than to default to dollars, have the visitor select his own currency, and wait for the page to reload with his own currency. The third option—and this is only acceptable if you tell the visitors up front that this is how you do things—is to show the currencies in U.S. dollars (or your local currency) on the product pages, then do all the conversions at the checkout page.

Check with your merchant bank and with your credit card processing software provider about getting real-time currency feeds. There are also commercial feeds available both from service providers and from free sources. Make sure you have a back-up solution in place in case your primary provider of real-time conversions goes down.

SHOW ALL TAXES, SHIPPING AND TARIFFS AT CHECKOUT

One major cause for chargebacks in international orders—when a customer contacts the bank that issued his credit card to contest a charge on his statement, and the merchant is left without payment—is miscommunication between merchants and customers as to the cost of shipping, taxes, and tariffs. Some merchants simply show the cost of the products, with their standard handling charges, saying they'll send the total later, or not even bothering to send the totals. It's not safe to assume that international customers are willing to eat the shipping costs and tariffs. Overseas shipping can be very expensive, and tariffs on some items are equal in cost to the items themselves—particularly for luxury items. If you have to collect these charges, you have to notify your customers while they can still make a choice. Because most overseas customers can't use the 800 number you provide on your site, they can't call you right away to cancel an order that has unreasonably high (to them) shipping charges or taxes. For many merchants, by the time they process the incoming e-mail saying to cancel the order, the order's already left the warehouse. This often leaves the customers with the option of paying to return something they thought they were no longer going to receive. No matter how this is resolved for the merchant, it's expensive. There's simply no excuse for not providing all the information relating to charges at the time of checkout.

> ### PROFILE: From2.com
>
> From2.com solves the problem of the need for real-time information at checkout. Merchants that sign up with From2.com can use the From2.com Global Delivered Costs Calculator,™ shown in Figure 10-1. This calculator gives the merchants a way to show customers all of the costs associated with importing and exporting goods, including freight, insurance, duties, taxes, value-added tax (VAT), and customs clearance fees. The merchant knows, so the customer knows, so there are no surprises and fewer chargebacks.

Figure 10-1. From2.com's Global Delivered Costs Calculator shows exactly what a customer will be charged.

Merchants who use From2.com's services work with From2.com to categorize their own products so that From2.com can accurately determine the fees related to shipment of those products to other countries. From2.com's calculator is an API that runs over the Web, so merchants only need to install the link to the calculator and don't have any tables of tariffs to keep up-to-date. From2.com guarantees that the amounts it shows on the calculators will cover all the charges and there won't be any surprises. From2.com also handles the shipping either itself or by using third-party carriers.

From2.com private-labels their solution so that customers don't see any From2.com fingerprints on the site. This is potentially one of the simplest routes a company can take to implement international shipping overnight.

UTILIZE LOCAL LOGISTICS COMPANIES FOR RETURNS

As much as possible, make use of companies in the countries in which you want to be a player to handle returns. Customers don't want to pay to ship back to the United States, and your chargeback rate will be lower if customers can return unwanted products without spending a lot more money. A chargeback is not a return. With a return the merchant refunds the money and usually gets the merchandise back. With a chargeback, the merchant eats the cost and simply never gets paid. Customers typically will initiate chargebacks in a couple of scenarios: either when they don't get the goods or when they can't get satisfaction from the merchant. Moreover, customers are far more likely to shop from companies with some local ties, since they rightly believe they'll get better service from them.

> ### PROFILE: E-Commerce Logistics
> In Europe, e-Commerce Logistics (eCL) provides all services connected to selling on the Web throughout Europe. The services that eCL offers to its clients make it possible for it to operate and sell its products in Europe via a variety of local networks.
>
> eCL has a number of clients, which provides an economy of scale allowing competitive pricing. The services that eCL provides include transportation, warehousing, fulfillment, distribution, payment processing, customer service, telemarketing, and return handling.
>
> With ten years of experience in B2B and B2C, eCL has a good knowledge of the different requirements in different countries regarding payments (e.g., credit card, COD, open invoice, direct debit), distribution (e.g., local post, UPS) and how the clients place orders (e.g., Internet, telemarketing, mail order). During year 2000, eCL will handle about 4 million orders all over Europe.
>
> So instead of building up an organization in every country, incurring significant costs, eCL can help you reach new markets with a local profile without you having to make the resource investment in each market.

How to Be a Major Player in a Market

If you implement the above steps on your site, you're going to be "open for business" in the markets you choose to sell in. However, you'll never be the first choice among merchants doing business in those countries. Any local company that comes along selling comparable products for comparable prices is likely to erode your market share in that country. Customers would rather shop in their own language, avoid seeing tariffs as a line item, know that customer service will be handled in their own language, and spend time at a site that reflects the colors and images that are familiar to them. Ecru and forest green may be comfort colors in the great Northwest, but to Latin American eyes, they reek of foreignness. Even within the United States, pastels are more a part of the local culture in certain cities (e.g., Miami and Los Angeles) than in other cities (e.g., Boston and Chicago). It pays to have a footprint that creates comfort.

To be a long-term contender in the international marketplace—which means maintaining sales even after local merchants have established themselves with an online presence—there is no shortcut for setting up a local site in the native language, with native language customer service. It's not enough, however, to simply translate your site into the local language. You have to create a new site that incorporates the culture, customs, and colors of the country in which you want to have a presence. For example, in the United States, we all know what a shopping cart looks like and what an icon of a shopping cart looks like. However, is that icon familiar to every other culture? Do their shopping carts look like ours? Unless you invest in local content developers to help you create appropriate icons, your icons might not resonate with your target audience.

ACQUIRE THE APPROPRIATE DOMAIN NAME

If you're going to be a player in a local market, you need to have a domain name that's appropriate for that country. The .com top-level domain was never intended to be the U.S.-specific domain, but it has turned out that way. There are 239 country-specific domain names. The first thing you want to do is to acquire your .com domain as a country-specific domain. For example, www.overtheweb.com, if it wanted to go into France, would need to acquire www.overtheweb.fr. This new domain name will serve the dual purpose of giving local visitors from that country a direct link to a localized home page and the local country search engines a way of knowing that this site is intended for their local audiences.

INTERNATIONALIZE YOUR ARCHITECTURE

Internationalized architecture and code means that nothing in your code is hard-coded for any particular cultural convention. For example, in the United States, dates are shown as month/day/year, but that's by no means an international convention. Date formatting, currency formatting, and money formatting should be parameter driven. A variable in your system should determine how these things are formatted, rather than having the formatting hard-coded into the system.

The other component of internationalized architecture is that your database can handle double-ASCII characters, which is how some other languages, such as Chinese and Japanese, are stored. ASCII only handles up to 256 characters, which isn't enough to display all the characters in many languages. If the database that supports your systems can't support double-ASCII, then you really have to start from scratch.

A final example of internationalized architecture is the ability for your database to sort a particular field by the appropriate language. For example, if you have a product description field in multiple languages, it would need to know the correct alphabetical order for English, Japanese, and Russian, in order to sort the field.

PROFILE: Uniscape

Uniscape is a best-of-breed solution for e-business globalization. Uniscape's technology platform and set of globalization services allow companies and dot-coms to cross linguistic, cultural, and national boundaries.

The Uniscape Globalization Infrastructure for eBusiness™ is a comprehensive globalization solution addressing the strategy, architecture, and business processes required to manage a global, multilingual Web presence. Together, Uniscape's technologies and services allow companies to manage the complex, distributed e-business globalization process.

Uniscape's Globalization Infrastructure is a technology platform for globalization that includes Uniscape Global Content Manager (GCM) and Uniscape.com.

The Uniscape Global Content Manager allows companies to coordinate content updates across multiple multilingual sites. Uniscape GCM detects changes throughout a network of globalized sites, automatically triggering localization of new content according to predetermined schedules, processes, and customer-defined business rules. For example, if a change is initiated in the United States, the system will know which sites should be updated, and then initiate the localization and posting.

Uniscape.com is Uniscape's Web-based localization solution. Designed to streamline the distributed localization process across more than forty languages, Uniscape.com automates and monitors the flow of content through each step of the localization process. Hosted by Uniscape, Uniscape.com ensures that content localization is an efficient, rapid process that meets time-to-market deliverables.

Uniscape also offers a full range of globalization services, including globalization strategy, internationalization, technology integration, and localization management services.

LOCALIZE YOUR CONTENT

Route customers based on the referring IP address, based on their selections on your home page, or (best of all) based on a domain name specific to that country to a site that's in their native language. Carry your logo through the local site—as long as you're sure it doesn't have some other meaning in that other country—but localize the colors. Some cultures prefer more subdued colors, some prefer more flamboyant colors. Find an editor in that country who can steer you right. Don't count on your graphic artist in Seattle or Manhattan to dictate the color scheme.

Retain the services of a translation company with reputable clients to handle the translation of the content and the message. There's more to translation than just converting word-for-word or sentence-for-sentence.

Translation must include cultural relevance. A good translation company will rewrite all your product descriptions to make them appropriate and appealing to the local country. For example, in Japan, American logos on merchandise sell well. The product description in English might read, "New York Yankees hat with white stitching on black canvas." In Japanese, the same product description would probably read more like, "Authentic baseball hat for the New York Yankees baseball team. Just like they wear in New York City! White stitching on black canvas reflects the team's colors."

Include relevant warranty and returns information for the local country. Although you may routinely pay for returns shipment with a return merchandise authorization (RMA) number within the United States, be sure your policies are legal and can be supported for international shipments.

Respect the privacy laws of the local country. Be sure you have a lawyer who's licensed to practice in that country review your privacy policy to make sure it's compliant. In the European Union, for example, the privacy laws are much tougher than in the United States. Be sure your site reflects compliance and that you are operating within local laws.

GET LOCAL TRANSLATORS

Studies show that visitors spend more time, view more pages, and make more purchases at sites in their own native languages, which doesn't really come as any surprise. There are many, many companies that offer language translation services, but there are major differences in how they deliver their services. Some international translation services contract with independent translators in the native countries, which means that there may be less consistency and reliability, or accountability. Other translation services contract with local companies to provide the translation services, and still others employ their own translators in each country. It is important that you avoid translation services that employ translators who are not local to the countries where the content will be seen. Even a few years out of a country can make the difference between current and outdated use of idioms.

TRANSLATION SYSTEMS

Since you're generally paying for translation by the word, you want to be able to take advantage of technology that reuses translation so that the same content never needs to be translated more than once. Some of the more sophisticated translation systems offered by the larger globalization services actually use a multistep process to translate text.

First they consult a dictionary that your company has compiled for the target language, which indicates the preferential translation for each company-specific technology or term. Every time there's a match, those terms are translated into the target language. This ensures that regardless of who's doing the translation, your own technological terms and business will be translated consistently.

Next the system reviews the text in need of translation to see if any parts of it have already been translated. If so, the system pulls the previous version of the translation directly out of the database and applies that. Since only finalized, approved translation makes it into the database of translated text, you're sure that the translation is one you can live with.

Finally, anything left in the document is passed to a human translator who translates anything that was missed. This approach to translation can address up to 90 percent of your translation needs from reused content.

WORKFLOW ROUTING

Regardless of how you elect to translate your site, you'll need an industrial-strength workflow routing system. Every time a page changes on the primary site (which, for the purposes of this example, we'll assume is in English) and that page is not specific to the U.S. site, then the page needs to queue up to get translated and ripple out to all the other localized sites. That page should go into a translation system, which takes note of the changes—since not all of the page has probably changed—and runs through the three steps described in the section above to apply the best translation with the least human intervention. Then, that page probably needs to be reviewed by an in-country editor, legal counsel for that country, and possibly the in-country site manager.

This review process can't be handled with Post-it™ notes or with e-mail. E-mail can certainly be part of the solution, but ownership of files has to be managed more stringently than that so that no content is posted until it has passed all reviews. Finally, the approved page needs to go live on the site, with the content and the original English content going back into the translation database for future reuse.

Going live on the site probably involves some sort of integration with your existing content-management system, so it's a good idea to make sure your CMS (see Chapter 14) integrates with the systems of the globalization vendor you select.

PROFILE: Welocalize.com

Welocalize.com is a multilanguage globalization services company offering Web-enabled, enterprisewide translation, localization, and internationalization solutions.

Welocalize.com offers organizations a way to accelerate global delivery of multilanguage products through a scaleable, Web-enabled, enterprisewide workflow system. The system includes the Extend Site Monitor for maintaining and updating multilanguage Web sites, the Extend Tool Kit for text extraction and translation database preparation, and the Extend Client Interface for real-time project tracking via any browser.

The company can also work with your existing content-management system, which is easier if it's already internationalized (see Chapter 12 for more information about internationalized CM systems).

Welocalize.com's process is quite formalized. The company handles everything from site translation through dynamic identification of a visitor's location, so it can show the right home page from the beginning, through automated content management. Most companies generate content in one primary language. So Welocalize.com monitors your site for pages that have changed. Then it runs the new content through the company's translation service and all other language sites get updated as quickly as possible.

Welocalize.com has its own translators, who are resident in the relevant countries, so quality control of translation services is strong. Translators make use of assisted translation tools and a translation database tool to expedite translation, maximize consistency, and minimize costs.

ACCEPT APPROPRIATE PAYMENT METHODS

Credit card penetration in most of the world does not come close to that in the United States. Investigate alternative payment options, such as eChargePhone (for delivery of digital goods), iPIN, InternetCash, and Global Internet Billing. You will find that certain countries favor certain solutions. Find the one that's got the greatest penetration in each local country. An excellent resource for current reviews and evaluations of payment options is the ECommerce Guide at Internet.com (http://ecommerce. internet.com).

HANDLE CUSTOMER SERVICE LOCALLY

To the degree possible, you want your customer service to be handled in the country where your shoppers are located. Find a customer service center that has local offices, to avoid having to evaluate different companies and contract with them in different countries. Your choice of customer service center should be seen as a strategic alliance, and it should be given a high level of attention. Incorporate real-time chat, if possible, but realize that in much of the world, local calls are billed by the minute, so a fast phone call may be cheaper for your customers than a chat session—which would be free in the United States for most people.

DON'T FORGET THE SEARCH ENGINES

Although it's not uncommon for people around the world to go to Yahoo.com, it's more likely that they're going to begin searches for local merchandise (where they don't have to pay for international shipping) at their local Yahoo.cc (where cc is their local country code). In addition to Yahoo!, there are many, many other country-specific search engines. Many of them don't even have U.S. counterparts. If you're going to be found in other countries, you need to be listed in the comparable places on sites that international visitors frequent, which may not be those where you're being found today.

Seek out search engines and directories for any countries in which you want to have a presence and get your company listed. You can use Media Metrix and Nielsen_NetRatings.com to find out which search engines in which countries have the most traffic. You'll often find that there are first-tier and second-tier search engines and directories that see far and away the vast majority of the traffic; there also are a lot of also-rans. Focus on where the traffic is, just as you would in the U.S. market.

RESOURCES

The easiest thing to find is translation services, but as you've read, that's only a very small fraction of your solution.

For fulfillment and logistics companies, start with:

From2.com (www.from2.com). Handles complete fulfillment solution worldwide, but its specialty is the Latin American world. Its solution includes a real-time cost calculator that you integrate into your checkout process so that your customers can see the final cost of having goods delivered to their doors.

E-Commerce Logistics (www.e-commercelogistics.com). Offers a complete fulfillment solution for Europe, including returns handling.

For globalization and localization services, there are many companies willing to assist. You can look at:

http://dmoz.org/Computers/Software/Globalization/Companies/ Localization_and_Internationalization/

Or if you need to make a phone call today, try:

Uniscape (www.uniscape.com). Offers full-service localization.

Welocalize.com (www.welocalize.com). Offers full-service localization.

Order Status 11

A LESS glamorous topic would be difficult to find, but success in e-commerce isn't about being glamorous but about meeting your customers' needs and exceeding their expectations. Profitability in e-commerce requires that you meet needs and exceed expectations at the lowest possible cost.

Some discount grocery stores require customers to bag their own groceries to save a few cents; self-serve gas stations require customers to do more work than they might prefer to do. The Web is a different environment altogether, however, because customers generally *prefer* to do the work themselves rather than have it done for them. Consequently, if you make the information that your customers need available to them, you not only satisfy their preferences (of getting the information without picking up the phone) but you also save the customer-service expenses of having everyone who wants to find out where their orders are calling your site. BizRate's research from December of 1999 shows that 55 percent of customers contact customer service *while waiting for their orders!* Imagine if you could reduce the volume of calls that are unrelated to additional purchases by half!

There are two components to the information customers need: enough information about the products, shipping time, shipping and handling charges, and taxes to make a purchase, and enough information about the status of a product that's been ordered to be confident that the order went through without any problems, the order has been shipped, it's going to arrive in a timely manner, and the customer can be there to receive the product (if a signature is required). Is this so much to ask?

PRODUCT INFORMATION

By and large, merchants do a pretty good job of giving shoppers information about a product. Generally, manufacturers see to it that merchants have all the specifications of a product in order to present it properly. However, merchants often fail to realize that the information provided by the manufacturer is not all the information a customer will want. In addition to the details of the product itself, including price, merchants should also provide—on every page on which details of a product are displayed—availability, time to ship, and delivery time for multiple shipment options, by zip code. Although some merchants provide some of this information today, very few provide it all.

INVENTORY

Customers want to know whether a product is available and in stock before they provide you their billing and shipping information. Don't waste their time by taking all this information, then informing them by e-mail in the order confirmation message, that some or all of their order isn't immediately available. Frequently, customers order products together that they're going to use together, so getting only part of an order might be as good as getting none of it, from the customer's perspective. Customers generally are unenthusiastic about providing all their personal information to a new merchant, and providing it only to have to cancel the order because something they've ordered as a gift for a birthday right around the corner, that they've now been told is unavailable, is reason enough never to return to that merchant. Providing shipping and payment details are the online equivalent of waiting in line in a bricks-and-mortar store. If customers wait in line only to find that the product isn't there after all the waiting, they are right in believing that the store doesn't respect their time.

If you don't have inventory information about a product because you might use someone else, such as a distributor, to process your fulfillment, you need to do one of two things. You need to find distributors who are willing to feed you real-time data about inventory status. Or you need to tighten up your fulfillment relationship with the distributor so that you can query its inventory levels with enough frequency that you can tell shoppers accurately *before they've committed to make the purchase* whether you have the products to sell to them.

As a merchant, you have a choice of methods of showing inventory for a product. If you keep inventory yourself, the easiest way to show inventory is to show the stock level or at least an "in stock" flag on every product page. If you don't keep inventory, you can have a "check inventory" button on every product page. Whenever customers click that button, it shows current inventory levels (or at least availability). Your Web site thus communicates in real time with your distributor to confirm that the product is indeed immediately available. At times, the products will still be sold out from under a customer, and you'll have to contend with the wrath of that customer, but more often than not you'll be able to answer accurately the customer's legitimate question: "Do you have that in stock?"

PACK AND SHIP TIME

My father needed a computer monitor overnight because a mission-critical computer monitor at his office had just failed him that day. Because we're in different cities, and he consults me for computer problems, I told him I'd order him one on the Web and he'd have it the next day. Of course, the site (which shall remain nameless) from which I ordered didn't publish the fact that even if you pay the premium for overnight shipping, you couldn't expect the product to ship that day, but two days later! Consequently, he paid the premium for shipping a 17-inch monitor to his office (no small sum), then ended up having to go out to Circuit City to buy one (and lug it back to his office) anyway. Then he found the site from which I'd ordered did not have an 800 phone number for customer service, it had shipped the computer monitor before his e-mail reached the company, and he had to pay to return the monitor! How many places in this book could I have used them as a case study for what not to do? As it turns out, the company is about to go under on its own merit.

As a merchant, you have two choices: either show the time it takes to get the product out the door, if you have reasonably consistent pick, pack, and ship times (as experienced catalog warehouses are likely to have) or publish the time to ship for each individual product. If there's a cutoff point during the day—anything ordered by noon Eastern Standard Time gets shipped the same day—then make that clear as well. Spend the time evaluating how long it takes each item to get picked, packed, and shipped, then make this information available to your customers. Some may never make use of it, but regular shoppers—and you'd like to have more of those—will eventually factor that data into their shopping habits, visiting your site to make a purchase before proceeding to buy that item elsewhere because they know your cutoff times for getting their products shipped today.

DELIVERY TIME BY ZIP CODE

Do you remember the days when anything ordered through the mail took six to eight weeks for delivery? That's how long the television ads told us to allow. Today we laugh at that number, but many merchants find it acceptable to offer shipping options that include the following text: "Standard Ground Shipping: 3 to 7 days." How useful is that? If shipping time is three days, then as the consumer I can make the decision not to pay for expedited shipping because today's, say, Monday and three days will get the product here before the weekend when I need it. However, if shipping time is seven days, then I probably want to pay the premium for two-day shipping so I have the product by the weekend. Empower consumers to make intelligent decisions about what they are willing to pay for speed and convenience.

Suppose I carry an item over to the local pack-and-ship retailer for United Parcel Service (UPS). There will be a big map on the wall telling me what zone each state is in and then a chart converting UPS zones to the number of days it takes for a package to arrive there from where I am. Every year at Christmas, the UPS pack-and-ship retailer near me tapes a large number into each of the zones—12, 13, 14, 17—telling its customers the cut-off date after which packages shipped standard ground won't arrive in time for Christmas. You have access to the same data. By simply asking a customer for his zip code (or the ship-to zip code), you can do the calculations to tell him a far more accurate range for delivery time than three to seven days. Of course, if you're shipping via the U.S. postal service (USPS), then all bets are off. But most merchants do not ship to domestic addresses via USPS because package tracking is not available for standard first-class shipping.

ORDER INFORMATION

Customers want to know how much an order will cost—with all shipping, taxes, and tariffs applied—before they place an order. BizRate's research from the fourth quarter of 1999 shows that 75 percent of online buyers have abandoned a shopping cart within the last three months (an average of once per month). Twenty-five percent of online shoppers said they'd abandoned the cart because shipping and handling charges were too high. BizRate's data also shows that merchants erroneously believe that high shipping and handling charges are only the cause of an abandoned cart half as often as they actually are.

If the customer were to call you on the phone, you'd be able to tell him as he's shopping what his shipping and handling charges are, yet how many Web sites give him that data on the site while he's still adding items to the cart? The nicer interfaces keep the customer informed at all times about how many items are in the cart and what the total is. Why is that nice? For one thing, it's reassuring to new shoppers that actions they've already taken are sticking. Remember that today's Web shoppers aren't necessarily completely confident of their ability to "do it right" and are likely to blame themselves for any site errors.

In addition to showing customers the number of items in the cart, the total value of those items, and the shipping, find out right up front what their zip codes are and include the tax on the order, so they can see what their order totals truly are as they are shopping. Reduce your shoppers' incentive to abandon the cart by telling them everything they need to know right there on the product information page.

INCLUDE ALL TAXES AND TARIFFS AT CHECKOUT

The issue of taxes and tariffs is particularly important if you're selling to customers outside the United States. In the United States, unless the merchant and the customer are in the same state, the customer does not pay sales tax. However, when the sale is across international borders, tariffs can come into play, and they're often not trivial. Tariffs are affected by ship-to country, product category, and designation of use, either personal or business. Because shipping is usually also a larger component of the total order size in international orders than it is in domestic orders, it is essential that all the amounts that go into the order total be presented to the customers before they abandon the cart in horror at the order totals they've racked up.

There are vendors who will help you provide tax and tariff information by product category by country to your shoppers; Chapter 10 profiles one. It's nearly impossible for you to stay on top of this information on your own unless you're shipping to very few foreign countries and you're only operating in a very limited number of product categories. I know of one site that ships internationally, indicating during the checkout that it's the customer's responsibility to handle tariffs, but I don't think that's a very responsible approach—nor one conducive to customer loyalty. In fact, management at this site has lamented the high rate of refusal to accept goods overseas, resulting in high return-shipping costs for the merchant.

ORDER CONFIRMATION

Every order should be followed up with an e-mail message confirming that the order was placed, with all the details of the order except for payment information. There are still major sites sending out order confirmations that confirm only that there was an order without confirming what was ordered, what the total amount spent was, or what the shipping expectations should be.

Order confirmation e-mail is a frequently missed opportunity to build a relationship with the customer. The problem is that the merchant sees this correspondence as postsale correspondence, as if to say, "there's nothing more I can get from this customer right now." However, the customer sees this mail as the cementing of a relationship. Falling down on the job here can result in the customer having less confidence in the merchant's competence, and it will almost certainly result in more calls to customer service confirming that the customer actually ordered what he thinks he ordered.

Every order confirmation e-mail should have the following information in it:

→ Thank you to the customer for placing the order

→ Merchant's name—particularly important if the e-mail is being handled by a third-party fulfillment house

→ Contact information for customer service by phone and e-mail

→ Order confirmation number

→ Itemized list of what was purchased with prices by each item

→ Tax

→ Shipping costs

→ Order total

→ Billing information with specific account information omitted (or all digits but last four shown as Xs)

→ Shipping information

→ Date and time of order

→ Expected date and time order will be shipped

→ Expected date and time order will arrive

→ Specific instructions, ideally with direct link to where on the merchant's Web site the customer can track the order status

→ Instructions to customer on how to cancel the order or to correct the order if it's in error, and what the consequences are, particularly for items that haven't shipped yet (better to find out not to ship an item before it's left your warehouse than to have to deal with returns and restocking after it's gone out and come back)

→ Thank you to customer for placing order

If the merchant has any updated information about any items ordered, such as the fact that one of the items won't ship with the other items, this is the time to share the information with the customer.

The order confirmation e-mail, which is frequently read by customers because it addresses something they presumably care about, is a good place to offer a promotion on the next order. The promotion could consist of exclusive access to a "members-only" Web site through a link in the order-confirmation e-mail, a coupon code the customer can use for his next purchase, or a "refer-a-friend" promotion. Customers are often most excited about your site and your merchandise when they've just completed a purchase. Capitalize on that.

SHIP NOTIFICATION WITH ORDER TRACKING LINK

When the order, or any part of the order, ships, you want to take advantage of the opportunity to communicate with your customer again. The ship notification should include the following information:

→ Thank you to customer for placing the order

→ Merchant's name—particularly important if the e-mail or the shipping are being handled by a third-party fulfillment house

→ Contact information for customer service by phone and e-mail

→ Order-confirmation number

→ Itemized list of what has shipped with package-tracking information for each separate box

→ Itemized list of what has not shipped, with anticipated ship dates for each item (otherwise expect the customer to call customer service to see what happened to the rest of his order)

→ Shipping information, so that the customer is reminded where he told you to ship the merchandise

→ Link to package-tracking site for the carrier you're using with instructions if the first page customer sees won't show him the details

→ Specific instructions, ideally with direct link, to where on the merchant's Web site the customer can track the order status

↪ Instructions to customer on how to cancel the order—particularly the pieces that haven't shipped yet

↪ Thank you to customer for placing order

This is another frequently missed golden opportunity to build customer loyalty at almost no cost to you. Use a recommendation engine to personalize a special offer for this customer, based on his shopping history with you, his demographic profile, and his click-stream data. Look into his "wish list" and see what else he'd like to buy at a later date, then make a personalized offer for a discount on one or more of those items.

The problem many merchants have with this forum for ongoing sales is that the content of order-confirmation and ship-notification e-mails has traditionally been determined by the operations department, instead of by the marketing or merchandising departments. You need only look at the presentation of a typical targeted e-mail promotional message and an order-confirmation e-mail message to see that they're clearly designed in different departments. Marketing—the department that's otherwise responsible for the brand of the merchant—should participate in dictating what the content of these messages is and what the presentation is.

Customer Information

It's pretty typical for a Web site to ask customers for many details of their lives, especially during the checkout process. Studies consistently show that customers will provide personal information if they believe they will reap some benefit from providing that information, such as receiving relevant newsletters or an expedited checkout process. However, many sites that take great pains to ask customers all about themselves and their preferences never give their customers a chance either to view what's on file or to make changes later on.

AVAILABLE ON THE WEB

Any customer information the merchant has access to should be available on the Web site for the customer to view and edit. If the merchant's privacy policy is tough enough—meaning that the merchant promises not to divulge data to third parties without clear consent of the shopper—then customers are going to be happy to be able to see what their files look like and to remove data that's too personal or inaccurate. A customer's shopping profile isn't like a doctor's patient profile. If you think about it, it's rather patronizing that doctors do hold patient information so close to their vests—even preventing the patients from seeing what's in their own files. If a merchant is taking action based on information it has about a customer, that customer should have the chance to provide input into the accuracy of that information.

One site I mention elsewhere in this book has the most extensive opt-in page I've seen anywhere. It asks customers exactly what they'd like to know about with what frequency. However, there's no way for those customers later to come back to the site and change the requested frequency of communication. Once the customers opt in at any level, and return to the site to make a modification, they are given strictly an opt-in/opt-out option. Clearly, they should be given the same flexibility when they want to modify their communication options as when they want to create them.

Another type of customer's information that sites sometimes hold onto too zealously is payment information. It's understandable and admirable that a merchant would want to protect a customer's payment information, once that information has been stored for future expedited checkout, but many merchants don't give customers any way to remove a credit card, once the merchant has the information. For example, say I shop with my Visa card, then cancel that card, and return and shop with my MasterCard. I should be able to remove the Visa number from my profile so that it doesn't ask me if I want to use that number every time I check out. Worse still, if both the invalid card and the valid card are issued by the same company, then I need to pull out my card to see what the last four digits of that card are before I know which one of the card numbers on file to select. That really hasn't saved me any time at all.

AVAILABLE TO CUSTOMER SERVICE

Any customer service person who has contact with the customer, whether that person be on the phone, via real-time chat, responding to an e-mail inquiry, or in a store processing a return, should have access to all the customer's information he needs to handle an inquiry, complaint, or return. Customers will expect to be asked for payment information when talking to a live person either on the phone, by real-time chat, or in person in a store. Otherwise, they can't understand why information they know is "in your system" somewhere needs to be provided again.

I had the experience of shopping online with one of the larger mall merchants. I purchased several items at once, one of which was a gift. As a result, I asked for a gift box. The merchant was smart enough to send the entire order without a packing slip with a price, since they didn't know (and didn't ask) which item was the gift. One of the items I purchased for myself was not the color I'd hoped it would be, so I took it, with the packing slip without prices, to the mall store to return it. The sales staff, which was very interested in resolving my return accurately, despite the large postholiday crowds at the store, was simply unequipped to assist me. I waited almost forty minutes while I watched the sales clerk and the store manager trying to find the accurate presale price for the sweater in question.

Although I was impressed by the conscientiousness of the staff, I was annoyed that I had to wait that long to make a simple return. The store, in the meantime, could have used those two people to sell a lot of merchandise to everyone who was waiting in line behind me. I hoarded two people to resolve what should have been a simple transaction for them. If they'd had an Internet connection, or if I'd had a Web-enabled wireless device with me, I could have gone to the site and pulled up the receipt from my purchase, showing exactly what I'd paid. There were any number of ways the return could have been expedited, but the merchant didn't make any of them available to the sales staff.

IN-STORE KIOSKS

Ultimately, the marriage of online and offline will take place at in-store kiosks. In the example just above, an in-store kiosk would have allowed me to pull up and print the receipt for the sweater I wanted to return, without wasting any time of the sales staff. Kiosks have typically been failures in open environments, such as at visitor information centers at highway rest stops, or in university settings or building lobbies. Why? Maintenance. Kiosks require a lot of supervision to stay functional. Automatic teller machines (ATMs) prove that customers are willing to do much of the work associated with having transactions processed on their own. However, ATMs also need regular care and feeding.

In-store kiosks are an ideal hybrid of online and offline for customers. The physical downsides of kiosks—keeping them clean, keeping the printer stocked with paper, keeping them functional, and reporting and monitoring malfunction—are mitigated by the fact that store clerks can keep an eye on them and clean them and refill paper as needed. The possibility of abuse or vandalism is also significantly reduced in an in-store setting.

All customers won't use kiosks, but the success of ATMs tells us that many will. Customers frequently value their own time more highly than they value personalized human service. If I know I can go to the kiosk located next to your checkout counter and order a sweater that goes with an outfit, the rest of which you have in the store in my size, then I'm likely to do that myself. Chances are, no one in the store helped me find the first two pieces of the outfit. Why would I expect or want to wait for someone in the store to help me find the sweater? I can see from the mannequin in the window that the outfit has three pieces. I can also see that my size is not on the rack. Adding an additional incentive, such as offering free shipping if I place the order from your in-store kiosk, will help close the sale, because I've already made the trip to your store, and I will resent paying shipping when I see it as your fault that you don't have adequate inventory in stock.

Kiosks also offer the merchant the opportunity to customize the shopping experience in the physical store in a way that it has never been able to do before. If you ask customers to sign in at the kiosk and you print them personalized coupons that are based on their order history (see Chapter 8 on personalization), then you can begin to add some of the value—and create some of the loyalty—that you had previously only been able to do on the Web site. When you can save a customer time and money, reduce the involvement of your own in-store staff in sales, and increase order totals, then you have a truly fabulous solution that will keep customers coming back.

RESOURCES

The vast majority of the suggestions in this chapter involve changes to your own order-management system or Web site. There aren't any turnkey solutions out there for fixing those. However, you will need to work with the shipper you use in order to provide the shipping information I suggest on your Web site.

> *UPS (http://www.ups.com/bussol/solutions/index.html).* Start here to find the software you need to integrate their shipping information with your site.

> *Federal Express (http://www.fedex.com/us/ebusiness/eshipping/).* Start here to find the tools you need to provide integrated shipping information on your site.

Kiosks should be part of your business plans if you're a bricks-and-clicks merchant. One of the top producers of kiosk shells, the outside attractive and protective housing for the kiosk's computer innards, is Factura, http://www.factura.com, located in Rochester, New York. They have hundreds of kiosk enclosure styles, including a weather-resistant enclosure for outdoor kiosks. Factura merged with Microtouch, http://www.micro touch.com, one of the eminent touchscreen manufacturers. They offer a variety of touch-sensitive surfaces, including one that allows car shoppers to input data through the window of a dealership to the computer inside when the store is closed! A number of exhibit houses will build custom kiosk enclosures as part of a show or exhibit. Exhibit Works and ExhibitsNow!, both located in Detroit, Michigan, are two companies with extensive experience building kiosks.

If you want to outsource your kiosk development, look for someone who has been in the business for a while, such as The Technology Applications Group of Sequoia NET.com. Located in Auburn Hills, Michigan, this company has created kiosks for diverse applications, such as the Detroit Pistons at the Palace of Auburn Hills, the Detroit Zoo, and the Metropolitan Detroit Convention and Visitors Bureau. Business and commercial applications include transactional kiosks in the cities of Livonia, Novi, and

Sterling Heights and a number of credit unions in Detroit and surrounding suburban areas.

Several companies provide kiosk development software. One of these is Degasoft (www.degasoft.com), an Icelandic company with an award-winning product called Kudos. Another kiosk software company is Kiosk Software, www.kioskco.com, which uses standard Web languages including XML to develop kiosk applications.

Other larger development organizations include US West and IBM Global Systems.

Robust Content-Management Systems (CMS) 12

THE DAYS when serious Web merchants can rely on homegrown content-management systems are long gone. There was a time—not that long ago—when most merchants had their own content-management systems (CMSs), which were integrated with their own shopping cart systems. Slowly, merchants saw the value in using packaged shopping cart solutions, and many migrated to commercial shopping carts—used only for the checkout tunnel—but stuck with their own CMSs, also known as merchandising systems. Today merchants have no choice but to abandon—as one would abandon an albatross around his neck—their homegrown solutions for one of the many robust, stable, full-function CMSs on the market.

There is no bigger burden for an e-commerce site than that of keeping content fresh, prices accurate, specials timely, and sales relevant. For most merchants, this is a double-pronged burden. First, they have to manage the business relationships with vendors and manufacturers to make deals that are attractive to their customers. Then they have to fight with tools to get their content taken live on their site—tools that often required assistance from IT staff. The commercial CMSs available today take IT out of the loop altogether when it comes to publishing content. They keep IT busy integrating the CMS with other systems, rather than making highly paid, difficult-to-find developers slaves to content publishing.

Many software vendors have found that repackaging their products, which were formerly mere HTML editors, as *content management systems*, has given them new shelf life. Be warned, however, that not every software system that calls itself a CMS is of the caliber discussed in this chapter. Some truly are *industrial-strength* and meet the requirements set out in this chapter. Others, however, are little more than glorified HTML editors. To a large degree, you get what you pay for. You should, however, plan to negotiate for the best deal.

CUSTOMIZATION

While most CMSs promise out-of-the-box functionality, that's a goal that none meet. Your CMS needs to work with your order-management system (OMS), your business intelligence software, your inventory-management software, your enterprise resource planning (ERP) software, if you have it, and your customer database and personalization software. How could any software possibly do that "out of the box?" When you're evaluating CMS vendors, talk to the vendors of your existing software to see if they already have prebuilt interfaces with any CMSs.

You need to make sure you are fully aware of what's involved in customization and what the consequences of customization will be on installing future upgrades. When you see a vendor demo, be sure to ask what kind of customization was required to get it to operate as you saw. Get your systems architect involved in vendor meetings right from the beginning and give him the go-ahead to ask the tough questions. Be sure that the strategic decision-makers in your company don't purchase any software that hasn't been reviewed by someone technical who knows what will be involved in customization.

Baseline Features

There are more than a handful of top-notch CMSs available commercially. Whatever solution you opt for should include all the features listed in this section.

CONTENT INDEPENDENT OF PRESENTATION

The goal of hypertext markup language (HTML 4) and cascading style sheets (CSS) was to permit content to be independent of the presentation of that content. In fact, they fell far short of that lofty goal because not all browsers displayed content the same way.

Today's good CMSs store content in such a way that it can be retrieved when needed, and will match the presentation of that context— desktop browser, mobile device, Web appliance, etc.

The key to an efficient CMS is the ability to repurpose content. Let's consider how a CMS would handle the data related to a promotion for a closeout special for a fishing rod. There would probably be a title for the promotion, a short description, a long description, a photo of the fishing rod, a price, and possibly links to related merchandise, such as tackle, lures, and waders. There would also be data that wouldn't be displayed, such as the date on which the promotion ends, or a link to the products database with inventory so that once inventory fell low enough, the promotion would be pulled.

The merchant might want to display only the title of the promotion with the price on a list of specials on the home page. Then it might want to send e-mail to customers who have indicated an interest in fishing items and include in the message the title, price, and short description of the fishing rod. On the category page for fishing merchandise, it might be appropriate to include the title, the price, the short description, and a photo. Finally, on the product description page for that item, customers probably need to see all the fields.

A good CMS will only require content creators to provide each of those data items once, then will use templates and logic to provide the correct item in the correct place at the correct time.

CONTENT STORED IN NONPROPRIETARY FORMAT

How the data is stored in the CMS is as important as that it's stored independently of the presentation. Some of the content that will be stored is inherently tied to a format, such as images, which will likely be .png, .jpg, or .gif files, or audio, which would probably be .aif or .wav. However, the majority of content will be text, and should be stored in a universal, nonproprietary format, such as ASCII or XML. Regardless of which tool a CMS uses—or permits content creators to use—to import and format data, data should be stored in such a way that there's an easy migration path between the current system and a future system—whether it's needed as an upgrade or as a result of an acquisition.

CONTENT UPDATABLE FROM CLIENT TOOL BY CONTENT CREATORS

Content creators can be marketing staff, freelance writers located around the globe, or merchandisers. Where the content originates should be irrelevant to the CMS. A good CMS provides multiple options for getting content into the system. One user-friendly solution should be the Web browser.

When evaluating a CMS, have your content creators evaluate the client interface that they'll be using daily to update the content on the site. Make sure it's intuitive and fast and doesn't require excessive clicks. If it's not intuitive, then your training costs will be substantially higher, which should be factored into the negotiated price.

Some CMSs permit content creators to use plug-ins for common desktop software, such as the popular Microsoft Office suite of products. If your content creators use the tools that have the plug-ins and can continue to work in their favorite tools, and if those tools can communicate with the CMS, then you can expect productivity to be higher.

PROFILE: NCompass Labs

NCompass Labs provides a powerful Web site design, content authoring, publishing, and site management tool in its Resolution software. You can use it to deploy and manage sophisticated, dynamic Internet, extranet, or intranet sites. It can be integrated with an organization's existing infrastructure and allows content owners to be fully engaged in Web and e-business initiatives.

Resolution's Web Client allows nontechnical authors to use their browser interface and common desktop applications, such as Microsoft Word,® to create Web content without requiring the installation and maintenance of desktop software. This browser interface, combined with support for all of the world's major languages and time zone synchronization (shows application content for the time of day where the browser is), permits authors easily to contribute and to schedule posting of up-to-date content, regardless of their geographic location. Resolution's Publishing API and a content component architecture together permit the personalized, on-the-fly delivery of content to audiences with different interests and language requirements using any of a diverse set of wireless and wired browsing devices.

NO PROPRIETARY CLIENT SOFTWARE REQUIRED

There are four reasons why the client should run in a browser rather than in separate software: location of content creators, compatibility issues with proprietary software, training costs, and version control.

1. Because content creators can be anywhere—and not necessarily within the reach of your IS department—the client interface should run from any of the major Web browsers (or at least one of them).

2. Because proprietary client software is tested and installed on fewer hardware configurations than the major browsers, it is more likely to have compatibility issues that are either undocumented or unknown. How many IS and content producer hours and how much frustration is it worth to find them and document them yourself?

3. Proprietary client interfaces increase training costs, because users of the tool have to learn a new interface.

4. Finally, if the client tool is a separate piece of software that has to be installed rather than an application that runs within a browser, then users of the client tool have to be sure that the version they have is the most current one so that they can always connect to the CMS. All these issues amount to an additional burden and expense for the IS staff.

WORKFLOW RULES MANAGE CONTENT APPROVAL

Once the content is brought into the system and stored in a nonproprietary format, how does it get onto the site? Generally, there's an approval process for each piece of content, but that approval process probably differs for each type of content. Prices might need to be approved by the vice president of merchandising. Product descriptions might need to be reviewed by a lead writer in the marketing department. Images of products might go through merchandising, while site graphics would go through the multimedia or marketing department.

Good CMSs provide an intuitive interface that allows workflow rules to be defined in a graphical environment or by using a wizard, assigning workflow based on either role (e.g., manager, vice president, lead writer) or user ID (e.g., "all rebate offers go through Jane"). Content might be assigned for approval based on the role or user ID of the creator, or based on the type of content.

The approval process might use an internal routing system, which relies on each of the individuals charged with approval responsibility checking into the system often, might send e-mail seeking approval (receiving e-mail responses as approval or rejection), or might use text paging or some other real-time interaction to expedite approval. Additionally, each component of content should be able to be assigned a priority so that higher-priority content can be approved ahead of lower-priority content, even if it enters the approval queue later.

CONTENT CAN GO LIVE WHILE SYSTEM IS LIVE

It almost goes without saying that a good CMS should be able to take content live while the system is operational. However, I've seen systems that required the site to shut down while content was refreshed. In order to avoid any confusion on the part of those who are using these dinosaur systems, I want to be perfectly clear that taking content live while the system is operational is a feature that industrial-strength CMSs have.

Of course, there's more to taking content live in today's distributed, multiserver environments, where cached content often resides around the globe, than just updating a single server. Make sure the CMS you select can handle updating content across servers in the architecture you use or are planning to use. It should be able to flush cached content selectively so that no one sees out-of-date content. It should also know when some servers are having trouble taking the update—for whatever reason—so that it can roll back the content (remove the new content and replace it with the old) if an adequate number of servers can't accept the update.

VERSIONING AND ROLLBACK

Version control is the accounting of the IT department. Most of us who have a formal education in computer science vaguely remember the topic being covered in classes, while our eyes glazed over. Be that as it may, sometimes even the most elaborate and carefully constructed approval process fails to catch bad content, or inadequate testing fails to catch poor functionality, and the only choice left to us is to revert to the previous version of content or software.

A good CMS manages version control both by content creation/ approval date and time, by author/approver, and by type of content. Even if prices have to be rolled back because an expected shipping contract that would have allowed free shipping to be included on a line of products falls through, do all graphics for those products have to be rolled back? How about the product descriptions? Possibly, but probably not. All-or-nothing rollbacks cost more time, as everything has to work its way through the approval process again—wasting management time disproportionately.

Finally, can the rollbacks easily be effected against a distributed multiserver environment? Again, these issues need to be discussed between your architects and the engineers from the CMS vendor. Different architectures require different rollback approaches. Make sure yours is supported by any CMS you seriously consider.

TEMPLATES MANAGE CONTENT DISPLAY

Part of what makes sites easy to navigate is that they rely on relatively few page designs—frequently as few as three or four. All site content falls into one of a few formats, each with its own template. For each format, navigational elements are consistently located in the same place. Not only do templates make sites easier to navigate, they also make them easier to build.

Graphic artists can create the few templates that are needed to display any page on a PC-based browser, the few templates that are needed for WAP devices, possibly the few that are needed for Web-clipping devices (namely the Palm VII), and templates for any other devices that are anticipated to load the site. By relying on templates that are browser/platform driven, each visitor sees what he needs to see given the real estate limitations of his device.

Perhaps more importantly, templates give designers the ability to alter the display of content, regardless of the content being displayed (the flipside of the section above about content being independent of presentation). Presentation independence allows a site to give itself a makeover—based on acquisition or whimsy—with great facility.

PERSONALIZATION ENGINE

Personalization is something that most of the heavy-hitting CMSs claim to do. How they do it differentiates the vendors. You'll want to find the approach that meshes with the way your organization makes merchandising decisions. Chapter 8 discusses site personalization at length.

A personalization engine is usually defined—by the vendors—as the ability to create business rules that include such variables as visitor behavior (click-stream analysis), a shopper's previous purchases, day of week, time of day, and available inventory. A personalization engine allows merchandisers to say that, for example, a shopper who's looking at a golf shirt on Friday, Saturday, or Sunday should be shown a special offer for khaki shorts, but a shopper who's looking at the same shirt on Monday through Thursday should be shown a special offer for khaki slacks.

The key to a personalization engine is that it changes what a visitor sees on the page, depending on variables. Usually, the rules and recommendations that a site uses must be developed by merchandisers, rather than based on data mining of the site by the CMS. The business rules are generally defined through a user-friendly wizard with no intervention by the IT department.

BUSINESS RULES MANAGE VISITOR EXPERIENCE

There are many variables that factor into a favorable Web-site experience for your visitors. One biggie is that the content be relevant. The bigger your site and the greater the choice of products, the more important relevant content is. In a store with a physical presence, managers make decisions about how to display inventory in such a way that customers will be able to find what they were looking for quickly and that customers will easily find accessories and outfits, increasing the total value of the purchase.

In order to make content relevant, you have to know something either about the visitor or about the merchandise. Most CMSs assume you know something about the merchandise. Chapter 8 covers how to make your site compelling when you know something about the visitor. The more merchandisers can control what products are displayed with what other products—and under what circumstances—the better they can create a relevant shopping experience for visitors.

A good CMS will enable merchandisers to create complex business rules to manage what products display with what other products. These business rules will probably be created with the help of a wizard. A user-friendly interface makes it easier for merchandisers to create rules, test results of businesses rules, compare rules and results, and modify rules—all without the intervention of IT, and without trepidation that they're going to break something.

CENTRALIZED MANAGEMENT OF DESIGN ELEMENTS
Design elements affect the way a site looks. It's imperative that not just anyone have access to graphical elements and templates that affect the site. By managing the elements centrally, small or large changes can be made in one place by someone with authorization that will automatically ripple through the content, affecting the appearance of all instances of that item wherever it may be displayed.

SUPPORT FOR CONTENT AWARENESS ACROSS LOCATIONS
Many merchant sites have distributed architectures with servers located in multiple locations—to improve connection times and avoid known bottlenecks in the Internet's structure. Because CMSs have to deliver content updates in real time to each of these servers, the CMS should have a way of tracking which servers it had trouble updating, if any. That way, if an inadequate number of servers are updated, the updates can be rolled back off

all the servers and any servers that aren't accepting updates can be taken out of the rotation so no visitors will receive content from them. Finally, once a server is contacted to receive new content, the CMS should have a record of which updates it missed, apply them, and bring the server back into the rotation.

No manual work should be required to accomplish any of this. An administrator should be able to indicate what percentage of servers must be able to accept an update before it's applied to them all, and some warning and logging should take place to keep the administrator apprised on how updates are proceeding.

CHECKOUT PROCESS INTEGRATES WITH PAYMENT PROVIDER NETWORKS

Part of the CMS's job is to allow a customer to check out with the merchandise he's selected. Whichever CMS you select should have modules that will allow you to connect seamlessly to the payment-processing network. This is an area where no downtime can be permitted, so it's imperative that the CMS you select has been rigorously tested, and that there be a backup plan—such as queuing credit card authorizations until the network is back up—should the interface with the payment network go down.

EXTENSIVE METRICS TOOLS FOR IT, MARKETING, AND MERCHANDISING

The good CMSs give you access to data about your site, about your marketing campaigns, and about how the merchandise is moving. This data should be easily reported out of the system so users at all levels can see how decisions (business rules) they've made are affecting profitability. These reports should allow filtering and be appropriate for the information each of these groups is trying to extract.

Merchandisers should be able to see the degree to which the personalization business rules are affecting the products customers are purchasing. Marketing folks should be able to monitor the closure rates of visitors coming into the site from ads and links on other sites. Finally, IT people need to know how much traffic each server is seeing, which servers are having trouble, the average load time for the home page, and a host of other facts about the network configuration.

PROFILE: FatWire

FatWire.com's UpdateEngine is a 100 percent pure Java™ platform for content delivery. Using the Java Database Connectivity (JDBC) drivers, it can talk to any database. Merchants can build any application on top of the platform, or it can use the various applications that FatWire provides, such as the e-commerce track suite, the sales track, and the press release track. There's a business-rule-driven personalization engine built in, too.

Business rules are defined in wizards, or they can be written in Java-based FUEL (Fatwire UpdateEngine Language), and allow the CMS to create content on the fly. Figure 12-1 shows a dialog box for creating business rules in the UpdateEngine.

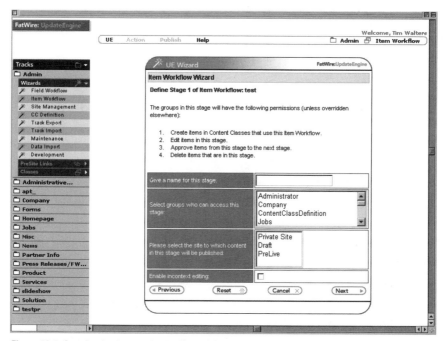

Figure 12-1. Creating business rules in the UpdateEngine.

The e-commerce track suite can deliver content in multiple languages and multiple currencies. Additionally, merchants can program an event engine so that pricing can be dependent on pricing from another site in real time. The system can deliver to WAP devices and can output in any markup language. Templates determine what content is displayed for each device. Additionally, members can be grouped and sent bulk targeted e-mail promotions directly from the UpdateEngine.

Differentiating Features

Frankly, the features list above is extensive enough that any site that implements a CMS with all those features will do well enough to compete with other well-equipped sites. That said, there are other features that distinguish the best-of-breed solutions. The list in this section isn't comprehensive—and of course, new versions are constantly being released, so the features list is a moving target—but these are among what I believe are the more useful differentiating features.

TAKES CONTENT FROM DESKTOP APPLICATIONS

While it is imperative that the CMS have an intuitive, browser-based client tool, some CMSs go beyond that. By providing a plug-in that works with common desktop software such as Word, Excel, and PowerPoint, content creators can create and edit content in their favorite desktop applications, then simply click a button in the toolbar to export the data into the CMS. If your content lends itself to creation in these desktop applications, this can be a real time saver. If your content creators use desktop applications for which the CMS provides plug-ins, this capability can dramatically increase productivity. Check on those two big "ifs" before insisting that your CMS accept content from desktop applications.

PROFILE: BroadVision

BroadVision offers a suite of integrated applications that provide an end-to-end e-commerce solution. All the applications are built on top of the BroadVision One-To-One Enterprise foundation; they include One-To-One Retail Commerce, Business Commerce, Financial/Banking, and Billing. Each of these applications provides functionality appropriate for high-end, scalable Web applications.

BroadVision's content management solution, One-To-One Publishing, allows content to be stored in XML, with templates and style sheets (XSL) used to format the content for the appropriate output format or medium, including PC browsers, mobile phones, PDAs, and print. One-To-One Publishing accepts content directly from desktop applications, such as Word, PowerPoint, and Excel. Workflow, routing, access management, and the ability to check out and check in content items (get permission from the system to change items) are all built into the system.

From One-To-One Publishing, final content is staged to the One-To-One Enterprise server, which delivers it to the Web. There, the integrated personalization engine uses business rules that merchandisers build using a graphical user interface. The interface is intuitive and simple to use, enabling nonprogrammer business managers to adjust business rules such as pricing, discounts, and featured items in real time to meet the needs of a dynamic marketplace. Because business rules can rely on user profiles, click-stream analysis, and other factors, they can apply to all users or all products, to particular communities of users, or even to an individual user.

WAP is supported, as are multiple languages and currencies. Because the system stores content in XML and uses templates with style sheets, BroadVision can deliver content to hundreds of platforms, and BroadVision is well-positioned to take advantage of entirely new, emerging classes of client devices such as 3G mobile phones, Internet appliances, and the like.

DELIVERS TO WAP AND OTHER NON-PC BROWSERS

The number of people currently using WAP devices in the United States is small—under 1 million by even the most aggressive estimates—but the day will soon arrive when WAP devices constitute a significant portion of your site traffic. Especially if you expect to see much traffic from Europe and Asia, you can't really afford to invest in a solution that doesn't deliver well to WAP and I-mode.

Most CMSs that deliver to WAP require you to create separate WAP templates, which is a good design decision, since navigation via WAP is entirely different from navigation via a wired browser. Be sure to test out the interface you get from a number of WAP-enabled devices before you select one to meet this criterion.

RECOMMENDATION ENGINE

A recommendation engine can increase your average basket size, improve your conversion rate, and increase customer loyalty. Very few CMSs offer recommendation engines of the type discussed in Chapter 8 on personalization. However, some CMSs have already been integrated with recommendation engines such as the top-of-the-line Net Perceptions solution. If possible, evaluate recommendations concurrently with CMSs, and keep in mind whether they've already been integrated, to save yourself the trouble of making them work together.

IMPLEMENTATION TIME

One major consideration when implementing a CMS should be how long it takes to implement the system. Ask the vendor, then ask the references. Of course, part of implementation will be integrating the system with your existing back-end systems, but try to find references who have had similar integration scenarios so that you can get a realistic assessment of the total time of implementation. The cost of implementation can grow dramatically if the implementation timeline slips, since you may be paying for vendor staff to be on site during implementation. Negotiate a fixed fee for implementation costs associated with the technical staff of the vendor so that the vendor will be highly motivated to meet or beat the deadlines established. What you want to avoid is having the vendor's staff become permanent residents of your office—especially when you're paying for them by the hour.

EASE OF INTEGRATION WITH EXISTING BUSINESS SYSTEMS

Your content-management system clearly needs to be able to communicate with existing back-end systems. To the degree possible, find a CMS for which the interface has already been built, and for which the interface is available. Most CMS vendors will tell you that they have an API library or that their systems are built with open standards so that you can "easily" write the interfaces from your system to theirs. If you must, you can, but it's never easy and then you have the challenge of keeping interfaces in sync after upgrades to your other back-end software come out and upgrades to the CMS come out. If you have the option, you definitely want to find a CMS that already has a partnership and integration with the back-end systems you have in your company.

HARVEST CONTENT FROM OTHER SITES

Some CMSs will harvest pricing or other content from competitors' sites in real time. You can use this information to offer the lowest price on every product or to display price comparisons on your site. I'm certainly not recommending that you base your price on your competitors' prices minus some amount, but there are sites that include features like side-by-side price comparisons as part of the product information pages, and this feature is clearly of value to them.

THE IMPORTANCE OF YOUR VENDOR RELATIONSHIP

For the most part, CMS vendors offer the same baseline features—the crux of your system. Each, however, offers a different approach, style, or architecture. When making your selection, be sure to evaluate multiple vendors. Your CMS vendor is as close to a roommate as you're going to get in e-commerce. Before you decide to move in together, make sure you've checked out references for the vendor thoroughly. If the vendor gives you a list of ten, ask for five more, then start checking references from the bottom of the list. You might not find a vendor that's perfect, but you should be aware of what issues other merchants are having with the vendor.

Make sure you have an account manager you like, who's responsive, and who understands your industry. I strongly encourage you to make your satisfaction with your account manager's performance part of the terms of your contract. Make it clear that if you're not happy with the performance of your account manager—or if your account manager leaves or is promoted—you have the right to a new account manager. Insist on veto power over the replacement and that you don't have to pay maintenance fees while your site is in limbo.

WHY NOT CUSTOM-BUILD?

The old question to "build or buy" becomes almost a no-brainer on the Internet. The pace of change and the importance of being first to market within your own industry with new solutions, products, and features, make it nearly impossible for any company to do everything. No company can keep up with the technological demands of growing a business in every direction at once. The problem of keeping up and growing in every direction at once is solved in one of three ways: strategic partnerships, reliance on third-party software solutions, and application service providers.

Strategic partnerships allow merchants to offer complimentary products and services without having to ramp up in every direction at once. Third-party software permits a company to implement a solution in a fraction of the time it would take to develop that solution in-house. It also allows a company to pay for only a fraction of the development costs of a solution, since the total cost can be spread among several customers. Finally, making use of a best-of-breed software solution helps guarantee that a company will have access to the latest and greatest features without a significant additional development cost.

Making use of an application service provider can be the very best option, depending on the application provided. In the case of a CMS, unless the ASP is also hosting the site and maintaining all customer information for the merchant, it's likely that any larger merchant will want to own the CMS.

INTERNATIONALIZED SOLUTIONS

Chapter 10 discusses the three phases to operating a merchant site in multiple countries. The first is internationalizing the software architecture. If you're planning on operating multiple stores in multiple languages, you need to make sure your CMS platform is fully internationalized. The cost of re-engineering your CMS platform is high, so it's definitely better to make sure this is part of the solution you're purchasing.

Internationalization includes the inherent ability in a database to sort a database file based on ASCII characters or double-byte characters so that if a field of data is in Japanese, for example, the data in that field can be sorted alphabetically for Japanese. Internationalized code uses switches to dictate the date and time formatting, the currency, comma and period placement in prices, phone number formatting, and a host of other variables, rather than hard-coding date formatting as month/day/year, as we expect to see in the United States.

Welocalize.com, which is discussed in a profile in Chapter 10, offers a CMS that is fully internationalized. There are other CMSs that support multicurrency capability, but check to make sure all the internationalization features are covered before believing that the ability to handle multiple languages or multiple currencies constitutes a true internationalized solution.

RESOURCES

The field of CMSs is growing so fast that the list below is necessarily out of date by the time you read this. Your best bet is to talk to as many vendors as you have time for to make sure you're not missing any important features. Even if you're leaning toward a vendor without quite as many bells and whistles as another vendor, consider the plans of the vendor for software enhancements.

WHITE PAPERS

Far and away the best white paper available is from Ncompass Labs and is entitled *Untangling Web Content Management*. Read it before you start inviting any vendors on site to demonstrate their wares. It is gratefully free of self-promotion.

MAILING LISTS

There is one mailing list for the discussion of CM that's hosted out of Ireland. The traffic is surprisingly low. You can subscribe by sending mail to listserv@listserv.heanet.ie. Your message should include "subscribe Content firstname lastname."

Another mailing list is cms-list@camworld.com. You can subscribe from the CamWorld Web site (http://www.camworld.com/cms/). This site is generally an excellent source of information on CMSs.

A third resource site for CMSs is Digital Insider (www.digitalinsider.com).

VENDORS

Blue Martini (www.bluemartini.com). Offers its own suite of products for everything from CMS to merchandising to order management and CRM.

NCompass Labs (www.ncompasslabs.com). Offers Resolution, which works seamlessly with Microsoft products.

FatWire (www.fatwire.com). Offers its Java-based UpdateEngine.

BroadVision (www.broadvision.com). Provides an end-to-end CMS that's XML-based.

Zope (www.zope.org). Offers a free open-source CM solution that's Unix and WinNT compatible.

Roxen (www.roxen.com). Provides a free CM solution.

The Stibo Group (www.stibo.com). Offers a cross-media information and publishing system, which extends beyond what most CMSs will do, but it includes many of the features I've recommended earlier in this chapter.

Finally, a consulting firm dedicated to helping you install a best-of-breed system is Accelerus.com.

PART IV

TECHNOLOGIES FOR CUSTOMER SERVICE

Chat

WHERE ARE you sitting when you make an online pur-chase? Chances are, you're either at home in the evening, or you're making a quick purchase during your lunch break at your desk. In either case, if you have a question about a product before you make a pur-chase, how convenient is it to pick up the phone and call customer service?

If you're at home and *if* you have a second phone line, it's probably no big deal to get your teenager off the phone to call customer service, but you may be reluctant to call, even if you can get the phone to yourself, since you don't know how long you'll have to wait on hold.

If you're shopping from work, you're probably a bit more reluctant to pick up the phone because your office, or rather, your cube, isn't quite as private as you might like and it's not really anyone else's business that you're buying boxer shorts, and that the Gap Web site doesn't list the size chart for men's boxers.

What other options do you have? You can certainly send e-mail to customer service at the merchant at which you're shopping, but how long it will take to get a response is anyone's guess, and online shopping isn't supposed to be about waiting on hold, or waiting to get customer service e-mail back. You want to make your purchase, and you want to make it now, and if this merchant doesn't meet your need for enough information to make the purchase, then you're off to a site that does.

ONLINE SUPPORT OPTIONS

Who contacts customer support, when, and why? Without answers to these critical questions, it's difficult to decide what types of support a site should offer. BizRate.com, the leading provider of data about buyers' actual behavior, collected immediately after the sale, from 850 merchants, has hard data to answer these questions.[1]

WHO CONTACTS CUSTOMER SUPPORT?

One in five customers contacts customer support about any given sale, according to BizRate. Buyers whose order totals are larger are more likely to contact customer support. In the fourth quarter of 1999, the average order total of a customer who did not contact customer support was $83; for customers who did contact customer support, the average order total was $121. First-time buyers to a site are more likely to contact customer support.

Because customer support experience is critical to creating customer loyalty and repeat customers, it is vitally important that these first-time buyers from a site have a favorable customer support experience, or they won't become regular customers. The two factors most highly correlated with a buyer's likelihood to purchase from a merchant again are level and quality of customer support and on-time delivery, in that order.

WHEN DO CUSTOMERS CONTACT CUSTOMER SUPPORT?

As shown in Figure 13-1, the most common time to contact customer support is while waiting for an order. Chapter 14 addresses solutions to reduce the postsale support burden while increasing buyer satisfaction.

The most startling thing about this data is that only 12 percent of those who did contact customer support did so during the purchase. That's 12 percent of the roughly 20 percent who contacted customer support, or only 2.4 percent of all shoppers who were making purchases! Is it realistic

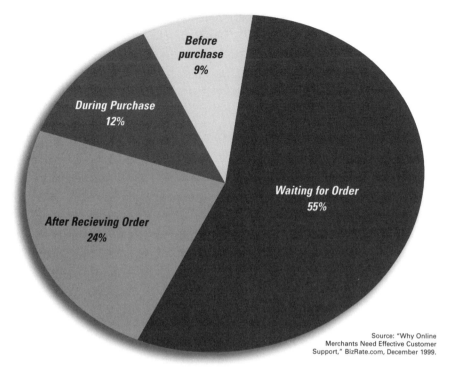

Figure 13-1. The majority of customers contact customer service while waiting for an order.

to think that only 2.4 percent of shoppers had questions? This during a quarter when almost 62 percent of sales were to customers making their first purchase from that merchant? Combine these numbers about buyers with shopping cart abandonment rates of 75 percent.[2]

What the 2.4 percent number probably shows is that only a small fraction of customers with questions about products, shipping, prices, or site policies actually went on to complete the sale on the Web. The rest either abandoned their carts or made the purchase from the merchant on the phone (if the merchant offered that option).

WHY DO CUSTOMERS CONTACT CUSTOMER SUPPORT?

Most customers who contact customer support do so while waiting to receive their orders. Unsurprisingly, this corresponds with the top two reasons buyers list for contacting customer support: late delivery of an order (24 percent) and to get status of an out-of-stock or back-ordered item (21 percent). The next most common reason to contact customer support corresponds to the number of customers who contacted customer support after receiving their orders: incomplete, incorrect, or damaged order (16 percent). Finally we come to the interesting number: 15 percent of those customers who contacted customer support who made a purchase indicated they asked about an item for sale.

MORE TELLING: HOW MANY SHOPPERS DIDN'T CONTACT CUSTOMER SUPPORT?

Shouldn't it be the case that 40 percent or more of customers contact customer support *during the sale?* What percentage of the time do bricks-and-mortar customers ask for help during their purchase? Wouldn't that be a better measuring stick to use?

What percentage of customers *who did not make a purchase* had a question about a product, but because they saw contacting customer support as too inconvenient, too time-consuming, or too public, they didn't seek presales support and didn't make a purchase? The customer support options available at most sites—phone support (70 percent) and e-mail support (96 percent)—don't address the immediacy of shopping on the Web.

Consider whether you'd return to a physical store if the only help you could get was by completing a questionnaire and returning days later to read the answer posted on a bulletin board. What if the only assistance you could get at a physical store was to be secured by taking a number but then not be told which number was currently being served? As absurd as these options seem, these are the bricks-and-mortar equivalents of trying to provide presales support to customers online using only e-mail and phone banks.

DEARTH OF TWO-PHONE-LINE HOUSEHOLDS

What percentage of households in the United States has more than one phone line? I asked the vice presidents and directors of e-commerce of many companies I interviewed for this book, and to a person, they thought the number was around 50 percent. The truth is that fewer than 23 percent of U.S. households have more than one phone line, according the most recent estimates from the Federal Communications Commission.[3] How can so many Web sites decide that the best way to handle customer support, especially presales support, is by asking customers to phone them, when phoning customer service will, for the vast majority of the U.S. population, require the customer to disconnect from the Web?

U.S. VERSUS GLOBAL STATISTICS

In the case of many statistics, I limit myself to the U.S. population—a fact for which I apologize. As you saw in Chapter 10, I believe that the Web is an international phenomenon, and that all sites that are serious about e-commerce, except local sites, should plan to operate in a global market-place. My only excuse is that getting at most of this data is difficult enough for one country and if I waited to complete this book until I had data for every country, the rest of the book would be obsolete.

AMERICA ONLINE (AOL) QUANDARY

In my extensive interviews, I routinely asked executives whether they used America Online (AOL). Not a single one said he used it with any regularity or had used it recently. Most had *never* used AOL. I can't blame them; I'm not favorably disposed to the way AOL foists ads on me, but I do use it when I visit my parents. If these decision-makers had used AOL, they would know that when an AOL user disconnects his phone line and hears that distinctive "good-bye" message, all AOL browser windows close.[4]

For those of you who use AOL, you might be surprised to learn that that's not how the Web works for the rest of us. If you connect to the Web just about any other way—and there may be Internet Service Providers (ISPs) that also close your windows when you disconnect, but I'm not aware of any—the browser window stays open even after you disconnect, which means that you can connect to the Web, pull up an article, discon-nect, and read the article at your leisure offline.

What this AOL-windows-close issue creates is a situation in which AOL users with only one phone line cannot look at the product they're calling customer support about, should they choose to contact customer support with a question about a product before they purchase it, unless they print out the page! Worse still, if they do call customer support about a product, and the support representative tells them they should really be looking at a different product, and begins to give instructions on finding that page, the caller can't follow along. Of course, this last problem is common to any household with only one phone line.

PRESALES SUPPORT VERSUS CUSTOMER SERVICE

Until now in this chapter, I've referred to any contact between a customer and the merchant outside of the published material on a site as a *customer support contact*. For the rest of this chapter, I'll distinguish between *presales support* and *customer service*, which is any contact between customer and merchant that takes place after a sale is made.

INCREASING PRESALES CONTACTS

It's very counterintuitive, because customer service is overhead. An e-commerce site should try to increase the number of presales contacts and reduce the number of postsales contacts. Presales contacts indicate interest in purchasing. Customers who contact a site for presales support can be sold, up-sold, and cross-sold. Customers who contact support after a sale are either already disaffected or can easily become disaffected by a negative customer service experience.

THE INTIMACY OF SHOPPING ONLINE

When online shopping first started taking off, everyone talked about the anonymity and solitude of it all. All alone, the shopper clicks around the site, reading product descriptions, adding products to his cart, eventually checking out, without ever making contact with another human being. For every shopper, it's as if he's the only one in the store.

With few notable exceptions, online shopping should be a very personal experience, and sites that have had the most success getting shoppers to complete the process have introduced the feeling of community to shopping.[5] Amazon was the first to permit the online version of soliciting the opinions of others at the video rental store—"Have you seen this one? Is it any good?"—with reviews by other readers. Lands' End (www.lands end.com) has since begun offering "Shop with a Friend," which allows two different shoppers (who agree to meet there at the same time) to hook up on the site, evaluate the same pages and products, and communicate in real time about their choices—all the fun of shopping at the mall without the hot pretzels.

THE COMPETITION OF E-COMMERCE SITES IS THE CORNER MARKET

Let's compare shopping online to going to the grocery store. There's a particularly charming grocery store in Charlottesville, Virginia, called Harris Teeter. Walking through the store on an average visit, it's difficult not to come across six to ten employees. Even if, say, the woman behind the deli counter isn't particularly helpful, the impression made on you by the others at the bakery, the seafood counter, the customer service desk, and the checkout is likely to sway your overall impression toward the positive. This would be especially likely after one of the friendly bag boys—or grown men, more likely—carries your bags to your car and loads up your trunk.

Don't Web merchants realize that shoppers like these little inconsequential relationships? They like being recognized when they return to a store, participating in polite banter about the weather, feeling like their business is appreciated. If you don't have a grocery store in your neighborhood that offers this kind of service, think of your favorite family-owned restaurant, where you know the owner and he greets you by name with a handshake.

What happens when you sign onto the Web to make a purchase? For the sake of comparison, let's say you're not buying a big-ticket item or a financial product, like a mortgage, that might require human intervention and follow-up. Should you need to contact customer service for assistance, your overwhelming impression of the store would be from the contact with the one individual who responded.

How long does it take to get a response (other than from the autoresponder that says the mail's been received)? Do you have to wait on hold so long that you finally hang up and give up? If an e-mail inquiry takes too long to get an answer, you've probably either bought the merchandise at a physical store or at another online merchant or decided you didn't need it after all. If the merchant does respond in a timeframe that's useful to you, is the response warm and personal? Do you feel (and that's the right verb for the relationship the merchant ought to be creating: *feel*, not *think*) that the merchant is trying to establish a personal relationship with you?

COMPETING WITH THE BAG BOY

Merchants need to remember the bag boy who carries groceries to customers' cars at Harris Teeter—that's their competition. The minute or two of chitchat on a weekly basis forms a relationship that customers are reluctant to give up for nothing or for a cold, impersonal reply. This impression that customer service makes is likely to overshadow the customer's experience with the search tool, the prices, the interface, and the quality of the merchandise offered. Reflecting the importance of the initial customer/customer service interaction, BizRate reports that customers who avail themselves of customer service are less likely overall to return to merchants, no doubt as a result of dissatisfaction with that service.[6]

So, then, how can online merchants create an intimate shopping experience for their customers by making friendly, helpful presales support available around every corner, as it is at Harris Teeter? There are a couple ways. One is clearly real-time chat with knowledgeable, friendly staff. Another is having every message answered by a person who signs with at least his own first name. A third is permitting (and even encouraging) customers to contact the same staff member again by e-mail, if they have more questions, and making sure that the e-mail lands in the right box.

PERSONAL NOTE

I had the good fortune to answer Web master e-mail for a client for about three months. I was both helping them to catch up on a backlog of mail and reviewing their mail-processing systems to help them improve the way they filtered and responded to e-mail. I made a point of putting my first name and title at the bottom of every message. Some of these messages I was answering were a month old, and some of the people writing were angry in the first place, but still I never had anyone answer my reply angrily—and I replied to over 1500 messages. Frequently, customers—and the inquiries were overwhelmingly from men—would apologize to me in their responses for having flown off the handle in the first place. One gracious lady from Latin America was so grateful for the help I provided—and this was over the course of probably eight messages that went back and forth—that she invited me to come stay in her home if I were ever in Brazil. I'd like to add that this company did not ship to Brazil. I was confident that when my client did ship to Brazil, she'd be their best customer, and in the meantime, a garrulous Web-savvy woman like this one would be an excellent advocate in public and private forums alike for the stellar customer service my client now offered.

REAL-TIME CHAT: HELP WHEN IT'S NEEDED

The only realistic options for presales support that don't require the customer to disconnect and offer assistance in those critical moments when a customer is interested are real-time chat via a tool on the merchants' site and instant messaging on the order of Yahoo! or Netscape Instant Messengers. In order for instant messaging to work, the customer must have the software installed.

The real-time chat tools that merchants provide on their own sites don't usually require that any additional software exist on the customer's side—although one does require the customer to accept two applets—while the functionality is nearly identical to instant messengers. According to Datamonitor from June of 2000, less than 1 percent of e-retailers offer live customer service as an option on their sites.

REAL-TIME MESSAGING: A BIG LOSER

In the course of researching the tools for this chapter, I came across what appeared to be an alternate form of real-time chat: real-time messaging. With this tool, the customer sends a single query to a *virtual salesperson* who responds with an answer based on natural language processing and artificial intelligence. I don't want to pick on the company where I had this exchange, because by now I hope their tool has been improved, but the responses by the virtual salesperson were completely nonresponsive, to the point of being absurd. I felt like I was talking to a self-absorbed person at a cocktail party, with every response being the equivalent of "enough about me. What do you think about me?"

WOULD YOU LIKE SOME FRIES WITH THAT?

Presales support, which includes the opportunity to up-sell and cross-sell the customer, perhaps highlighting complementary products (e.g., recommending a carrying case to a customer inquiring about a notebook computer, or mentioning a sale on children's nightwear to a customer purchasing children's slippers), is a sorely missing component of online sales. Car dealers employ salespeople who are trained to offer floor mats and undercoat rust protection, shoe stores train their sales staff to recommend shoe maintenance products at the sale, even fast-food restaurants offer you "fries with that." What is wrong with online merchants that they are willing to forgo this tremendous opportunity to assist customers while increasing the basket size?

It's clearly a win-win proposition for them and the customers, who are getting a new level of customer support previously unavailable to them on the Web, and not usually available to them in large department stores or superstores. Table 13-1 shows the average order size by industry for Web orders in 1999, and the same figures for only the fourth quarter of 1999. Overall, Web order sizes have been falling over the past year or so, as customers become more comfortable with the idea of placing orders for smaller items, become more accustomed to paying a shipping charge, and take advantage of the free shipping being offered with greater frequency by merchants.[7] The fourth quarter saw a spike in average basket sizes that is probably related to holiday shopping.

Category	Average Purchase Amount for Fourth Quarter of 1999	Average Purchase Amount for 1999
Total retail e-commerce	$103	$92
Apparel	$114	$101
Computer goods	$228	$207
Consumer goods	$128	$134
Entertainment	$55	$55
Food/wine	$72	$71
Gifts	$61	$58
Home and garden	$91	$88
Toys	$62	$64

Table 13-1. Average basket size by industry. (Source: "Consumer Online Report: Total Retail E-Commerce," BizRate.com, Fourth Quarter 1999.)

Before real-time chat, the cost of that opportunity was high: phone support. Phone representatives are expensive at around $25 per hour, which includes the cost of connecting them to the Internet, the cost of the support software, and the long-distance charges. Table 13-2 shows how phone support and real-time chat compare.

Factor	Phone Support	Chat Support
Single-threading vs. multithreading	Can handle only one call at a time	Can handle multiple contacts at once
Closing the sale	Can close the sale by taking payment information on the spot	May or may not have access to credit card information (depending on whether support is presales or postsales)
Location	CSRs generally need to be located in the same physical location for the phone system to work	CSRs can be located anywhere (even working from home with good connections)
Connection	Customers must change gears from hands on the keyboard/mouse to hand on the phone	Customers continue to type/ click; customers with only one phone line not required to disconnect from Web

Table 13-2. Comparison of phone support and real-time chat across several areas.

AVERAGE BASKET SIZE COMPARISON

Merchants that offer a choice between closing the sale on the Web site and closing it over the phone find that the average phone order is larger than the average Web order. This is potentially a huge opportunity that many merchants are missing in trying to reduce their perceived customer service costs.

SERVICE WITH A SMILEY FACE

Customer service online is like that old joke about the weather: "Everyone talks about it, but no one ever does anything about it."

The grim truth about customer service is that most sites don't do a particularly good job of it. A Jupiter Communications survey from 1999 showed that 46 percent of major Web sites surveyed didn't respond to customer service e-mail within five days. Even worse news is that this number is up from surveys conducted a year earlier.

Why are so many sites falling down on the job when it comes to offering such seemingly basic support? Two reasons:

1. *They don't offer enough channels for customer service assistance.* Far more people than necessary end up sending e-mail, which is a highly inefficient means of communication.

2. *They're unequipped to deal with the high volume that results from the increases in traffic and sales on their sites.*

Both of these problems could have been solved with better planning. The first—specifically the inefficiency of e-mail for customer support—can be remedied by offering real-time chat on a site. The second is a reflection of poor capacity planning or poor communication about capacity planning.

CAPACITY PLANNING

Web sites typically have substantial technology organizations that are responsible for, among other things, capacity planning. As early as January, large Web sites that host their own servers begin to perform rudimentary calculations to estimate what kind of traffic they expect to see during their holiday shopping season, which typically peaks on December 14. These estimates will dictate how many and what kind of servers to purchase, what kind of connectivity and redundancy they need to the Internet, whether the database they used last year will be able to support this capacity, or whether an upgrade in the next six months will be necessary, among others. What these capacity planning figures don't usually do is migrate over to the customer service organization, where they're sorely needed.

Why not? Typically, these capacity figures are phrased in terms of number of page views per month/day/hour/second, both peak and average, and number of orders per month/day/hour/second, both peak and average. Technology professionals often don't realize that customer service can use these numbers and that customer service doesn't necessarily do its own capacity planning. Communication should be the easiest technology problem to solve!

Finally, most sites live in denial of the fact that so many customers make use of customer service at some point in the buying process. Few sites are willing to make the investment in equipment, technology, and people that will be required to stay on top of these customer service demands. Sites begin by setting customer service goals, such as "all e-mail will be answered within twenty-four hours" or "hold times will be limited to three minutes," and they end up conceding that these standards are simply too expensive to meet on peak days and during peak hours.

Poor capacity planning and inadequate customer service channels force customers to pick up the phone or send e-mail when an online FAQ or knowledge base might provide the answer in a timely manner.

WHY NOT E-MAIL?

E-mail is my least favorite support option, yet it's the one that most sites rely on most heavily. Ninety-six percent of Web merchants offer e-mail support.[8] Start-ups live under the delusion that this is the easiest kind of support to handle, because they don't need to invest in additional phone equipment or incur long-distance charges; they assume that because they can already handle e-mail from their desks, handling customer-service e-mail will be a bearable burden. Established sites are usually so inundated replying to e-mail that they can't get their heads above water long enough to plan for alternative support channels.

E-mail isn't timely enough. Even sites that manage to respond during the same business day are unlikely to find the shopper still in buying mode when the response arrives. The result may be that the customer has a favorable impression of the site but may not return to buy that item. The goodwill shouldn't be discounted, but the sale might have been lost.

E-mail begets more e-mail. This can be both good and bad, but generally when customers write with inquiries, the complete answer can't be provided in a single response, because the customer doesn't give enough information. In some cases, merchants end up with dialogues with customers. Instead of one e-mail to answer an inquiry, there may be four. Either a single phone conversation or a single chat session would have been able to answer the question.

Providing quality assurance is more difficult with e-mail than with other channels. Why? Most sites that rely heavily on e-mail are so overwhelmed by the volume they receive that they couldn't possibly find the resources or the time to audit the mail they're sending. I once received a scripted response from a major Web site that had four grammatical errors: two spelling errors and two homonym errors. One of the errors was using *sight* instead of *site* when referring to the company's own Web site.

MAKING THE MOST OF E-MAIL

Excellent tools are available on the market that can help to alleviate the problem of proofreading e-mail responses. They filter e-mail carefully, if the site sets up the business rules correctly, by using natural language processing and artificial intelligence to answer requests without any human intervention. They also provide an easy way for support representatives to send scripted responses to a large number of inquiries. These tools can take a site a long way toward making a customer service organization more efficient. However, if e-mail is to create any kind of bond between the sender and the site, then a warm human touch is needed. No automated solution is going to compete with the bag boys at Harris Teeter.

Knowledge(Base) Is Power

Knowledgebases and comprehensive FAQs have their places on Web sites. I prefer the knowledgebase format because it gives me the chance to type out my questions. Knowledgebases also give the illusion of having nearly infinite answers, whether they do or not.

Sites that cater to more technically savvy crowds do well to offer knowledgebases. 3Com hosts one about its products, which contains very technical answers—the kind that actually solve the problems you might come across when installing the company's networking products at 9 p.m. at home.

Knowledgebases and FAQs rarely offer a substitute for personalized customer service. If the site offers a product or service for free, the only cost being the time it takes the visitor to master it—such as a free download site, a community site, or an information site—and if the site limits itself to knowledgebases and FAQs, that's understandable. However, if a site wants to part a customer from his money, personalized customer assistance of some sort is essential.

INSTANT KNOWLEDGEBASE

Some very strong tools are on the market that will parse through a site's existing e-mail archives and strip out frequently asked questions and answers, then index the content so that site visitors can access a knowledgebase without the site ever having to sit down and write one. Additionally, these tools will work concomitantly with some e-mail software, growing richer in real time—as questions come in to e-mail support, they are automatically added to the knowledgebase.

HOW REAL-TIME CHAT WORKS

When a customer clicks on a text or graphic link on a merchant Web site, the request is instantly queued in a customer service tool. If a support representative is available to handle the request, a greeting from the support representative, with his name, will appear in a text box that has appeared on the customer's screen. Figure 13-2 shows the chat box the customer would see if the site were using HumanClick for chat support.

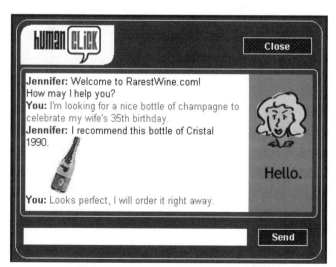

Figure 13-2. The chat box that HumanClick offers is one of the nicer ones.

If every rep is tied up, the customer will see the same text box, but instead of a greeting, the customer will see a message indicating that someone will be with him shortly. Once a support rep is available, the dialogue can begin. Some real-time chat tools, such as WebLine, ask for a name and/or phone number from the customer before the chat can begin. I imagine it's less confusing for a support representative to have the names of the six or so people he's chatting with concurrently than it is to have chat sessions simply identified by number.

After the chat session is initiated, the customer chats with the support rep in real time.

ENHANCING PRODUCTIVITY

Better chat tools give the support representative a big advantage in productivity because they have hot keys for specific expressions, such as "Please wait a moment while I look into that." While the customer is busy typing, the support representative can be responding to other customers. Support reps can handle up to four to six concurrent chat sessions, depending on their experience, the complexity of the products being discussed, and the tools they use. Figure 13-3 shows the data flow in a chat session.

MUST-HAVE FEATURES

In addition to basic chat, some tools offer the ability for the support representatives to push Web pages (referred to as URL push) to the customers so that the reps can show customers the featured specials they mention, or visit particular pages together, with clicks by either the rep or the customer taking effect on the screen of the other. This is a minimum requirement for a presales tool.

Particularly important to productivity—and the cost of live support is directly related to the length of each incident and the number of incidents a representative can handle concurrently—is the ability to script the tool used by the support rep to send polite, but common follow-up questions to the customer without excessive typing. The support tool you choose should be programmable by the merchant to add scripted responses that can be sent by hot key or menu clicks.

Another useful feature to look for is the ability to monitor a customer as he moves about the site. A natural follow-on to this is the ability to define

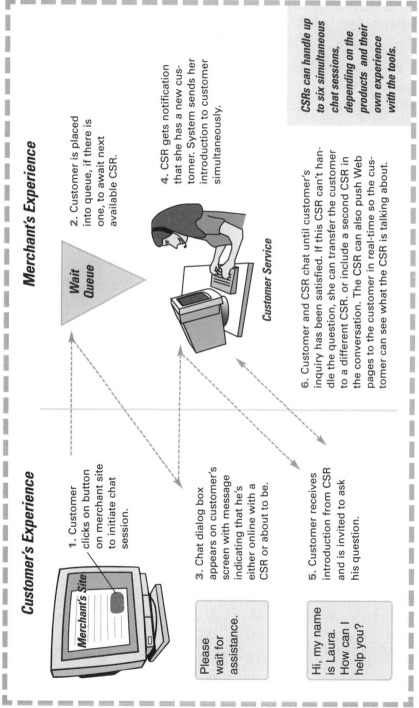

Customer's Experience

1. Customer clicks on button on merchant site to initiate chat session.

Merchant's Site

3. Chat dialog box appears on customer's screen with message indicating that he's either online with a CSR or about to be.

Please wait for assistance.

5. Customer receives introduction from CSR and is invited to ask his question.

Hi, my name is Laura. How can I help you?

Merchant's Experience

Wait Queue

2. Customer is placed into queue, if there is one, to await next available CSR.

4. CSR gets notification that she has a new customer. System sends her introduction to customer simultaneously.

Customer Service

6. Customer and CSR chat until customer's inquiry has been satisfied. If this CSR can't handle the question, she can transfer the customer to a different CSR, or include a second CSR in the conversation. The CSR can also push Web pages to the customer in real-time so the customer can see what the CSR is talking about.

CSRs can handle up to six simultaneous chat sessions, depending on the products and their own experience with the tools.

Figure 13-3. Data flow in a presales chat session.

business rules that proactively offer live support when a customer takes certain predictable action—such as beginning the checkout process, then backing up a screen, or returning to a product page to view the product information again—based on available support staff. A site would be foolish to offer live support if the representatives were all overloaded with sessions and a prospect who took the site up on the offer found that he did not have the attention of a salesperson after all.

Because of the number of technology neophytes coming online every week, I believe plug-ins are something you want to avoid in a real-time chat tool. Only one of the tools mentioned in the resources section requires the customer to accept plug-ins in order to use the product. As more and more security-related issues surface, customers will become understandably more suspicious of accepting plug-ins. Applets, as the plug-ins are called, have free reign of a user's hard drive, which is why Web site browsers should be cautious about accepting them. The job of a merchant should be to sell products, not to reconfigure the customers' computers. Requiring that the customers accept plug-ins is an unnecessary hurdle.

URL PUSH

Just as when shopping in a department store, a sales clerk can show a customer where a particular item is located or find a coordinating item for the customer, when using real-time chat with URL push, the sales representative at your site can push a Web page out to the customer's computer, displaying an item that might solve the customer's problem or showing the page with return policies for the customer to read. Not all real-time chat tools offer URL push, but in order to assist a sales representative in cross-selling and up-selling, they should. It's important that URL push open up a new window of a browser for the customer, not take over the existing window, or the customer might lose view of the product that spurred him to contact customer service in the first place.

PROACTIVE PRESALES SUPPORT

If a merchant really wants to reach out and touch the customers, it should consider providing proactive presales support. Remember the days of old when you'd walk into a clothing store and the salesperson would ask: "May I help you find something?" Sure, folks who had no interest got annoyed that they were being hassled, but serious shoppers were relieved not to have to wade through seemingly unlimited inventory trying to determine if what they sought was somewhere to be found.

Proactive presales support has its risks, namely the feeling by some that their privacy is being encroached upon when they innocently click into a site, only to have a chat box appear on the screen with Melissa or David offering to help. This feature can be especially disconcerting for shoppers sitting at their computers at home in their pajamas at 1 a.m., feeling like they suddenly have uninvited company.

Providing proactive presales support should be done strategically. When deciding at what point to get involved in a customer's private interactions, factors such as some indication that the customer is ready to buy should be taken into consideration. One logical place to intervene to save a sale might be when a customer begins the checkout process, then either backs out or decides to return to a specific product in the cart for more information.

Wherever a site decides to interpose itself into the customer's buying experience, the business rules that are applied should be carefully considered. The goal is not to frighten off browsers but to help provide crucial data so that the site closes sales with those ready to make the purchase.

Another feature that seems obviously necessary, but isn't available in any chat tool as of this writing, is the ability to begin a secure chat session, in midconversation, so that the salesperson can actually take the order without sending the customer back through the site. No one would expect a phone representative to answer customer inquiries, offer complementary products, then send the customer to the site to place the order. Why do chat products fail to take the last step and close the sale?

IN-HOUSE OR OUTSOURCED

When choosing a chat tool, sites need to decide the degree to which they want to integrate the chat tool with other systems versus the degree to which they want to be rid of all support for hardware and software. Tools are available that require in-house installation. Other tools include hosting the software in the price. The latter option gets a site up and running more quickly. The former option permits the chat tool to integrate more tightly into the other customer service channels that the site provides.

In the name of customer relationship management (CRM) many sites will opt for the in-house solution, but outsourcing the hosting has definite advantages:

→ Instant set-up—often within a day.

→ No hardware to buy, install, support, back up, upgrade, etc.

→ Capacity planning and support is someone else's problem.

WHAT SHOPPERS SAY

As recently as September of 1999, it would have been difficult to find more than a small handful of sites using real-time chat to provide pre-sales and customer service assistance to their customers. Fortunately, the number of sites that have added this service multiplies every month. The first site of which I'm aware that provided this service (and a suite of other customer service options) was BuyNow.com. The site that probably sees the most traffic through its real-time chat service is Lands' End (www.landsend.com).

According to Cyber Dialogue's American Internet Usage Survey, 63 percent of shoppers say they find live help with a customer service person via the computer either helpful or very helpful.[9]

RESOURCES

Owing to the fact that really smart developers are working furiously, even as you read, to make everything in this book obsolete, and because of the lag time in producing a book, the list below isn't comprehensive. These vendors, however, do represent the range of types of real-time chat software available and a handful of customer service outsourcing companies that work with them.

REAL-TIME CHAT SOFTWARE

→ *eShare (www.eshare.com)* offers NetAgent Live! if you want it to host the software, or it will license the software to you to host in-house. No downloads are required by the shopper. Major clients include TheStreet.com, Bluefly.com, and Linkshare.

➔ *FaceTime* by FaceTime Communications *(www.facetime.net)* is a business-to-business and business-to-customer real-time instant messaging business platform and applications that can then be hosted on the company's servers or hosted on your own servers. Other features of the software include URL push, monitoring of customer traffic around the site, the ability to create business rules to optimize the quality of service and the user experience, private labeling of the chat window, customer service tool configuration so that sales reps can send scripted responses and inquiries with a single click or hot key, and secure chat (optional).

➔ *iServe 3.0* by SneakerLabs *(www.sneakerlabs.com)* offers a free-for-one product but charges for additional seats. SneakerLabs hosts the software. iServe includes the ability to push URLs to customers. Software monitors movement of visitors around the site with the sales rep able to proactively offer support at his own discretion. No customer downloads are required.

➔ *iSession* by Sessio *(www.sessio.com)* hosts the software for the merchants. The chat client can be customized by the merchant to include requests for shopper information (e.g., names, e-mail addresses) and private labeling. No downloads are required. The client supports URL push. The customer service tool supports the ability to have quick responses of programmed text.

➔ *HumanClick (www.humanclick.com)* offers real-time chat software, which is hosted for free by HumanClick on its own servers. This start-up from mid-December 1999 had over 10,000 clients by February 2000. HumanClick was purchased by LivePerson in October of 2000. No downloads are required by the shopper. The software monitors the movement of shoppers around the site, permitting customer service representatives to offer their services at appropriate times. The Pro version, which will be a for-free service beginning in January of 2001, offers URL push, private labeling of the chat window, and a full-featured customer service tool, including scripting and hot keys. Major clients include mostly smaller Web sites that offer their own customer service.

→ *LivePerson (www.liveperson.com)* offers a real-time chat service, which is hosted by LivePerson. Because there's no hardware to acquire and install, and no software to install and configure, merchants can be up and running in a matter of hours. No downloads are required by the shopper, but the chat box does ask for the customer's first name. The customer service tool has the ability to build in quick responses and to send URLs out to customer's computers to open in their own browsers. Major clients include iQVC.com, proflowers.com, and E-LOAN.com.

→ *WebLine (www.webline.com)*, owned by Cisco Systems, offers a real-time chat system that is hosted by the merchant, on the merchant's own hardware. It integrates tightly with other Cisco products. The site offers a range of real-time products including the "Shop with a Friend" functionality, found on the Lands' End site, and two-way browser synchronization. Depending on the suite of services the merchant installs, two plug-ins may be required by the shopper to use these services. Major clients include Lands' End, Fidelity Investments, and Hewlett-Packard.

Other vendors include:

Blue Martini (www.bluemartini.com)

cs-live.com (www.cs-live.com)

Groopz.com (www.groopz.com)

Lucent (www.lucent.com)

Webhelp.com (www.webhelp.com)

CUSTOMER SUPPORT CENTERS THAT CAN HELP

The number of customer support centers grows exponentially with each passing week. Many more should be available by the time this book is published, but the ones listed below are a good place to start.

If a merchant wants a turnkey solution for real-time chat, nothing beats outsourcing to a customer support center with already trained representatives. Turnkey solutions provide for instant growth, and that's part of the solution that most merchants need.

APAC Customer Services, Inc. (WebLine)

E-ComSupport.com (E-Share)

PeopleSupport (NetEffect)

Precision Response Corp (WebLine)

TeleSales, Inc (WebLine)

VSI Holdings, Inc. (WebLine)

WebConverse Inc.

Systems 14

CUSTOMER service is much more than an overhead expense. It is a strategic advantage for your company. Whether your company is a pure-play dot-com, a bricks-and-clicks store, or something else, you cannot afford to ignore customer service. In fact, I'd argue that your competitors with less selection, higher prices, and better service ultimately will take your market share if you don't give your customers a reason to stay with you.

Customer service is about knowing your customers and serving your customers. Customers don't want you to be the KGB and dig up information they've never given you or that's not directly relevant to their shopping at your site or stores, but they do want you to remember their behavior at your site or stores. Unless you're selling products that people are ashamed to be purchasing, most customers don't want to be anonymous when they return to your site or store.

Knowing your customers is about half of the challenge for most sites and stores. Providing what they want based on what you know about them is the other half. Technology cannot address the biggest part of this challenge for most merchants—a positive customer service culture can, and that's much less expensive than technology in most cases, as well.

The old way of thinking of retail—from a product-centric perspective—is dead. Customers don't usually go to a site to find a product but to solve a problem. If you design your site and your customer service system around products and moving products, you will fail to respond to customers' needs for solutions. Smart sites will look at customers both individually and in clusters and recommend appropriate products for their expressed and unexpressed needs.

Customers' expectations are higher than ever. They expect you to know all about them and to use that information to serve them better. Other merchants are reaching into their customers' mailboxes offering targeted relevant offers, displaying compelling ads for products they're in the market for on their home pages, and delivering targeted offers by postal mail to encourage them to visit their stores or their Web sites. Compete, or risk being left behind.

Customer relationship management is a big umbrella. Several of the technologies already discussed in this book are as much about knowing and serving customers as about moving products—personalization, targeted EDM, and real-time chat, for example. This chapter focuses on the customer service component of CRM.

CUSTOMER SERVICE AS DIFFERENTIATOR

Surveys consistently show that customer service is the most important factor when it comes to turning a one-time customer into a loyal customer. BizRate's data shows that customers who contact customer service are less likely to return to that site, so it would appear that most sites are missing opportunities to turn one-time customers into customers who will return.

That begs the question: Which is more cost effective, spending money on customer acquisition or spending money on customer service? Because an average customer service phone call (the most expensive way to respond to a customer service inquiry) costs $3.20 and the cost of acquiring a new customer is around $38, it's an easy answer. It's more cost effective to take eleven customer service phone calls than to acquire one new customer, all else being equal. You need to determine your own customer acquisition costs and your own customer service costs in order to see how many customer service contacts a single customer can make before it is more cost effective to replace him.

Customer satisfaction must be a strategic goal of your organization. It's typical in a retail establishment for advertising and marketing to be above customer service and operations in the corporate pecking order. (The former are thought to be revenue generators, while the latter are always classified as overhead.) The name of the game has always been to reduce the amount of money that has to be spent on operations and customer service to make that money available to be used by advertising and marketing. The problem with that model is that it assumes that once a company acquires a customer, it doesn't need to spend any more money to keep him. In fact, with communications on the Web being nearly free, the viral consequences of a bad shopping experience can snowball. It has the effect not only of antagonizing the customer (who was acquired, then neglected) but also of having him tell two friends, who in turn tell two friends (and so on and so on), that a site is to be avoided.

BUILDING A CUSTOMER-CENTRIC ORGANIZATION

Making the customer the center of your business is bigger than any one technology, bigger than your Web site, and bigger than offering the right promotion at the right time. Many of the technologies in this book are components of building a customer-centric organization. Providing the right e-mail offers at the right times to customers is one component of a customer-centric organization. Recognizing customers when they come in the door (both the Web site door and the store door) and identifying them by name is another component. Customer-centric organizations try both to bring the right people to the products they're already selling, through appropriate marketing, and to identify the right products for the customers they're already serving, through appropriate merchandising. In neither case is a shoehorn a necessary tool. Many sites get whatever deals they can from their distributors and hawk them on their sites without any idea of whether their existing customer base will want them.

Who runs a customer-centric organization? In a typical product-centered organization, merchandising is frequently steering the ship. Marketing takes direction from merchandising based on what products and promotions merchandising can line up with distributors and manufacturers. Customer service is like the cleanup crew after the party. If customers are dissatisfied with the quality of a product or service, or if the enormous success of a promotion leaves some customers without access to the product or service, then merchandising and marketing celebrate their success, and customer service apologizes and tries to appease customers.

In a customer-centric organization, marketing should be directing merchandising as to what kinds of products and promotions the existing customer base wants. If the existing customer base isn't the optimal customer mix for the company's long-term plans, then marketing should be working with merchandising to determine how to meet the needs of the optimal customer mix. Finally, marketing should work with customer service proactively to anticipate what customer service has to be prepared to deliver. Because customer service is likely sitting on one side of a two-way, real-time chat with customers, and ideally offering personalized recommendations to e-mail, phone, and chat inquiries, customer service representatives need to be part of the planning process for promotions and new product offerings.

WHAT "MULTICHANNEL" REALLY MEANS

Merchants frequently give lip service to the concept of multichannel support. They offer e-mail support and phone support for their Web orders, and if they have stores, they accept returns there. Multichannel support should actually cover all touch points between a merchant and a customer. These points would include such seemingly obscure ones as:

→ Having an in-store sales clerk know what offers were made by e-mail to customers who are either making a purchase or returning a product, including what offers the customer responded favorably to

→ Putting kiosks in the bricks-and-mortar store so that customers can order products that may be out of stock in that particular store—to complete an outfit or provide an accessory for a barbecue grill, for example

→ Making coupons available via wireless devices such as phones, PDAs, and pagers when customers "sign-in" at the bricks-and-mortar stores

→ In-store clerks being able to pull up an online customer's shopping history to know what was purchased, either to execute a paperless return or to coordinate an ensemble or to locate an accessory

THE ISOLATED DATA PHENOMENON

In fact, much of the data that's needed to have customers feel recognized wherever they come into contact with a merchant already exists within an organization. The problem is that the data that exists isn't available via the application to the interface (human or digital) at the time and place at which it's needed. Most of the following data is available from somewhere within the bowels of every organization.

CUSTOMER HISTORY

→ How long has this customer been shopping from this merchant?

→ What brought her here in the first place? Was she referred by a friend, or did she come in via some cross-marketing promotion; if the latter, what has the company done to cement the three-way relationship?

→ What types of products does the customer typically purchase?

→ What's her average order total?

MARKETING HISTORY

→ What types of promotions has the customer received from the merchant?

→ Does she typically respond to them?

→ What types of promotions have actually prompted her to make a purchase (e.g., dollars off, free shipping, percentage off a future purchase, sales)?

ORDER HISTORY

→ How many visits does it take to have the customer place an order?

→ Does she click through a promotion and make the purchase, or does she look around, returning later to make the purchase?

→ What types of purchases has she made?

→ What complementary products has she been offered?

→ What types of products are purchased by others who have purchased what the customer has purchased?

CUSTOMER SERVICE HISTORY

→ How often has the customer contacted customer service?

→ Were they able to satisfy her concerns?

→ Has she returned anything?

→ Is she a high-maintenance customer?

TRAFFIC HISTORY

→ How often does the customer visit the site?

→ Does she come via promotions, via a bookmark, by typing the site name into the browser, via an affiliate link, or some other way?

→ What are her shopping patterns?

→ Does she keep a wish list?

→ Does she fill and abandon a cart regularly?

→ If she abandons the cart, at what point does she do that?

GETTING DATA WHERE YOU NEED IT

It would be useful for a store clerk or a phone representative or a real-time chat rep to know that the customer has items on her wish list so that she could cross-sell them, or offer them as today's "featured products." Conversely, any of the above-mentioned service people should also know if this customer routinely returns every product she purchases, making her a high-maintenance customer, in which case, trying to sell her more merchandise might not be in the interest of the company. If any of the three service people mentioned above knows that this customer's average order total is twice what she's about to purchase, then trying to cross-sell her makes sense, because the customer is clearly comfortable spending the extra money—and may, in fact, not be comfortable placing only a small order. As a final example, offering whatever type of promotion has worked in the past may be exactly what this customer needs to close the sale. Only with the information at their disposal can the assorted service people who come across the customer's path offer the most attractive deal to her.

Much of this data and customized offers can and should be part of the business rules of the content-management system (CMS) (see Chapter 12), which will ideally be driven by personalization (see Chapter 8). All of this data should be evaluated when customers are aggregated for purposes of sending out personalized targeted e-mail (see Chapter 6). Customer loyalty, however, still hinges on the personal experiences of shoppers with a merchant's customer service team—whether that contact comes by phone, by e-mail, in a retail establishment, or via real-time chat (see Chapter 13). Only a multichannel, integrated CRM system can put the information in front of the eyeballs that need it for human contact.

WHAT IS CRM?

CRM is estimated to be a $6.5 billion business by 2003, according to IDC. With that kind of revenue potential, it's no wonder that every company that sells any products even vaguely related to customers touts its solution as a CRM solution. CRM is a suite of software that, at its core, includes an order-management system that tracks and makes available what a customer has purchased, so that phone, e-mail, chat, and store salespeople can answer questions about previous purchases and handle returns. It is crucial software to have, because BizRate reports that 24 percent of customer service contacts take place after an order has been received. CRM also needs transactional capabilities so that sales and service representatives can resolve issues related to orders and returns such as refunding shipping, determining the status of open orders (the same BizRate research shows that 55 percent of customer service contacts take place while waiting for an order to arrive), and handling exchanges. A good CRM system will have all the informational capabilities of a Web site with additional empowerment to change customer and order information for the sales and service reps working on the system.

But there's more to CRM. The software is practically the foundational platform for an online merchant. Your CRM system will provide the basis and the data for your personalization engine, which will feed your targeted EDM campaigns. The data in your CRM system will feed your content management system with a customer's profile and order history. CRM may not be quite as broad as marketers of quasi-CRM solutions claim it is, but it's pretty big, just the same.

CRM VERSUS ERP

Enterprise resource planning (ERP) was the buzzword of the 1990s. It relied on supply-chain management, the idea that companies could save their way into profitability. CRM systems are about demand-chain management, if such a thing can exist. Managing your relationship with your customers, partners, bricks-and-mortar outlets, and salespeople is managing the demand side of the equation. Some CRM systems also claim to be ERP systems, but ERP tends to focus on procurement, manufacturing, and billing to a degree that CRM does not.

---->

Inbound E-Mail

Companies have been "handling" inbound e-mail from customers for so long that everyone seems to assume that this is one area of the Web where the dust has settled. There's nothing new here, right? Wrong. There are many decisions that merchants need to make when it comes to responding to inbound e-mail. The first question is whether to use an auto-responder to acknowledge that e-mail has been received. The next question is whether to use a natural language processing system to try to respond to customer inquiries without human intervention. The third question is how to create business rules so that mail ends up in the appropriate in-boxes and your own people don't need to spend too much time rerouting mail. Finally, you need to decide the degree to which you're going to track e-mail conversations between your customers and your employees so that you can maintain a history of a customer's complaints.

I would recommend that you use an auto-responder, because sending e-mail to a merchant often feels to customers that they are putting a message in a bottle and casting it out to sea. An instant response gives them some confidence that someone really is on the other end of the communication. However, if you have a five-day backlog of messages to deal with, don't use an auto-responder with a friendly message assuring customers that their query will be handled promptly. Set realistic expectations so that you can meet or exceed them.

SELECTING A CRM VENDOR

Selecting a CRM vendor is a critical decision. While you probably can't expect any single product to have all the features you want in a CRM solution, you can expect the best CRM vendors to have relationships in place so that you don't have to patch multiple products together. Consider not only who the CRM vendors are but also where they have alliances.

The big decision in the CRM industry today is whether to go with Siebel or not. Siebel is the clear industry leader in CRM solutions—the only software provider with double-digit market share according to IDC. While Siebel is the gold standard against which other CRM vendors are measured, there are other vendors worth considering. Smaller vendors, which have only provided a small piece of the pie until now, are adding more features so that they can offer full CRM capability.

While Siebel arguably handles enterprise resource planning, not every ERP vendor truly handles CRM. To make matters even more confusing, some vendors are referring to their own offerings as ERM (enterprise or e-business relationship management). Because CRM predates the "e" revolution, CRM is seen as referring to a less hip technology.

Whichever acronym you settle on, realize that the selection of CRM vendor is every bit as important as choice of CMS vendor (see Chapter 12), because extricating yourself from a relationship with a subpar vendor will be expensive and time consuming. Review the following guidelines to make sure you haven't overlooked anything obvious:

→ How many channels are you operating or should you be operating? The software you select should address all the channels you need without being overly focused on one of your less important channels. If your call center handles only customer service and not sales, you probably don't want to select a CRM solution that was originally built for call-center sales.

→ Does the CRM software offer the features you need?

→ Does the CRM software interface with your other systems? In theory, all digital systems can work with all other digital systems, but do you have to build the interface? Look for a CRM solution that has prebuilt interfaces to your back office and CMS. The less customization that's required, the better. A reduction in customization will both speed implementation time and reduce the lifetime cost of the solution, because you won't need to customize every software upgrade to work with your other systems.

→ Does the CRM vendor have strategic relationships in place to provide features that its own software doesn't include? Frequently, you'll find that a well-integrated partnership will serve you better than one system that tries to do everything. Just make sure the relationship between the vendors is more than a press release deep, that you're not the beta client for implementation, and that you're not paying for all the features of the partner's software if you're only using the subset necessary to complement your CRM software.

→ Are the vendor's other clients satisfied with the level of support they receive? Some vendors frontload support so that during the honeymoon, everyone's satisfied; then after that, newer clients take precedence over older clients.

→ Does the vendor take enhancement suggestions from clients? Check with other clients to see what they've found on this front. A smart vendor will listen to its clients to see what they need and use that kind of front-line experience to stay ahead of competition.

↪ How are you paying for the implementation, and what are you paying for? Is the cost of implementation fixed or do you pay for the professional services of the vendor's people on your site forever? Some vendors make more from consulting services than from the software. Where is the incentive for the vendor? Does the package include strategic consulting? Is that what you want? I've seen two-month implementations drag on for six months when the vendor had no incentive to wrap things up and move its people onto another client. Billing by the hour or the day doesn't always give the vendor the proper motivation to transfer skills to your team.

↪ How do you *feel* about your vendors? Ask key participants in the negotiations, including architects, vice presidents, and others on your team whether they have a good feeling about working with these people. In my experience, whenever we've brought in a bad vendor, there were many red flags that we ignored, either individually or collectively, along the way. Companies that aren't going to deliver what they promise usually give you lots of warnings along the way. Unless you ask your people, you may be ignoring these warnings.

CRM AT WORK

In most of the chapters in this book, I've relied on case studies to show one element of a technology at work. CRM is just too big to demonstrate using a real case study, so I've created the following scenario featuring a fictional company, The Leaf, which sells garden supplies and plants and flowers through catalogs, bricks-and-mortar stores, and an online site. Any relationship to any real company is coincidental, although I hope there are real companies that are implementing what I consider to be these best practices.

The Leaf uses a CRM system that permits it to track customers across all its channels. They've recently implemented kiosks at their bricks-and-mortar stores, on which customers can find targeted promotions, print care instructions for plants, and look up their own profiles and purchase history. Customers are identified uniquely by their e-mail addresses and passwords. Customers without e-mail addresses can use their phone numbers as identifiers (the phone number instantly becomes the e-mail ID "@theleaf.com").

At checkout, customers are asked to provide their e-mail addresses so that their purchase histories are kept up to date and they can look up their purchases later when they wonder whether they planted heliopsis or coreopsis, so they know when and how to prune and fertilize. Of course, The Leaf also benefits when it can link offline purchases to online purchases.

Customers can seek support via any channel for purchases made through any channel. This means that gardeners who find themselves with a pruning question can phone the call center while standing in the garden trying to identify the type of insect devouring their hostas. Alternatively, catalog customers can turn to the search tool of the Web site to see what insects are likely to be the culprits and what pesticides are recommended to eliminate the problem.

Targeted e-mail is delivered to customers based on online and offline shopping behavior. In addition to e-mail promotions being mailed to the customer, a copy is also filed with the customer's profile, so that the customer can retrieve an online coupon from a kiosk at the store, print it out, and take it to the register. Additionally, the sales representative at the phone center will be aware of any promotions in the customer's profile so that a customer making a purchase over the phone will be able to use the promotion there, as well.

Covert personalization is used in all channels to make the right offers at the right times. The sales rep who's taking a catalog order can offer a customer a special deal on something she already knows is on her "buy later" list or on something she's visited on more than one occasion on the site. Shipping offers are also customized for the gardener. A customer who typically spends $75 each transaction can be offered a "free shipping for purchases over $85" offer when he visits the site, to try to increase his order total by a nonthreatening amount.

If a customer has a complaint or return that is in process, the sales rep at the store can inquire at the checkout whether the incident was resolved to the customer's satisfaction. After The Leaf believes the issue has been resolved, it can use the same information online to survey the customer about whatever the complaint was. Phone representatives are trained to inquire about recent customer service complaints as well, so that when a customer interacts with any touch points of The Leaf, he'll know that they care about his previous unsatisfactory experience.

Customers like the overt personalization features of The Leaf's Web site, including the ability to indicate what zone they're in, so as to receive newsletters particular to their climate and gardens. They also like having the ability to keep a garden portfolio in their profiles so that they can look things up at the stores and find solutions and recommendations specific to their own gardens. They even have the ability to record the names and locations of plants they already have or plants they've purchased elsewhere, so they have an integrated garden portfolio. Of course, The Leaf uses all this information to up-sell and cross-sell customers on organic fertilizers, pruning tools, garden equipment, and patio accessories.

In addition to selling garden plants, The Leaf also sells floral arrangements and plants as gift items. There is no place on the site for a customer to indicate his anniversary to be reminded to send flowers. Once he has sent flowers as a gift for a particular occasion, however, he will be reminded annually at that time of year that a possible gift-giving occasion is around the corner. Then, if he's in the market, in relatively few clicks he can have a comparably priced gift shipped in time.

BUILDING THE RELATIONSHIP

The Leaf clearly has its act together more than most multichannel operations. Fictional enterprises can afford such luxuries. However, the key to all the promotions, personalization, and features of The Leaf's multichannel experience is that they all focus on giving the customer more. Why would a customer shop anywhere else? Being queried via one channel—in the store, perhaps—about a customer service issue raised in a different channel—via e-mail or real-time chat—is not something the customer would soon forget. The customer doesn't get the feeling that he is dealing with different companies—as you probably have if you've ever noticed a price discrepancy between different channels of the same merchant, or had to repeat all your purchase information to a salesperson, or had to produce a paper receipt when you know the company should have a record of a product purchase "in their system." Instead, the customer knows that the company is one integrated unit and that his business matters to this company.

Customer relationship management is ultimately about developing a relationship with the customer that serves the customer's needs. After all, a customer doesn't want a relationship built on your convenience or your quarterly sales goals. If you can address the customer's needs before he can identify them, then you've truly added value to his life. You've saved him time hunting for solutions to his problems, money purchasing incompatible products, and possible embarrassment by missing an important occasion. And customers will reward merchants who add this kind of value to their lives with lifetime loyalty.

 ## Resources

WEB SITES

CRM Supersite (www.crmsupersite.com)

CRM Assist (www.crmassist.com)

VENDORS AND INTEGRATORS

Siebel, E.piphany, Kana, IBM, HP, Oracle, and Onyx are but a few. Most of the larger consultancies offer CRM solutions—either their own or implementation and integration of a major third-party provider. Ask around within your industry to find integrators with experience so they don't have to learn at your expense.

WHITE PAPERS

Siebel has some excellent white papers, as do some of the other vendors. I recommend that you check the Web sites of all the vendors to see what white papers are available. You'll often have to provide personal information or talk to a sales rep before you get one, but the white papers can be very informative.

PART V

TURNKEY GROWTH

Outsource Everything 15

THE WORLD of e-commerce is moving too fast for any business to excel at everything. The only way to succeed is for a business to focus on its own business, which is probably *not* technology, and to find hosting services, application service providers, customer service centers, and technical contractors that it can ramp up or down at the drop of a hat. Businesses should think in terms of the services they need rather than the resources they need to deliver services. The only way to move quickly enough in this environment is to rely as much as possible on services provided by others.

This chapter will discuss the reasons why relying on others to provide the technology solutions is a good idea, followed by some techniques for selecting those vendors that will fill out your business.

WHY OUTSOURCE?

There are eight excellent reasons not to develop the software yourself:

→ To have the time and energy to focus on your business

→ Because the software development lifecycle is too slow relative to the speed of the Web

→ To speed time to market of your ideas and services

→ To get more features than you could afford to develop in-house, in terms of both time and money

→ To avoid having to find, hire, train, and retain scarce technical resources

→ To remain nimble and not be weighed down by your technology choices

→ To be able to change the direction of your business quickly, should market forces necessitate

→ Because customer loyalty doesn't depend on writing your own software

WHAT BUSINESS ARE YOU IN?

Focus is the name of the game in e-commerce, and very few companies seem to be able to keep their eyes on the ball. It brings to mind a basketball game, with a player at the free-throw line and the fans of the other team wildly gesturing, waving flags, foam sticks, and signs behind the backboard, in clear view of the player, trying to distract him from making what would probably be an easy shot in an empty stadium. If the player looks at anything the fans are doing, instead of at the hoop, he's sure to miss.

You as the merchant are the player. The opposing team's fans are the hype of new sites, the buzz of new advertising techniques, and the reports of other sites' IPOs and takeovers. Today you need to focus on the goal, which is unrelated to any of those things.

Another thing that can keep a merchant from focusing on the business of his own business is an undue focus on technology. Without the technology, the business isn't possible, but the merchant has to be wary not to focus too much on the technology. It would be like focusing on the car instead of the road when driving. Ideally, the car would be so well designed you wouldn't need to take your eyes off the road to change the radio station. In the same way you shouldn't need to take your eye off your business goal to get a new feature added to your systems. ASPs can facilitate this in a way that in-house software cannot.

THE SOFTWARE-DEVELOPMENT LIFE CYCLE

Developing software in-house, unless you're in the business of selling software and support services or you're an ASP, is probably a mistake. Even hiring a consulting firm to develop the software for you is probably a mistake. What you want to avoid is owning a static version of software. What you want is to have access to the services the software provides without being wedded to the software. If you develop in-house or if you hire someone to develop it for you, you're stuck with the software and the cost of ongoing upgrades and enhancements. And you get to pay for the entire solution yourself.

The optimal model is to rely on an ASP and have the services hosted elsewhere. The next best thing is to license the software, install it on your own servers, and pay for it monthly or annually, complete with a service agreement.

It's not the fault of any particular software, but even your most ingenious architect can't create software that anticipates your needs. The software-development life cycle relies on the fact that needs must be identified and requirements defined *before* software can be written. If it's your needs that are identified, then there will be long gap between when you feel pain and when the cure—in the form of software—is available. If you use software that's also used by dozens or hundreds of other sites, then there's a good possibility that one of the other sites has already felt the pain of a missing feature and made its case to the software vendor, and the solution might be in the works before you identify the need and begin to make your case to the vendor. Occasionally, you will be the first client of a software vendor or ASP to identify a need, but even on those occasions, you won't pay for the cost of the enhancement, except as part of your monthly or annual fees.

TIME TO MARKET

Time to market is important on the Web. Even if you won't be the first in your industry to have a solution, you can't afford to be perceived as a laggard by your customers. From simple things, like offering expedited shipping options, to more sophisticated services, like real-time chat and wireless access, he who hesitates is lost.

Using the services and software of an ASP or vendor can get your solution onto your site more quickly than any other way. If, for example, you've decided to ship internationally, the time it would take you to develop the relationships with vendors, tax specialists, and logistics companies would strip you of any competitive advantages associated with the fact that you've made the decision ahead of your competitors. If the competitors could take advantage of the services of a company like From2.com and implement a turnkey solution, then even if they waited four more months to decide to ship internationally, they might still beat you to market with their solution.

YOU CAN'T AFFORD TO DEVELOP IN-HOUSE

When you purchase or license software from someone else, you not only get a solution right away but you also share the cost of development with all the other companies using that solution. The cost associated with getting the rich features set of tested, installed software would be prohibitive for the vast majority of businesses, even if the software could be developed expeditiously. For example, you might find, when you're talking to vendors, that no one has exactly what you wanted when you began your investigation. You would still be better off, however, going with the solution that solves most of the problems than building a solution from scratch that will cover what you know you need today but won't be in place for four to six months. By that time, you most likely would have an entirely new set of needs.

SCARCE TECHNICAL RESOURCES

It's not news that technical people of all stripes are in short supply. Computer science graduates from most institutions can expect to start new jobs, with no experience, at $60,000 per year. Graduates expect to have multiple offers from which to choose. Developers with only six months to a year of Java, ColdFusion, or SAP experience can expect to be recruited away from their current employers with juicy salary increases. Nationwide, the need for developers and the cost of those developers has increased enormously.

When you rely on ASPs and vendors to deliver your software, then you find that you need only a fraction of the technical talent in-house—just enough people to integrate the acquired solution with existing systems. Many companies don't value the "soft dollars" of developing in-house as highly as the "hard dollars" of finding a commercial solution. That's a mistake because the rule of thumb for new development is that the cost of development is 10 percent of the cost of the entire solution. The cost of maintenance is the other 90 percent.

JACK BE NIMBLE

Even when merchants do understand what businesses they are in, they need to stay nimble. The days of being able to stick to five-year business plans are long gone. Although software should enhance a business's ability to move swiftly, more often it's like an anchor, keeping the business from moving at all. Even for the most traditional of businesses, industries are changing rapidly and no one can be sure exactly what an industry will look like in three years.

The grocery business is one excellent example. When you think of groceries, do you think of a mom-and-pop grocery store with shiny apples on display as you enter the store and hand-lettered signs in the window? Do you think of a megagrocery store where you can also get a haircut, buy hot food, and drop off your shoes for repair? Or do you think of placing your order online for delivery the next day?

Your industry might not have been that dramatically affected by technology yet, but that doesn't mean it's immune to change. By not binding yourself to technology, you are nimble enough to move with or ahead of the rest of your industry.

JACK BE QUICK

Some of the more successful Web businesses have had to abandon their initial industries—or at least change the focus of their energy—to fill a niche that they identified, even if meant working with their competitors. Part of the reason you don't want to be weighed down with technology—unless you absolutely can't find any commercial provider selling that particular software—is that you may find the opportunity exists just outside of where you've been focusing your energy. Two examples of this are Paytime, which is a currency platform that spun off of the Cybergold loyalty program when it was acquired by MyPoints, and the Ask Jeeves corporate solution engine, which I discuss in Chapter 9.

In both these examples, the companies had technology that they couldn't afford to keep to themselves. They realized that if they went into a service provider role, they could continue to maintain the software while sharing the costs of the software upgrades with multiple partners—their clients. Because they already had money and people wrapped up in the technology, it was the best move to make.

CASE STUDY: Paytime

Nat Goldhaber:

"Paytime is a company that was spun off from Cybergold, an Internet site that pays Web surfers for their attention. The 'pay' they receive is in the form of real cash that they can use in a variety of ways: as money to deposit into their checking or Visa accounts, as spendable cash for buying goods and services from name-brand merchants on the Internet, or as donations to the nonprofit or charitable organization of their choice.

"To track member activity while they surf the Web and maintain accurate records of the earnings they accrue for their attention online, we developed our own proprietary technology (as described in our 'attention brokerage' patent #5794210) for paying Cybergold members their cash rewards. We called it Paytime. And it proved so successful for Cybergold, we decided it could serve as a valuable 'back-end' redemption tool for other Internet companies that specialize in incentive reward marketing. The beauty of Paytime is that, as a payment platform, it need not be limited to the redemption of incentive rewards. We believe it can serve as a general payment platform, offering redemption services to many incentive companies, and payment services to multiple merchants. So we decided to spin out Paytime as a separate entity.

"Shortly after we made this decision, Cybergold and MyPoints entered consolidation talks, and MyPoints agreed with this strategy. The combined incentive companies will be the largest online incentive company by far, and will be able to concentrate on its marketing strength, rather than on software development and merchant cultivation.

"Paytime will be the largest alternate payment system by far, with more online consumer accounts than the five leading online banks combined. As a result, Paytime expects to become the standard payment system not only for loyalty programs, but for all Internet merchants who for various reasons need alternatives to the credit card networks."

CASE STUDY: Ask Jeeves
Steve Roop, Director of Product Management

"Ask Jeeves was founded in 1996 as a consumer search tool. A bunch of our own people came from the CRM field, and we knew very well that in the call center environment you'd get the same questions over and over again. It's very frustrating when you get 15,000 calls a day with the same questions. If a Web site had a Q&A system that was easy and convenient, it could reduce all these extra calls. We also knew from the success of ATM machines that people are comfortable with self-service.

"By 1998 we had corporate sites like Dell, Microsoft WebTV, and AltaVista coming to us to ask whether we could help them make their own content more accessible using our services. What we saw was that there were many new Internet users coming online. Content was exploding on corporate sites. But the average customer's ability to find the content [he was] looking for was decreasing dramatically. We saw a critical need for an intuitive natural language Q&A system.

"Companies thought when they went to e-business, their phone calls and e-mail would go down, but what happened was that it caused a rise in their offline communication channels. Because of our initial experience as a consumer search tool, we understood how people asked questions and what kind of metrics we could provide to Web sites. Now we're able to reduce the number of offline communications for corporate sites that use our systems, which lowers support costs. More importantly, we help people find what they're looking for."

CASE STUDY: eWonder.com

Fayad Syed, Vice President

"In May of 1999, we launched RatingWonders. The idea was to show the capability of merchants, as well as their performance. We manage over 85 parameters for each merchant that deal with customer service options, checkout options, ordering options, privacy information, product information, restocking fees, gift services, express checkout, etc.

"At this point, aggregating data became the core business. We have people doing that in an office in India; we also have consumer reviews. We combine ratings with performance. We were doing all this work to make RatingWonders a destination site, but then we realized that we didn't have the money required to get that kind of branding out there to generate the traffic. So we shifted the business model.

"We changed the model to be a content service provider to portals, merchants, and shopping bots. We license our database to them. It took about a year and a half to aggregate the data. Every thirty days we review the ratings of every merchant. In the short span of two months' time we've got four clients signed up already.

"We have a completely internationalized database. We will have 80 percent of merchants in the other five countries we're going into rated by third quarter 2000, and the entire system is completely WAP compatible."

CUSTOMER LOYALTY: THE DIFFERENCE BETWEEN SUCCESSFUL AND UNSUCCESSFUL SITES

Rarely in e-commerce is technology a strategic advantage per se. Aside from the site working, and the site being reasonably fast—two factors that, when they're not working as intended, shoppers regularly identify as turn-offs to shopping and buying—no survey has ever shown that buyers return to a site because of the *technology*. They might return to a site because of features offered by the technology, such as a shopping wizard, great search tools, ease of checkout, or any of the other site features I recommend you implement earlier in this book, but they don't care how or where these services are running.

BizRate has research from the first quarter of 2000 showing once again that the most often listed influential factor in deciding to buy (by buyers immediately after the sale) is a good product search tool (40 percent) followed by expedited checkout (34 percent). Do customers care whether the services that make your site a pleasure to shop at and a breeze to purchase from run on your own servers or on an ASP's servers? No.

What's the number-one factor listed by customers for returning to a site? Customer service. Customer service is only loosely related to technology at all. Services like real-time chat and click-to-voice make customer service more immediate, but it's still the job of the merchant to keep the customer service representatives assisting customers with a good attitude and a willingness to help. These elements can be communicated very well with real people in adequate supply answering e-mail queries the same day. As of the middle of 2000, some of the sites with the best customer service and customer loyalty records hadn't implemented anything other than e-mail and an 800 number to handle customer service. Winning customer service is a strong indication that the merchant understands what customers want, and customers know and appreciate that.

The Ins and Outs of Outsourcing

Once you've made the rational decision not to do all your development in house, the real work begins. You still need to do a needs assessment to determine what the criteria for selecting a vendor or ASP will be. The process of selecting a vendor is fairly standard, but the rest of this chapter discusses some techniques that are unique to selecting technology solutions for the Web that might help you avoid picking a lemon.

BE BUSINESS DRIVEN, NOT TECHNOLOGY DRIVEN

Something about the Internet has turned businesses upside down. I talk with other technology folks like myself, and we lament the fact that companies—usually the company my colleague is working for—aren't focusing enough on the business that they're supposed to be in. They're too caught up in the hype of whatever the new technology or promotion is that promises to fix all ills, whether it be language-filtering e-mail systems that send automatic replies based on the questions asked by the customers, incentive programs that are supposed to bring in loyal customers, or sweepstakes that are going to grow the customer base. When I talk to exec-utive-level and marketing people at the same companies, they go on and on about the technology, and are not adequately critical of the business cases behind the technologies. Why is this?

My theory is that technology people love technology, but they also understand it well enough to know that technology alone is not a business or a business plan. Ultimately, technology should be like the roof of the building: if it's doing its job, no one thinks twice about it. In my opinion, technology people are less inclined to be snowed by the technology. There's no mystery, so we question the business case behind decisions in a way that businesspeople often do not. Businesspeople, particularly marketing peo-ple, aren't skeptical enough of what the technology can do *for the business*. Sure, the technology might be able to deliver 1 million e-mail messages to women in your database reminding them to shop for Father's Day, but what will happen then? Do you have any evidence that the ads you're send-ing are going to get a response from people? Do you have any empirical data about the clickthrough rate for this campaign or the clickthrough or conversion rate for this type and length of e-mail? Or for the clickthrough rate or conversion rate for this particular audience? The success of this campaign doesn't rely on the e-mail software—carrier pigeons might deliver the message more effectively—it relies on the way the business side of the business does its job.

I've sat in on countless "dog-and-pony" shows with dot-com clients at which the business and marketing people were nodding along with the presentation. The technology people, on the other hand, were more likely to ask, simply, "how's it done?" and then move onto the business justifica-tion for making the decision to implement this technology.

I'm not suggesting that technology people are smarter than people from the business side of the company, just that they're less likely to be taken in by the allure of the technology. Businesspeople need to know that the technology is the method, not the goal. The business decisions and business case justification should drive the decision to ally with one provider of software or solutions over another. Even in the Web economy, business cases must be made for all technology decisions. The law of gravity applies to dot-coms just as it does in the offline world.

INCLUDE ARCHITECTS IN ALL MEETINGS

Decisions about creating new partnerships are often made by business development people. Even when the decisions involve technologies, technologists are often left out of the discussions at the "whether" point and only included at the "how do we do this" point. Frankly, that's too late. You might be expecting a certain amount of negative feedback from most technical people when an out-of-house solution is being considered, and you might want to avoid that type of confrontation until the deal is done. However, you really can't afford to forgo the experience of your senior technical folks—and that's not just your CIO or CTO who may not understand the architecture of your systems. System architects are perfectly situated to participate in negotiations with vendors and ASPs and should always be included at dog-and-pony shows with vendors. They can help you determine the limitations and capabilities of the technical service for which the company is negotiating and modifications your systems need to implement to integrate with that solution.

Most people who have spent many years of their lives in front of computers have a different set of social skills—they're more direct—than marketing folks and others who make a living with words and ideas. You can therefore usually rely on technical people to tell it like it is and to ask tough questions of vendors while it's still early enough in the process to use the answers as part of the decision-making process.

IT'S ALL ABOUT PARTNERSHIPS

The Web is built on partnerships. When you sign up to receive services from an ASP or vendor, because your own functionality relies so heavily on its success, you're essentially going into business with the company. I often chuckle when I go to a smaller site and see that it lists Oracle or Microsoft as one of its "partners," because I know that means that it's simply buying software from them. It's no joke, however, when you sign on with a customer service center to provide customer service to your site or a wireless aggregator to deliver your products to wireless shoppers. You really are partnering with them, which means you're relying on them, and if they fail, you're sunk.

I realize that my recommendations may seem paradoxical. On the one hand, I'm recommending that businesses hire others to provide these services so they're not as vested in them and in the technologies that facilitate them. On the other hand, I'm recommending that businesses see their easily dissolved relationships as partnerships. In a way, the situation with Web partnerships is like a wealthy individual courting for marriage: Assume it's going to last forever, but get the prenuptial agreement, just in case.

GET REFERENCES

Partnerships assume you can trust the other party in the agreement. The only way you can get to that point with your business is for you to conduct extensive reference checks before you sign up with any vendor. This should go without saying, but I've seen too many clients make snap decisions based on vendor presentations—assuming that the world couldn't wait for reference checks. Although this isn't always a recipe for disaster, it certainly can be. There are a lot more people promising solutions than delivering. Until recently, the standards for performance have been relatively low, because the number of players in each field has been small. Now that each niche of technology services has multiple players, the bar has been raised and competition has forced providers to deliver more than promises. Use reference checks to make sure you end up with the best solution in the field.

Also, don't hesitate to post (or have a consultant post) to e-commerce and more specific newsgroups and mailing lists asking for both positive and negative experiences with any or with specific vendors. If there are train wrecks in a vendor's recent past, you need to know about them.

In Celebration of ASPs

My bias for ASPs goes way back to 1997, before there was an acronym in place to describe Web sites that provided a service that was strictly Web based and didn't require any special software or configuration on the part of the user other than a Web browser. In fact, in 1997, ASP meant something entirely different: Active Server Pages, a programming language developed by Microsoft that permitted a Web page to talk to a database.

Back in 1997 I created a service that permitted a site owner to add a sign-in page to his site then send mail to anyone who signed in based on information the visitor provided. The information could be data, such as a zip code, or simply an expression of interest in specific topics. The interest areas were configurable by the administrator (my user). At the time mine was the only system of its kind. Today ListBot and others offer the same functionality. The system I built is almost identical to the one I recommend merchants use to find out from visitors what they're interested in hearing more about (see Chapter 6). When the user was ready to send mail to his list, he signed onto my server, indicated which targeted groups should receive the mail, composed the mail, and sent it.

The beauty of my system and other ASP solutions is that the site owner had only to add a button on his site to get his visitors to his sign-in page, which resided on my servers. Everything the visitors saw was configurable on my servers by the site owner. All the data about his visitors resided on my servers, to which he and only he had complete access, and to which he had a right when he terminated our relationship. For a nominal monthly fee, he added a valuable service to his own servers without any development cost, without any additional fees when I upgraded the software. Best of all, he could discontinue the service and switch over to another service with relatively little effort. He'd probably have to pay a couple hundred dollars as a set-up fee to get his data imported into the new service, but he had no investment in hardware, software, or training, so the cost of changing gears was relatively low. Had he invested in development costs, he'd have to rework his requirements and pay for developers to add the new features he wanted. Then he would have to endure the delay of testing and the inconvenience of implementation—or abandon his investment in his current tool and move his data over to a service that had all the features he wanted. Clients of my service automatically took advantage of upgrades because the software being upgraded was on my servers. The next time the site owner signed in, he'd simply see an enhanced features set. He was free to focus on running his own business.

ASPs provide all the functionality on their own servers, generally not requiring the user to install any software at all on either his client computer or on the servers. Sometimes, when the ASP is providing enhanced server functionality, such as real-time click-stream analysis for the user, the user will have to install small snippets of code on pages or APIs on the server. This code or these APIs send relevant data to the ASP in real time, allowing it to remain in sync with the server.

NO LONGER VOGUE WITH THE VENTURE CAPITALISTS (VCS)— SO WHAT?

The measure of an industry's success and utility is not whether venture capitalists (VCs) think it's the greatest thing since sliced bread. What VCs are looking for in an industry is not necessarily the same thing that merchants or other users of a service should be looking for. In the summer of 2000, I was told by a Web-savvy entrepreneur that VCs are no longer impressed by ASPs. They've moved onto other hot areas. He was clearly telling me this to impress me with the fact that he was no longer enamoured of the ASP model.

Rumors and reports about what VC firms are investing in today are among the visual clutter that can keep you from focusing on your businesses, like the signs and flags behind the backboard in the basketball game. Unless you're a VC yourself, you shouldn't be worried about what the next buzzword will be.

ASPs offer the best model for delivering technology-based services to Web businesses in a turnkey manner. The alternative to ASPs, once you've decided you're not going to develop in-house, is a software vendor. If you're in this for the glamour, you're not going to find the term *software vendor* on any list of VC-accepted buzzwords.

Feed THE Lions

FOR MANY merchants, this book will be a reality check. This book will make them realize that they've neither the stomach nor the budget to run with the big dogs in e-commerce and implement all of the technologies listed in this book. This doesn't mean that there's not a place for them in e-commerce. There is still a need for service providers to offer services to the companies that will be competing for e-commerce traffic and e-commerce dollars. There are tremendous opportunities for niche players to provide pieces of the infrastructure to the companies that ultimately decide to duke it out online.

THE EVOLUTION OF SHOPPING ONLINE

When the Web was in its infancy, merchants assumed that shopping online would be like shopping in a bricks-and-mortar store. Customers would rather make fewer trips to the store and would thus prefer to find a single store where they could get everything they needed from office products to baby care products to shoes. Value America opened its virtual doors in February of 1998 on that model. By the end of 1999, it had come to realize that selling Bonzai trees and jogging strollers probably wasn't part of what its core constituency of shoppers really wanted.

Near the end of 1999, all merchants began to realize that they'd need to offer free shipping to compete with the bricks-and-mortar merchants, because that was one of the factors that shoppers indicated led them to buy at that moment, rather than wait. A Forrester's report from December of 1999, "Free Delivery Is Here to Stay," helped make that fact clear. BizRate's data had been showing the same thing for several quarters, and results from the 1999 holiday shopping season confirmed it for individual merchants. The most successful promotion merchants could offer was free shipping.

With shipping being free, the incentive that previously existed for shoppers to load up their carts before leaving the store—to the extent that there was any—completely disappeared. Suddenly the cost to shoppers of purchasing a single printer cartridge, for example, went from around $24 plus shipping and handling of $6 to just the cost of the cartridge. Basket sizes fell as customers started to move toward purchasing individual items from individual merchants based on cost, available promotions (such as $5 off coupons), and their need for only that item at that moment. Unlike shopping in a physical store, the hassle associated with shopping on the Web is trivial—I don't have to pack my children up into the car, drive over to a store, keep them occupied while we shop, bribe them not to be too loud in the checkout line, get them back into their car seats, and return home just to purchase my print cartridge. Consequently, I don't feel a need to keep a list of what I need before I shop. When I need something, I sign on and purchase it.

All these factors conspired against merchants toward the beginning of 2000 to keep ever-larger inventories and move into ever-more product categories. Lean and mean became the name of the game. However, there were also factors working in the merchants' favor. Most notably, the holiday shopping season brought millions of new buyers to online stores. Surveys showed that the overall shopping satisfaction of these shoppers wasn't necessarily high. Slow Web sites greeted many of them, as did fulfillment problems with oversold merchants and difficulty reaching customer service to find out where, say, little Johnny's Pokemon toy was. But this foray into online shopping was sure to turn some until-now-only-lookers into buyers who would return again later.

Also working in the merchants' favor was an increased sense of security and confidence about how merchants were handling personal and financial data—or if not more confidence, at least less concern. The message seemed to be getting out to shoppers that if they purchased with their credit cards, even if the merchants' servers being hacked compromised customers' credit card information, those customers wouldn't be responsible for any false charges against their accounts. The widespread appearance of privacy policies and the increased appearance of privacy assurance seals such as those from TrustE and BBBOnline also added to consumers' confidence that their data wouldn't be widely distributed—whether this perception was accurate or not.

So, with more shoppers online, with greater confidence in the privacy and security of being online, with no disincentive to making small purchases, and with the necessity of offering free shipping to shoppers, merchants found themselves in 2000.

Guard Your Crack in the Sidewalk

The Web is no place to try to be all things to all people. Amazon continues to walk a very fine line with investors because it continues to dilute its name recognition for selling books—a niche it filled splendidly—by expanding into ever-more categories. At some point, expansion ceases to be a business decision and becomes an ego decision on the part of management.

A wise merchant will find the narrow niche he serves best and try to serve it as completely as possible. When he finds that the cost of acquiring new customers becomes prohibitive, he'll look for the best way to move inventory—presumably the source of his profitability—not for a way necessarily to acquire more customers. In many cases, moving inventory is best done by partnering with other companies that are already seeing the traffic, such as Amazon's zShops or AltaVista's Shopping portal.

There is, however, another way to go to where the traffic is, and that's to become an invisible provider of products or services to a merchant or a

portal that can't or (more likely) doesn't single-handedly want to solve all
the problems associated with being a merchant online. A generalist might
have been the thing to be for merchants in the 1980s, but moving into the
twenty-first century, the need for specialists has never been greater.

THE SERVICE ECONOMY

Not that long ago, when we thought of providing services to companies, we
thought of either off-the-shelf software or onsite consulting contracts.
Today the larger void is being filled by providing a department's worth of
services offsite. The first to fill this space were those companies that provided the most standard of business services—those that varied little from
business to business and had little to do with a company's core compe-
tency—such as hiring, personnel and benefits management, and payroll
services. Today, smart companies feel comfortable relying on partnerships
to provide everything from basic Web site hosting to fulfillment, returns
processing, customer service, and private-labeled customized services.

GETTING THE GIG

The best way to break into this industry is to fail at being a merchant and
find that your one area of excellence is a narrow niche of services that you
can provide to other merchants. Because everyone doesn't have the time,
money, or inclination to try to be an e-commerce merchant, then fail,
however, it's okay to begin with a plan to provide a narrow range of services to merchants.

DOMAIN EXPERTISE. There's no substitute for knowing what you're doing,
if you're going to solve a problem for a merchant or a lot of merchants.
The best way to know and to be able to prove it to the merchants you
approach with your solution is to have extensive previous experience in
that industry. This means that if you've got experience as a network
administrator, opening up a Web hosting service might make sense. If
you've got experience handling returns for a large catalog house, opening
up shop as a reverse-fulfillment service would be a good fit.

As a columnist for Internet.com and Office.com, I receive many
questions about e-commerce technology from readers. One day a post

came in from a man who wanted to open up a Web hosting service. He wanted to know how he should go about deciding whether to host on NT or Unix and how to know what equipment to budget for. He clearly had no experience administering a network, and he was planning to do things himself for a while. Even if I'd answered his questions (and there were many) in laborious detail, I couldn't have given him the expertise and experience he'd need to operate such a service effectively. And he certainly wouldn't be able to sway many sites to move their hosting to him unless he had the lowest prices and that factor was their only consideration. Of course, without any experience in maintaining servers, he'd be unlikely to succeed at keeping the servers running, and would probably lose even the price-only sites as a result of bad service. All in all, it was a losing proposition.

When I talk to venture capitalists, I hear the same thing. After a solid business idea, the first thing they look for is domain expertise. They want to see a track record in the industry in which the company seeks funding among senior management. Industry experience is valuable for many reasons. First, it's going to be easier to form partnerships with complementary companies if you've already got the names and numbers of their senior executives in your Rolodex and you're on a first-name basis. Second, you're unlikely to be taken by others who offer to partner with your company to provide a part of the services you need because you already know who's effective in that space. Finally, you've learned the ropes and made mistakes on someone else's dime. Experience is what you have when you've already made the mistakes.

PARTNERSHIPS. Once you have a winning management team with experience in the field, you need some good strategic partnerships to put your company on the radar and legitimize yourself. Because your management has contacts in the field, lining up partners shouldn't be that difficult. Your partners could be companies from which you acquire services or products and should definitely include at least one big-name company in your target market. Overlooking this crucial step can set your company back or put its growth on hold indefinitely.

The important thing to note is that these relationships really are partnerships. Merchants can't simply outsource these services, making selection of vendors or service providers strictly on the basis of price or proximity. Merchants have to believe that your service is an extension of their own business, and you have to offer adequate integration between your own systems and theirs to make it the case.

EVERYONE'S DOIN' IT

Enough with theory on providing services for merchants that are willing to spend the money to acquire customers, keep them satisfied, maintain their sites, and provide after-the-purchase service. This section profiles four companies that are filling a valuable niche. Some of them are quite young, less than a year old (one used to sell its software and now provides the service as an ASP), but all of them have major name clients and management with expertise in the field. Each one is meeting a need its merchant/clients would just as soon not have to meet on their own.

Some of these categories are huge and probably will eventually vertically differentiate into more than one field, with multiple service providers in each niche.

CASE STUDY: WebTrends Live/Click-Stream Analysis
Jeff Seacrist, Product Manager

"WebTrends has been around since 1995 providing products for Web masters: primarily log file analysis software. Our basic software addressed the technical needs of most sites for information, including page views, browsers being used by visitors, referring sites, and other information that helped Web masters manage Web servers.

"We realized there are more people within an organization who are interested in seeing information related to visitors and traffic, and that their requirements are becoming more and more detailed. They need to know in real time what kind of return they're seeing on their investments in technical infrastructure and in marketing campaigns. These people range from marketing directors to project managers to CEOs. They each have very specific needs for reporting, and the technology staffs are generally stretched too thinly to provide adequate reports for each of them.

"WebTrends Live (www.webtrendslive.com) is an ASP. There are several things that drove us to that. In most companies there's less IT time available to give more data to more and more people. WebTrends Live gives you fairly rich traffic analysis without a lot of involvement from IT staff. It relies on a pay-as-you-go model, so there's no up-front investment, which many sites want to avoid. Implementation is simple. On every page you add a JavaScript (usually into the template or include a file that runs on every page), that talks to our server. The visitors' browsers talk directly to our server, so we don't communicate with the Web servers at all.

"We opened our doors in March of 2000. We immediately had thousands of sites lined up. We were the first that could analyze e-commerce transactions. We can tell you a marketing campaign's success rate in real time. With the JavaScript, you're sending us your transaction data in real time so we can report to you real time. We're convinced this is just what e-commerce sites want, and what the future of software is."

CASE STUDY: E-Commerce Support Centers/ Customer Service

ECom presents companies with a plug-in, online support option. Customers get best-of-breed technologies, highly trained and skilled people, effective quality assurance processes, redundant systems, all in a 24 x 7 x 365 operation with flexible pricing. They support B2B and B2C (business-to-business and business-to-consumer) sites for clients ranging from Fortune 1000 companies to Internet startups.

Web site visitors who want phone support prefer the dial-around option (a support representative calls them), which avoids the queues and multiple select picks one deals with when dialing an 800 number. More and more Web users prefer not to use a phone at all, opting for live chat support which lets them avoid cradling a phone while following verbal instructions. ECom's online support allows an e-commerce support representative to take over the customer's browser and assist the customer with "follow-me browsing," assisted forms completion...even to working with the customer's desktop applications. Other aspects of its collaborative support enable it to converge traditional phone with online communications so one agent can assist a customer online or by phone (in many support center operations, phone and online customers need to be handled by separate agent groups).

Its IT staff and Web designers work with a client's IT department to add the help "button" to the site and to design the chat dialogue box so that it's consistent with the graphics of the site. The support function is completely transparent to the site visitor. The site visitor gets the help he needs via the communication he selects and never knows that someone in another company has helped him. He only knows it's been a good experience and one that encourages him to revisit the site. Needless to say, if the help needed was central to a purchase, that help meant the difference between a sale and an abandoned purchase.

ECom is over a year old. It is spun out of Gibralter Publishing, an active business with a strong direct marketing history. Its roots in direct marketing provide some unique advantages to its clients. It is a strong advocate of data capture and data mining to maximize customer profitability. As such, it views each customer interaction as an opportunity to enrich its clients' customer database and enhance its eCRM program. It can also proactively engage customers to gain cross-sell or up-sell opportunities in appropriate situations. It has partnerships in place to take a client into the entire eCRM value chain from data warehousing through sales support.

CASE STUDY: Digital Impact/E-Mail

Digital Impact is a leading provider of Internet direct marketing solutions or e-marketing solutions. The company sends personalized e-mail campaigns for clients looking to communicate more effectively with their customers. Digital Impact sends e-mails only to customers who have specifically requested to receive e-mails from its clients, a practice known as "opt-in," or permission-based, marketing. By tailoring e-mail content and format based on each customer's preferences and profiles, Digital Impact generates measurable results for its clients: up to double-digit response rates and triple-digit return on its marketing investment. Digital Impact works with over 120 clients, including industry-leading Fortune 500 companies to online e-commerce retailers. Digital Impact is a member of the TRUSTe privacy program [www.truste.org] and works only with companies that are advocates of strict consumer privacy guidelines.

Digital Impact's e-marketing services currently include direct e-mail marketing, customer acquisition tools, customer data analysis, and strategic consulting services and client support services. The benefits of Digital Impact's solution include:

→ *Targeted, relevant content.* Through its proprietary technologies and processes, the company can dynamically assemble and deliver millions of personalized e-mails based on recipient profiles. Digital Impact continually updates each individual profile with response data that is typically captured in less than one second.

→ *Personalized e-mail formatting.* Digital Impact's e-mail sensor technology enables the company to ensure that each recipient receives an e-mail that fully utilizes the graphical capabilities of that recipient's e-mail software, enabling e-mail delivery in one of several formats, including basic text, AOL format, or HTML, depending on the recipient's e-mail capabilities.

→ *Real-time performance tracking and campaign analysis.* Using its campaign management tools, Digital Impact can track and analyze large volumes of customer response data in real time, enabling clients to quickly execute test campaigns, gain valuable market research data, and evaluate the effectiveness of alternative e-marketing strategies. Clients can then launch full-scale campaigns based on these test results, all within a short period of time.

→ *Domain expertise.* The company's experience gained from designing and managing thousands of e-mail campaigns has allowed it to develop an e-marketing process built on best practices. This institutionalized process provides the company with a methodology to reliably execute each phase of a campaign, from initial setup to results analysis, and allows it to consistently deliver valuable e-marketing services to its clients.

→ *Robust, scalable infrastructure.* Digital's ongoing investments in hardware and software enable it to reliably assemble and deliver large volumes of client e-mails on a timely basis.

→ *Significantly improved time to market.* By leveraging Digital Impact's investment in infrastructure and technology, combined with Digital Impact's institutionalized processes and experience, its clients are able to deploy their e-marketing campaigns rapidly and reliably. This approach allows its clients to remain focused on their core business competencies and enhance their competitive positions.

Digital Impact's Merchant Mail service is the company's primary suite of e-marketing services. Sold as a single service, Merchant Mail currently consists of the following components: e-mail campaign management, targeting and personalization, media optimization, tracking and reporting, and data hosting and management.

Digital Impact also provides the Email Exchange Network, a service that helps clients acquire new customers by sharing e-mail addresses, with the consumer providing explicit consent.

CASE STUDY: The Kringle Company/Private-Labeled Personalized Letters

The Kringle Company (www.KringleCompany.com) is a privately held corporation based in North Pole, Alaska, which was incorporated in 1999. I was approached by the president of the Kringle Company in early fall of 1999 about assisting him with moving his personalized "letters from Santa" business onto the Web. I was so intrigued by the potential of this business, that I ultimately told him I would preferred to work for equity rather than cash.

The Kringle Company provides Web merchants the opportunity to sell personalized letters from Santa from their Web sites during the Christmas shopping season. Once the customer has made the purchase and paid it, he links through the order-confirmation screen directly into the Kringle Company personalization site, which is private labeled to look exactly like the merchant's site. To the customer, it looks as if he's made the purchase, now he's personalizing the card. Just as when he purchases a suit in a department store and walks down a hallway from the fitting rooms to have the suit altered by the tailor—it's a seamless experience.

Kringle doesn't sell any letters from Santa itself. It doesn't want to be competing with merchants, but chances are, if you purchase a personalized letter from Santa for a child during Christmas, Kringle Company is handling the personalization and fulfillment. These letters are an interesting novelty item for shoppers because there are eight different styles from which to choose—ranging from "Not Quite Coal'"for the child who's been more naughty than nice to "Sugarplum Fairy" for the sweet little girl. There's even a letter for a spouse. In addition to different messages, there is also a choice of color graphics to be printed on the letters. All letters are postmarked in North Pole, Alaska. Finally, each style of letter has at least five places in the text where the purchaser can personalize it so that the recipient receives a letter that's so personal that only Santa could know all the details.

For the merchant, the product is even more interesting because the merchant can add this product to his inventory without having to worry about holding any inventory or investing in any setup costs. The merchant processes refunds directly into the Kringle Company's Merchant system on a "no questions asked" basis. All the merchant has to do is add code on the order-confirmation page to pass the customer seamlessly through to the Kringle Company's personalization site, configure the Kringle Company's site to match its own, and send a nightly extract file to Kringle Company with orders placed that day. The merchant doesn't even pay Kringle Company until its collected from the customer, so there's absolutely no risk to the merchant.

Kringle could have opened up for retail business on its own, but the cost of acquiring customers—especially during the very competitive Christmas shopping season—would have been prohibitive. By

taking advantage of traffic the merchants are seeing anyway, the company is able to sell a lot of cards without a lot of overhead.

As you can see from the variety and range of companies profiled above, no niche is too narrow for a company with a useful service to offer to succeed.

And Finally . . .

Online shoppers are savvier today than ever. They know more and expect more. They are less impressed by fancy graphics and more interested in fast-to-load pages. They are less likely to click on banner ads and more likely to use a search engine. They're less likely to return to a site because of low prices and more likely to remember the experience they had with customer service.

They know what they want and they're willing to abandon a site that doesn't offer it, even if they're most of the way through the checkout process. It turns out that the Web is less about reinventing shopping than about doing away with the aspects of shopping that everyone hates—driving to the store, parking, waiting in line, bad service, unknowledgeable salespeople, inadequate selection. It's also about focusing on the features of shopping that people do like, such as being recognized, receiving good service, finding what you want at a good price, and knowledgeable salespeople.

Price is only a small component of the optimized shopping experience. In the early days of e-commerce, it was the component that too many sites focused on, too many sites that are no longer in business. Merchants who have survived through the early shakeout can use the technologies that I describe in Part II—search engines, affiliate programs, listfeeds, targeted EDM, and WAP—to attract and retain customers at the lowest possible cost. The technologies explained in Part III—personalization, shopping wizards, globalization, real-time access to inventory and order status, and a robust CMS—can help you anticipate your customers' needs and satisfy them. Finally, the technologies in Part IV—real-time chat and multichannel customer service—will make your one-time customers loyal customers.

Whether you decide to invest in the twelve technologies explained in this book or to direct your energy into providing services for merchants who do, I hope that the resources in this book help you capitalize on the innumerable opportunities to be a dot-com success story.

A Baker's Dozen

Alternative Payment Systems

MOST ONLINE merchants will not survive as such if the only payment systems they accept are traditional credit cards like Visa and MasterCard. Online fraud—or rather attempted online fraud—is a huge and largely undiscussed problem for the vast majority of online retailers. An entire industry has surfaced to meet the needs of online consumers for safety and privacy, and to meet the needs of merchants for assurances that the orders they accept and the products they ship won't later turn out to have been paid for with stolen credit card numbers.

When I drafted the outline for this book in January 2000, I did not anticipate the degree to which merchants' needs for payment alternatives would be met by alternative payment systems providers. Now, weekly, I receive press releases from new entrants into this space. As this book was going to press, long after all the other chapters were completed, I convinced the editor to let me add this thirteenth technology. This chapter discusses the problem that merchants (not consumers) have with the existing credit card payment system, and the vendors who are ready to provide safe, secure payment alternatives.

CONSUMERS ARE RARELY THE VICTIMS OF FRAUD

Visa, MasterCard, and the other credit card companies do an excellent job of protecting consumers from liability as a result of unauthorized use of their cards. They also permit consumers to contest charges when the goods ordered aren't delivered as promised. However, all these consumer-friendly policies come at the merchant's expense.

I couldn't find any published estimates of the amount of attempted or successful fraud committed against merchants. It would be a difficult number to determine because merchants are understandably reluctant to release any data that shows how easy they are to defraud. However, my own interviews with payment systems companies, merchants, and fraud-detection service companies indicate that between 10 and 55 percent of attempted transactions are fraudulent, with an average of around 35 percent. Few companies will talk about what percentage of their actual transactions turn out to be fraudulent.

The credit card companies, in an attempt to allay the concerns of consumers, have published statistics showing that online fraud is no higher than offline fraud. While this is probably true for credit card companies, as far as the risk that they bear, for merchants the risk associated with the *card-not-present* environment of the Web is bordering on untenable. Actions taken by the credit card companies to tighten the rules for companies that do business online reinforce the perception that there is a huge problem of fraud online. The credit card associations hear from their issuing banks, which hear from their customers who hold the cards. The card companies have also increased the fines that they assess merchants for chargebacks. *Chargeback* is the term for when a customer denies (or repudiates) having authorized a purchase. If the merchant can't prove the customer made the purchase (by having a signed receipt or an accurate PIN), then the merchant bank (a bank that authorizes merchants to accept credit cards and processes their charge requests) reverses the charge and it comes out of the merchant's pocket, along with additional chargeback fees.

Protecting the Merchant

Traditional credit card networks don't do a very good job of protecting the merchant. The authorization that you receive when you transmit a credit card number along with the amount of the purchase "for approval" to the payment processing network simply means that the card hasn't been reported as stolen, the number is valid, and the cardholder isn't over his credit limit (or the balance in the account will cover the purchase for the case of debit cards). You aren't protected by the credit card company against fraud.

There are steps you can and should take to determine what the probability of fraud is for an attempted purchase, but when it's risk that's being assessed, some apparently safe purchases will turn out to be fraudulent and some orders that are rejected will turn out to be coming from legitimate cardholders. Services like eFalcon and Retail Decisions can help you score the risk in real time of all orders placed online so that you can decide what risk threshold you're willing to accept and at what point you will reject the order. Even address verification service (AVS) doesn't guarantee that the transaction won't turn out to be fraudulent, since gifts are frequently shipped to addresses other than the bill-to address, and a criminal may well have the correct billing information for the credit card.

NONREPUDIATION

When a customer pays with a card number, but doesn't provide any physical proof that he owns the card, such as when a customer orders a product over the phone or on the Web, there's always a risk to you that he isn't who he says. The legitimacy of that payment hinges on the customer's identity. If you scan the card, then obtain a signature or a PIN from the customer, then you have nonrepudiable proof of the customer's identity. The customer can't deny that he made the purchase and have the charge reversed.

In order for you to be protected against orders placed with fraudulently obtained payment information, the payment system must support nonrepudiation. There are three kinds of nonrepudiation.

HARDWARE-BASED NONREPUDIATION. Hardware-based nonrepudiation relies on either a chip residing in the computer uniquely identifying the owner of the computer or a card or keychain containing a chip. In the case of the chip in the card or keychain, which is referred to as *smart-card technology*, the computer must have a scanner to read and act on the chip. Frequently, these chips actually hold not just the payment card information but the actual value in the account on them, so the scanner must both read and update the chip.

ENCRYPTED COOKIE-BASED NONREPUDIATION. Nonrepudiation can be established by a trusted third party (TTP), such as a payment system vendor, by having the TTP collect the identity and payment information and store it on the computer of the shopper in an encrypted cookie. Only a merchant in the network of that payment system vendor would have access to the key to decrypt the cookie to obtain payment when so authorized by the shopper. In some payment systems, the payment information is obtained by the merchant, but remains encrypted and is passed from the merchant to the payment system vendor. This system not only establishes nonrepudiation—the merchant could never get the cookie unless the customer visited its site and went through the checkout process—it also protects the payment information from the merchant, with the payment system vendor being the only party with access to it. The payment system vendor would then pay the merchant without the merchant ever needing to know the identity of the shopper, unless hard goods needed to be delivered.

SECURE CERTIFICATE NONREPUDIATION. Just like merchant Web sites, where consumers expect to see a locked lock in their browsers, proving to them that the merchant is using secure-sockets layer (SSL) for transmitting data encrypted and has a valid certificate from a TPP, such as Verisign, consumers can have secure certificates on their computers. When the merchant accesses the secure certificate, the TPP verifies the customer's identity. Secure certificates may be the ideal form of nonrepudiation for merchants, but because customers must install them and maintain them, keeping a copy on a floppy in case the operating system needs to be reinstalled or their computers need to be replaced, the success of client-side secure certificates has been limited.

A DISPUTE RESOLUTION SYSTEM THAT PROTECTS MERCHANTS

Customers should have a way to contest the charges made for purchases that aren't delivered, but they should be forced to take their issues to the merchants first. The merchants should have the opportunity to contest request for chargebacks by showing proof that the correct product was delivered. Payment systems without any consumer protection against fraud will never gain widespread acceptance in the United States, where customers are used to the consumer protection provided by the major credit cards.

NO RELIANCE ON TRADITIONAL CREDIT CARD NETWORKS

The alternative payment system must operate outside the traditional credit card networks or it will be subject to the same "no questions asked" chargeback policies for card-not-present transactions. Also, any system built on top of the traditional credit card networks will cost the merchant more because it will have to pay its merchant bank, then have to pay the alternative payment system as well.

NO REQUIREMENT FOR MERCHANTS TO HAVE A MERCHANT ACCOUNT

A merchant account is the account a merchant has with the merchant bank that allows the merchant to accept major credit cards. Merchant accounts, in addition to having a discount rate that's applied to every purchase, can also have an application fee, a monthly minimum service charge, a statement fee, and a per-transaction fee. On top of all those fees, chargebacks can result in additional fees being levied. The result for merchants who only transact a small amount of business by credit card is that the merchant account hardly pays for itself. Credit card issuer banks charge a discount rate to the merchant because they credit the merchant's account for the purchase before they've collected from the customer. Most alternative payment systems collect the money from the customer in advance of paying the merchant, so the payment to the merchant costs the payment system vendor the same amount whether the purchase is for $10 or $1000. In most cases, a flat per-transaction fee makes the most sense to the merchant with high-dollar orders, and a discount rate makes the most sense to the merchant with low-dollar orders. Some micropayments systems (payments of less than $5 or so; typically associated with digital goods like newpaper articles) do pay the merchant before they collect from the customer. In the case of micropayments, the merchant will prefer a discount rate to a per-transaction fee, since the per-transaction fee may equal or exceed the cost of the item.

COMPETITIVE PRICING

The amount that a merchant will pay to participate with an alternative payment system varies widely by vendor. Some charge setup fees, some charge strategic consulting fees, some charge by the transaction, some charge a discount rate, some charge an affiliate fee in lieu of or in addition to some of the above charges. With so many entrants in this area, merchants are able to negotiate. Only a few solutions will achieve critical mass—PayPal and QPass are probably the best-known alternative payment systems right now, each catering to entirely different audiences—and most of the solutions are competing for merchants. Take advantage of this fact and negotiate for a favorable rate structure.

EASY INSTALLATION

Merchants will have to make some changes to their checkout processes in order to participate in an alternative payment system. If you use third-party storefront software, check with the vendors or ASPs to see whether they have or are planning to implement an alternative payment system, because the payment system vendors that get integrated into the most popular storefront software will be more likely to succeed. Look for easy-to-integrate systems, but realize that the easiest to integrate are often the shopping-portal style vendors, which require shoppers to come through them. While integration may be fast with these systems, a merchant will likely pay an affiliate commission on every sale, which means that the merchant pays the acquisition cost every time. If the implementation is complex, negotiate to have the vendor come on site and do the implementation. It's a buyer's market for alternative payment system.

NO MONTHLY MINIMUM FEES OR APPLICATION FEES

Alternative payment systems should earn their keep by processing a lot of transactions as a result of having many merchants accepting their payment system and many customers using it. Alternative payment vendors should be advertising heavily to consumers. Monthly minimums levied on merchants or application fees make it neccessary for a certain volume of transactions to be conducted through the alternative payment system if it is to be cost-effective for the merchant. Payment systems with application fees are less likely to achieve critical mass unless they solve a very specific problem.

NO AFFILIATE FEES FOR RETURNING CUSTOMERS

Once the merchant acquires the customer, it should own access to the customer, rather than having to pay the acquisition fee (affiliate fee) to the payment network every time. If the payment system vendor requires that shoppers come through a shopping portal to use its payment system, the merchant will almost certainly pay an affiliate fee for every customer every time.

The other problem with payment systems that are only accessible through the payment portal is that other customers to that merchant never know that the merchant accepts other payment systems. Visa, MasterCard, American Express, and Discover get top billing on the checkout page and the alternative payment system remains a well-kept secret. Then shoppers, analysts, investors, and journalists believe that alternative payment systems aren't accepted by their favorite merchants and that the major credit cards are the only game in town. InternetCash, for example, is accepted by Overstock.com, a site I frequent. I first became familiar with InternetCash while checking out at Overstock.com. InternetCash has at least one competitor, CyberMoola. Because customers can only pay with CyberMoola by going through its shopping portal, I had to read about CyberMoola in a press release.

QUICK ACCESS TO FUNDS FOR MERCHANTS

Before you sign up with an alternative payment system vendor, make sure you know how long it holds your funds. It's certainly reasonable for the vendor not to pay you until the goods have been shipped, and to charge a higher discount rate if it is paying you in advance of receiving the funds from the shopper, but some vendors report payment to you (usually via online reports) long before you can get your hands on the money. Especially for prepaid payment systems, the money should be made available to you almost instantly after the sale is made.

LARGE NETWORK OF MERCHANTS ACCEPTING THIS PAYMENT SYSTEM

If few merchants accept the system, then few consumers will bother to participate. If few consumers use the system, then few merchants will bother to participate. It's a chicken-and-egg problem for the alternative payment systems. At this point, it's too early to tell which systems will become the dominant payment systems for people who don't want to pay with credit cards. However, you don't want to be the first merchant to accept a given payment system, no matter how attractive the terms are.

Regarding prepaid cards that are purchased at bricks-and-mortar retailers, which are usually aimed at shoppers who prefer to pay in cash, the number of retail outlets where the cards can be purchased is as important a factor as the number of merchants accepting a payment system. Prepaid online cash cards should be available at supermarkets and convenience stores, just as prepaid phone cards are.

NO HARDWARE OR SOFTWARE REQUIRED TO BE INSTALLED BY THE SHOPPER

Probably the very best system in terms of nonrepudiation is the secure electronic transactions (SET) protocol for online shopping. The reason it's so good is that it relies on secure certificates on the shoppers' computers or on smart cards. That's also the reason it hasn't caught on. Any technology that isn't delivered via the browser will be hard to sell. If a certificate or cookie must be maintained, it has to be transparent to the customer. Except for hardware-based payment systems, which haven't caught on to any significant degree outside of France, merchants should shy away from solutions that require the customer to download or install any additional software.

SHORT APPLICATION FOR CUSTOMERS TO OPEN ACCOUNTS

If customers come to your site with accounts already in place with the payment system vendor (as credit card customers do), then the length, complexity, or intrusiveness of the application doesn't matter to you. If, however, you expect to route people who are already in your checkout process to the payment system vendor to open accounts, and then return to your site to pay with that account, you better be sure the application process is not going to cause them to click away from the application and from their full carts. One of the payment systems mentioned later in this chapter, eCharge Net, is a line of credit to the customer, which means that it requires extensive personal financial information, including employment information.

EASY FOR CONSUMERS TO ADD ADDITIONAL FUNDS

While it seems attractive to the paranoid consumer not to provide any credit card or personal financial information to the payment system and still be able to shop online, in reality, many Web purchases aren't planned far enough in advance for consumers to want to send checks or money orders to the payment system to *recharge* (add additional funds to) their accounts. There are three ways to get money into a payment system account: credit card, direct withdrawal from checking or savings, and check or money order. The third option is the most private, but it is also the most cumbersome and the slowest for the consumer. If the only way to recharge an account is by postal mail and the shopper's account with a payment system is, say, $3 under what's needed to complete the purchase, chances are the cart will be abandoned forever. Since most online merchants also accept checks, wouldn't it make more sense for the customer simply to send a check directly to the merchant to complete the purchase than to send the check to the payment system to have the money sent to the merchant? Without an easy and immediate way for consumers to add funds to their accounts, impulse purchases—and the convenience of shopping online—are pretty much ruled out.

FRAUD PROTECTION FOR CONSUMERS

In the United States, consumers are spoiled by the fraud protection that comes with having a credit card. In other countries, there can be little or no protection with credit cards, which explains their lower penetration rate. Consumer protection laws in the United States protect cardholders from fraud after the first $50. Most issuing banks waive the $50, protecting consumers from all fraud. That's the level of fraud protection that consumers will expect. Any system that offers less is not likely to catch on in the United States.

IDENTITY PRIVACY FOR DIGITAL GOODS

There's no reason why someone purchasing a newspaper article, a song, or a screen saver should have to tell the merchant everything about himself, including his name and address. The ideal solution for purchasing soft goods, which often involve micropayments (the digital equivalent of loose change) is for the customer to be able to remain anonymous, providing only billing information. The most hassle-free system I've seen for purchasing soft goods, without being required to provide any personal information to the merchant, is QPass.

ALTERNATIVE PAYMENT SYSTEMS

Which alternative payment system a merchant should implement depends on factors other than the features described above, including:

→ *Type of goods being sold.* Digital goods versus hard goods.

→ *Types of customers.* Are the customers likely to own credit cards? Checking accounts? Do they prefer to shop with cash? Will they need to establish a line of credit before they can make a purchase? Are they most likely sophisticated Web users who would be comfortable downloading and installing software?

→ *Country of origin of customers.* Many alternative payment systems don't work outside the United States. Consumers in some countries rely heavily on bank drafts for purchases.

→ *Ease of cancellation of order.* Some alternative payment systems for digital goods permit the customer to cancel the purchase within 24 hours without any chance for the merchant to contest it. This sounds bad, but it can be very good if the cost of handling a complaint for a merchant is higher than the cost of the merchandise order being canceled. Payment systems that offer this feature typically let the merchant configure the parameters so that he can dictate the number of times a customer can cancel a purchase, the total amount a customer can cancel, and the window during which the customer can cancel a purchase.

→ *Expected purchasing frequency.* If the merchant sells goods that the customer will want to purchase over and over, such as CDs or books, then he won't want to pay an affiliate fee to the payment system every time the customer wants to shop from him.

However, if the merchant expects to see a customer only once a year, or even less frequently, such as when filling a prescription for eyeglasses, then he might not mind paying the affiliate fee, since the customer is likely to have forgotten about the merchant since the last purchase.

MAJOR PAYMENT SYSTEM VENDORS

I review alternative payment systems for Internet.com's ECommerce Guide (ecommerce.internet.com). The following list represents many of the major vendors in this field, but to see an up-to-date list, please visit the Payment Systems page at the ECommerce Guide. I have not reviewed every payment solution covered here, but I'm including some products I have not yet reviewed so that you can get a fuller picture of the vendors in each of the areas. You should make a point of talking to all the vendors in the category that is most appropriate for you. For solutions in this section, if the product name and the company name differ, the company name will be in parentheses next to the product name.

SAME-AS-CASH

These payment systems appeal to customers who can't get credit cards, don't want credit cards, or don't feel comfortable using credit cards online. In general, same-as-cash payment systems require the purchaser to go to a bricks-and-mortar retailer, like a grocer or a convenience store, and purchase a card. Same-as-cash payment is ideal for teenagers, for example. The potential fraud for consumers is limited to the face value on the card. Typically, the card must be activated at the vendor's Web site, where the customer supplies a password; then the money can be spent at any merchant in the network. When the card is activated, the vendor places an encrypted cookie on the customer's computer. This cookie provides non-repudiation to the merchant during a purchase. There is usually a way for customers to shop from other computers (without the cookie), but they must answer a series of questions to prove their identity to the vendor. Usually, the amount of money on the card, which is now associated with an account, can be augmented by credit card from the vendor's Web site.

INTERNETCASH. Cards are purchased at convenience stores and can be augmented online. Merchants install software on their own servers to communicate with the vendor's servers. The merchant's money is available quickly, and because of the nonrepudiation provided by the combination cookie and password, chargebacks are not an issue. Merchants pay a discount rate competitive with credit cards.

CYBERMOOLA. Cards are purchased at mall stores or online at the vendor's Web site and can be augmented online. Parents can limit the merchants in the network from which their minor children can shop. The merchant's money is available quickly, and nonrepudiation based on the encrypted cookie makes chargebacks a moot point. Merchant implementation is easy, but customers must come through the vendor's portal, and merchants must pay an affiliate fee to the vendor for every purchase. Merchants are paid by the vendor through traditional credit card networks, so merchants must still have a merchant account and pay the credit card discount rate on all purchases.

CHARGIT PREPAY (GLOBAL INTERNET BILLING). Not reviewed; solution introduced in Q4 2000.

PRAXELL. Not reviewed; solution introduced in Q4 2000.

POCKETPASS. Not reviewed; solution introduced in Q4 2000.

CUBECARD. Not reviewed; solution introduced in Q4 2000.

STORED-VALUE ACCOUNTS ONLINE

With a stored-value account, the customer goes to the vendor's site and creates an account, funding it with a credit card number, checking or savings account information, or a check or money order mailed to the vendor. In any case, the risk to the customer is limited to the amount in the account. The vendor then usually creates an encrypted cookie on the customer's computer that establishes the customer's identity and account information. The customer also has a password. When the amount in the account is spent, the customer must authorize transfer of additional money to fund the account from a credit card or checking or savings account, or must send another check or money order to recharge the account.

EZCMONEY (EZCARD INC.). The account is opened with a minimal amount of information. The account is funded by check or money order and recharged in the same way.

SELF-RECHARGING ACCOUNTS

Customers can create accounts that fund initially with a credit card or ACH transfer from checking or savings, but when they've spent the amount with which they initially funded the account, the payment system automatically recharges the account from the credit cards. The degree of automation of recharging and the involvement of the customer in the process vary among the solutions. Customers can then spend the money with any merchant in the network. Merchants install software on their servers and make minor modifications to their checkout processes to accept payments.

PAYPAL (X.COM). In addition to being used to purchase from merchants, PayPal is also a leading facilitator of consumer-to-consumer (C2C) money transfers, such as at auctions. X.com has over 4 million account holders.

iPIN. This solution is particularly popular in France, where purchasing via bank transfer is more common. It allows bank transfers from checking or savings from participating banks. Customers must enroll with their banks, so penetration is limited.

CHECKSPACE. This is targeted at the small business consumer. Not reviewed; solution introduced in Q4 2000.

QCHEX. Not reviewed; solution introduced in Q4 2000.

HARDWARE-BASED STORED-VALUE ACCOUNTS

Hardware-based solutions are very attractive in theory, but in practice they won't work until major hardware manufacturers agree to implement the technologies on consumer-grade equipment. Hardware-based payment systems also have the disadvantage of working only from computers on which the chip or card reader is installed. Accounts may be funded in the usual ways, then the merchant literally deducts the money from a prepaid account, with nonrepudiation provided by the hardware.

WAVE SYSTEMS. Stored value chip resides on customer's computer.

VISA SMART CARDS. Stored value cards.

MONDEX (MASTERCARD) Stored value cards require a card reader on the customer's computer.

PAYING VIA THE PHONE BILL

In countries where credit card penetration is low and among shoppers without credit cards, paying via the phone bill can be an attractive alternative to credit cards. In order to pay and have the charges billed to the consumer's phone bill, the shopper must access the merchant's site with a dial-up connection. Students in Ethernet-enabled dorm rooms, business shoppers, and consumers in broadband-enabled homes would not be able to use this mechanism to pay by phone. The way this system works is that when the consumer wants to pay during the checkout process, he clicks on a button to indicate that he wants to have his phone account billed. The vendor then initiates a software download that triggers his modem to disconnect from the ISP and connect to a 900 number. The phone call itself actually creates the entry on the phone bill. The software then disconnects from the 900 number and reconnects to the ISP, taking the consumer to the order confirmation page for the merchant.

ECHARGE PHONE. Permits online purchases to be billed to a customer's phone bill in the United States and a handful of other countries. The amount of purchase must be preprogrammed by eCharge, so it's not terribly flexible.

CHARGIT DIAL (GLOBAL INTERNET BILLING). Permits online purchases to be billed to customer's phone bill in any country.

MICROPAYMENTS

With micropayments systems, you might not need to store any payment information from your customers. Depending on which solution you choose, you may simply store a token returned from the payment processor, which confirms that payment was received. Alternatively, you can give the payment processor access to your servers, and they can both accept payment, and direct your customers to the digital content without your involvement.

Ultimately, you will need reports back from them showing what was sold. Ease of cancellation of an order is important so that your own customer service staff doesn't get bogged down resolving issues for $2.50 purchases of digital content that customers claim they couldn't access.

QPASS. This provides micropayments for *The New York Times* and *The Wall Street Jounal* online editions. A large strategic consulting agreement fee is part of the setup process.

MILLICENT. Not reviewed.

RESOURCES

The best source of up-to-date reviews of payment systems can be found at the ECommerce Guide (ecommerce.internet.com), where Mark Merkow— author of *The Complete Guide to Internet Security,* among other books, articles, and courses—and I review payment solutions. He also discusses trends in payment system technology in his EC Outlook column, which runs semimonthly. Mark's knowledge of smart-card technology and the industry is unparalleled.

Payment system vendors include:

InternetCash (www.internetcash.com)

CyberMoola (www.cybermoola.com)

QPass (www.qpass.com)

Millicent (www.millicent.com)

eCharge (www.echarge.com). Offers both phone billing and a line of credit.

Global Internet Billing (www.globalinternetbilling.com). Offers both phone billing and prepaid cards.

Praxell (www.praxell.com)

Pocketpass (www.pocketpass.com)

CubeCard (www.cubecard.com)

Qchex.com (www.qchex.com)

EZCard Inc. (www.ezcardinc.com)

PayPal (www.paypal.com)

CheckSpace (www.checkspace.com)

iPin (www.ipin.com)

Wave Systems (www.wavesystems.com)

Visa (www.visa.com)

Mondex (www.mondex.com)

Qpass (www.qpass.com)

Millicent (www.millicent.com)

Research firm for alternative payments:

Altamont Partners (www.altamontpartners.com)

NOTES

CHAPTER 1

1. Chris Nerney, "E-Tailers May Be Bottoming Out," *Internet Stock Report,* www.internetstockreport.com, March 9, 2000.

2. *Run-of-site ads* appear with equal probability on all pages of a site to all visitors. The alternative is *targeted ads,* which only appear two times. They appear when the visitor has indicated a specific interest, such as on a search engine. For example, if you type "home loans," the banner ads that appear on the results pages will likely relate to financing and purchasing a home. They also appear based on the profile of previous clicking behavior associated with the "cookies" on your computer.

3. Mary Modahl, *Now or Never: How Companies Must Change to Win the Battle for Internet Consumers,* Harper Business, 2000.

4. "75 Percent of Shoppers Abandon Carts," *Cyberatlas,* cyberatlas.internet.com, November 1, 1999.

5. "Why Online Merchants Need Effective Customer Support," BizRate.com, December 1999.

6. Forrester Research, "Free Delivery Is Here to Stay," December 29, 1999.

7. Modahl, p. 84

8. BizRate.com, *Consumer Online Report,* Fourth Quarter 1999.

9. Forrester Research.

10. Jupiter/NFO Consumer Survey, N: 1,817, January 2000.

11. IDC/Dataquest estimate that by 2003, 37 percent of online shoppers will reside outside the United States and Canada.

12. Web Presence Providers hosts your site either on your own server at its own offices or on its servers. The difference between ISPs and WPPs is that ISPs offer dial-up facilities, whereas WPPs expect you to have a connection to the Web.

CHAPTER 2

1. Modahl, p. 93.

2. According to Nielsen/Netratings from August 2000, the average clickthrough

rate for a banner ad is 0.45 percent. According to AdRelevance from August of 2000, the average CPM (cost per thousand impressions) for a banner ad is $30.52. The industry average conversion rate is 1.7 percent. Here's the math:

CPM	$30.52/1000 clicks
Cost per impression	$30.52/1000 = $0.03052 dollars/impression
Clickthrough rate	0.0045 clicks/impression
Cost per click	$0.03052/0.0045 = $6.782222/click (where a visitor is a click)
Conversion rate	0.017 purchasers/visitor (where a visitor is a click)
Cost of acquisition	$6.782222/0.017 = $398.9542/purchaser

3. BizRate.com, *Consumer Online Report*, Fourth Quarter 1999.

4. Jupiter Communications, *Creating Loyalty: Building Profitable Relationships*, April 2000.

CHAPTER 3

1. Directories such as the Open Directory Project (at www.dmoz.org) that accept volunteer editors will have instructions about applying to be an editor on the site.

2. Jupiter/NFO Consumer Survey.

3. Steve Lawrence and C. Lee Giles, "Accessibility of Information on the Web," *Nature*, vol. 400, no. 6740, 1999, p. 107.

4. Media Metrix, March 24, 2000.

CHAPTER 4

1. McKinsey & Company, "How E-Tailing Can Rise from the Ashes," *The McKinsey Quarterly*, 2000, no. 3, pp. 98-109.

2. "Bain & Company and Mainspring Conclude That Customer Loyalty Is the Key Driver of Online Retail Profitability," *Mainspring*, March 30, 2000.

3. Jupiter Communications, April 2000.

4. BizRate.com.

5. Ibid.

CHAPTER 13

1. Unless otherwise noted, all data in this section of this chapter is derived from "Why Online Merchants Need Effective Customer Support," BizRate.com, December 1999

2. "75 Percent of Shoppers Abandon Carts," *Cyberatlas* (cyberatlas.internet.com), November 1, 1999.

3. "Trends in Telephone Service," table 20.4, Federal Communications Commission, March 2000.

4. I realize that some savvy AOL users connect to the Web via AOL and do their browsing in a different browser, such as Internet Explorer or Netscape, but I don't think many AOL users realize this is an option, or what the advantages would be.

5. There are products that people don't want to buy in brightly lit stores. Pornographic materials and supplies come quickly to mind. Many pharmaceutical products carry a stigma, and sites that provide these products—such as bladder-control products, weight-loss products, impotence treatments, for example—should exercise extreme caution when trying to create an intimate shopping experience for customers interested in these products. Even in these environments, however, presales support can be valuable, if handled discretely.

6. BizRate.com.

7. Forrester Research.

8. BizRate.com, "Why Online Merchants Need Effective Customer Support," December 1999.

9. Cyber Dialogue, 2000.

ABOUT THE AUTHOR

Alexis Gutzman has been in IT since 1986 and has been developing Web technologies since 1993, when she was the director of the Multimedia Resource Center at the University of Virginia. She put up her first commercial Web site in 1997, and since then has worked for a number of dot-coms—both prominent and obscure—mostly as a consultant.

The author of *ColdFusion for Dummies, FrontPage 2000 Answers!,* and *The HTML 4 Bible,* Gutzman currently is a columnist for Internet.com and Office.com. She writes the weekly "ECommerce Tech Advisor" and "eBusiness Illuminator" columns, where she deals routinely and in-depth with the topics of wireless technology and e-commerce strategy, payment methods, security, marketing, research, and trends. Widely cross-posted by Internet.com and widely cross-linked by other sites, her columns are read by close to 100,000 readers on the Internet.com and Office.com sites, and by countless others on the other sites where they're distributed.

Based on the insightful analysis of her columns, Gutzman receives frequent requests for information and opinion from major media outlets in their coverage of e-commerce, as well as regular inquiries from directors, vice presidents, and CEOs of major corporations, dot-coms, and consulting firms. She is also a frequent speaker internationally on e-business and e-commerce topics.

Gutzman holds a bachelor's degree from Northwestern University and a master's degree from the Lyndon B. Johnson School of Public Affairs at the University of Texas. She writes from Bethel, Connecticut, where she lives with her husband and their three children.